"Kent provides a careful and comprehensive history of the development of the Wechsler Memory Scale. The clinical sections regarding memory difficulties associated with various forms of neuropsychopathology and the discussion of the clinical interpretation of the scale are unique and very valuable. There is a real need for this book."

—**Arthur MacNeill Horton Jr.**, Chief, Neuropsychology Section, Psych Associates of Maryland, Towson, Maryland, USA

The Wechsler Memory Scale

The Wechsler Memory Scale (WMS) is one of the most popular memory scales in the United States and much of the English-speaking world. This is the first book to systematically trace the evolution of the instrument in terms of its content and structure, whilst providing a guide to clinical interpretation and discussing its many research uses.

The Wechsler Memory Scale: A Guide for Clinicians and Researchers provides a comprehensive review and synthesis of the literature on all the major editions and revisions of the WMS, including the Wechsler Memory Scale-I, Wechsler Memory Scale-Revised, Wechsler Memory Scale-III, and the Wechsler Memory Scale-IV. It discusses major factor analytic studies of each version of the test, clinical interpretation of each version including studies on malingering, uses of each version with special populations, and makes suggestions for the next revision (i.e., the WMS-V).

This book is designed to be a go-to source for all graduate students, clinicians, and researchers who use the Wechsler Memory Scale, as well as to institutions offering formal training in adult clinical and neuropsychological assessment.

Phillip L. Kent, PsyD, spent over 40 years practicing in the field of psychology. He has worked in schools, public state psychiatric hospitals, mental health centers, nursing homes, and private practice. He holds five graduate degrees in general experimental psychology, clinical psychology, school psychology, and gerontological studies, and is a diplomate with the American Board of Professional Neuropsychology with added qualifications in geriatric neuropsychology.

The Wechsler Memory Scale

A Guide for Clinicians and Researchers

Phillip L. Kent

Routledge
Taylor & Francis Group

NEW YORK AND LONDON

First published 2020
by Routledge
52 Vanderbilt Avenue, New York, NY 10017

and by Routledge
2 Park Square, Milton Park, Abingdon, Oxon, OX14 4RN

Routledge is an imprint of the Taylor & Francis Group, an informa business

© 2020 Taylor & Francis

Library of Congress Cataloging-in-Publication Data
A catalog record for this book has been requested

ISBN: 978-0-367-46166-9 (hbk)
ISBN: 978-0-367-46165-2 (pbk)
ISBN: 978-1-003-02734-8 (ebk)

Typeset in Times New Roman
by Apex CoVantage, LLC

Contents

Acknowledgments

My first introduction to the Wechsler Memory Scale came in the late 1970s while I was working in a large state psychiatric hospital in Minnesota. Part of my job as a psychologist was to complete psychological evaluations on a wide variety of geriatric, chemically dependent, and neuropsychiatric patients who presented with memory issues. At the time, the original Wechsler Memory Scale appeared to be useful for this purpose. My interest in the scale gradually deepened to the point where I completed a dissertation on the theoretical adequacy of Wechsler's theory of memory and memory scales. By the time I completed my dissertation, the scale was in its revised edition. During the course of my career, which spanned over four decades, I was fortunate enough to use all revisions of the test in my clinical practice, thereby gaining first-hand experience with all versions of the test.

Throughout the time I used the scale, I read everything I could about the development, reliability, and validity of each test version. I was amazed by its wide range of clinical and research applications. I was also fortunate to have been able to discuss my interest in and concerns about the scale with two supportive and clinically astute colleagues, the late Leonard F. Koziol, PsyD, and the late Charles VanBuskirk, PhD, each of whom contributed to my understanding of the instrument in unique ways.

Despite the fact that the Wechsler Memory Scale has been the most used memory battery in the U.S. for the past 30 years and likely the most researched, there has never been a guide about the Wechsler Memory Scale similar to the series of volumes authored by David Wechsler and Joseph Matarazzo on the Wechsler Adult Intelligence Scale, which summarized the evolution and clinical and research uses of that test. This book was written to fill that void.

This book would not have been possible without the encouragement and expert assistance and guidance of Lucy Kennedy and Molly Selby, editors with Taylor and Francis. I would also like to thank my wife, Gertraud, who has been incredibly supportive of this labor of love and who put up with my long years in graduate school and the thousands of hours that went into this work. I dedicate this book to her and our two sons, Benjiman and Alexandyr.

Introduction

> Despite frequent criticism (Erickson & Scott, 1977; Lezak, 1983; Prigatano, 1978) and the introduction of the Wechsler Memory Scale-Revised (Wechsler, 1987), the original WMS is likely to continue to be used by clinicians and researchers. . . .
>
> (Sherer, Nixon, Anderson, & Adams, 1992, p. 506)

The purpose of this book is to provide a review and selective synthesis of the literature on the major official versions of the Wechsler Memory Scale, namely the Wechsler Memory Scale-I, Wechsler Memory Scale-Revised, Wechsler Memory Scale-III, and Wechsler Memory Scale-IV. It is designed to be of interest to and use by clinicians, researchers, and graduate students.

The origin of this book dates back to the 1980s when the writer was in graduate school. A proposal was made to write a dissertation based on a synthesis of the available literature on the Wechsler Memory Scale-I and the Wechsler Memory Scale-Revised. The proposal was not accepted, and the author instead pursued a delineation of the theoretical adequacy of structure of the Wechsler Memory Scales and Wechsler's implicit theory of memory (Kent, 1993). A second attempt to provide a literature synthesis in the late 1990s was derailed by a tornado, which interfered with efforts to collect the necessary literature to complete the project. At that time, there were approximately 900 published articles in print relating to the clinical and research uses of the scales. Since then, several thousand additional research articles have been published.

With each new test revision have come guides on the clinical use of the new scale. These guides tended to focus primarily on the new revision and were often authored by individuals associated with its development. Each revision was touted as "new and improved" by the publisher. As we will see, however, the essential core of the WMS has changed little since its inception. The new subtests introduced in each revision "disappear" when the next revision is published, suggesting they lacked clinical utility and validity.

In preparing for the present book, the writer completed multiple APA PsychNET Gold literature searches for the years 1945 through mid-2019. The searches yielded thousands of references, of which about 57% were deemed pertinent to the goals of this book. Additional references were obtained from other sources. Articles of interest were those that discussed the origins and evolution of the Wechsler Memory Scale, the many clinical and research uses of the scales, and articles addressing test interpretation.

Any literature review of this nature is bound to be selective and no doubt would result in a much different product in the hands of another writer or one with different aims. Nonetheless, an attempt was made to ensure it is generally reflective of the major uses of the WMS to date.

This book differs from others of a similar nature in that it is the first to address the use of the original scale and *all* its official major revisions in various clinical and research studies. It is also unique in that it was written by an independent researcher not affiliated with the development of any WMS revision and one who used all versions of the test in clinical practice.

Although the Wechsler Memory Scale was introduced to the profession in 1945 (Wechsler, 1945), the first official revision was not published until 1987 (Wechsler, 1987), 42 years after the original version and six years after the death of David Wechsler. Additional official revisions appeared in 1997 (Wechsler, 1997) and 2009 (Wechsler, 2009a). As this book is being written, it is anticipated that the Wechsler Memory Scale-V will appear in 2021 or 2022, assuming the 2020 census data is used for normative purposes.

Despite the fact there have been three official revisions of the original scale and dozens of unofficial revisions or adaptations, the most famous of which is Russell's (1975), a review of the literature reveals that the original scale and all official revisions remain in clinical or research use. For example, Gamito et al. (2014) used the WMS-I to investigate the cognitive recovery in stroke patients; Hiscox et al. (2018) used the WMS-R to investigate episodic memory in older adults; and O'Shea et al. (2018) used the WMS-III to investigate the memory performance of healthy adults.

The present publication focuses primarily on the official major versions of the Wechsler Memory Scale. It does not review the literature for the Children's Memory Scale or most published abbreviated versions of the WMS. It is significant to note that in conducting the literature review for the present project, relatively few research publications were identified that used any of the official abbreviated versions as part of their methodology, suggesting they have not had widespread clinical use. However, countless studies have used the Logical Memory I and II and Visual Reproduction I and II subtests, and, to a lesser degree, the Verbal Paired Associates I and II subtests from the three official revisions. The preponderance of literature cited in this book comes from research conducted within the U.S., despite the fact that the Wechsler Memory Scale and its various iterations have been used in such countries as

Brazil (Spedo et al., 2013; Bolognani et al., 2015), Greece (Efklides et al., 2002), Korea (Shin et al., 2016), Japan (Shimada et al., 2012), and Australia (Shores & Carstairs, 2000).

In this work, the acronym WMS will be used to refer to the original Wechsler Memory Scale (the WMS-I), a generic or unknown version of the original scale, or all versions of the WMS, depending on context.

Chapter 1

Methodology

In conducting background research for this book, multiple literature searches were completed using APA PsychNET Gold for the following periods: 1945–1949, 1950–1959, 1960–1969, 1970–1979, 1980–1989, 1990–1999, 2000–2009, and 2010–2018. Three types of searches were conducted for each period. The first procedure was Wechsler Memory Scale: Any Field and Years; the second procedure was Wechsler Memory Scale: Abstract and Years; and the third procedure was Wechsler + Memory + Scale: Abstract and Years. The searches yielded the following results (see Table 1.1).

As can be seen from Table 1.1, the correspondence is fairly close between the numbers of potential references identified using the first two procedures for the years 1945–1999. During this period, 1,872 potential references were identified using Procedure 1 versus 1,576 using Procedure 2. Once we get to the year 2000 and beyond, the relationship breaks down. For the years 2000–2009, 5,985 potential references were identified using Procedure 1 versus 819 using Procedure 2. And the difference for the years 2010–2018 was even greater: 12,073 potential references were identified using Procedure 1 versus 833 references using Procedure 2. The reasons for the dramatic differences in these literature searches are not clear, but may be partially due to the increase in neuroscience research during this period.

Procedure 2 identified fewer potential references than did Procedure 1 for each period, because with the latter, although the terms Wechsler Memory Scale needed to appear anywhere in the abstract, the term *Wechsler* could refer to any Wechsler test, *memory* to any type of memory, and *scale* could identify a particular test or method of analysis.

It is only with the use of Procedure 3 that the most pertinent results were obtained. However, this procedure has the potential for under-identifying potential references since the WMS may have been used as an investigatory tool not referenced in the abstract. In addition, Procedure 3 identified irrelevant potential references, such as in the situation where the author of the publication described a scale as "like the Wechsler Memory Scale" but did not actually use the WMS in the study.

Table 1.1 Research Protocol

Years Surveyed	Procedure 1 WMS: Any Field & Years	Procedure 2 WMS: Abstract & Years	Procedure 3 W+M+S: Abstract & Years
1945–1949	11	7	3
1950–1959	40	25	18
1960–1969	55	26	17
1970–1979	178	116	105
1980–1989	563	491	343
1990–1999	1,025	911	535
2000–2009	5,985	819	461
2010–2018	12,073	833	380
Total	19,930	3,228	1,862

All abstracts for all publications identified using all three procedures for the years 1945–1999 were read to identify pertinent references. A pertinent reference was defined as one in which the Wechsler Memory Scale was used in a study that was in accordance with the goals of the present project. If a potential reference was not available in English, the article was excluded from consideration. Articles were also excluded if they did not contain enough information from which conclusions could be drawn.

For the years 2000–2018, the author read all the abstracts of potential articles identified using Procedures 2 and 3 to ascertain which were relevant to the present project. It was not feasible to read abstracts of all potential references obtained by Procedure 1 due to the sheer volume of the publications identified (18,058). Using the results of Procedure 3 as a rough guide, the author estimated that over 95% of the articles identified using Procedure 1 would not be relevant to the current project.

About 100 additional references were obtained through Googling "Wechsler Memory Scale," completing an additional APA PsychNET Gold search for the first six months of 2019, searching for pertinent references on the ResearchGate and Academia websites, and obtaining pertinent references cited in various publications.

Although the aforementioned procedures did not identify all published research papers that could be pertinent to the present endeavor, it is felt by the present writer that they identified a representative sample of them, as APA PsychNET is the premier database used by psychologists and other behavioral researchers. Although the methodology used to identify pertinent references for this book was not exhaustive, it was felt to be comprehensive enough to accomplish the goals of this book.

Chapter 2

A History of the Origins and Evolution of Wechsler's Memory Scales

The purpose of this chapter is to provide an overview of the evolution of the content and structure of the Wechsler Memory Scale and a critique of each version. As we shall see, evolution has not always resulted in improvement. Since the purpose of this chapter is to provide a broad overview, it will not discuss the content of the subtests in detail.

Despite the fact that the Wechsler Memory Scale is presently in its fourth edition and the publisher is in the process of preparing a new edition, which is expected to be released in the next two to three years, all prior editions of the test remain in use. Because of this, it is important for the clinician and researcher to know how the version of interest relates to other versions, especially past versions. This is also important since the test publisher has often cited research on prior versions to support the validity of new revisions. In addition, in the real world, it is not uncommon for a clinician to have test results on a patient from a prior version of the test that have to be compared to test results from a more recent revision. Understanding the content and limitations of each test version and the continuities or discontinuities between test versions is important for valid assessment and making inferences about suspected changes in memory functioning.

Sound evidence-based psychological and neuropsychological assessment includes knowledge of the each test's reliability, validity, and shortcomings (Bowden, 2017a; Matarazzo, 1990) and a working knowledge of the research regarding the test. In addition, it involves considering the quantitative and qualitative information regarding the subject at hand and having a good working knowledge of psychological measurement, neurology, neuropsychology, and general psychology (Ardila, 1992; Matarazzo, 1990; Wechsler, 1939). As many researchers have pointed out, test scores in themselves do not mean much. A specific configuration of scores on a test can imply vastly different clinical conditions, depending upon the background and presenting symptoms of the person being evaluated. For instance, on the Minnesota Multiphasic Personality Inventory, peak scores on scales 4 and 9 can be manifested by (1) a person with an antisocial personality; (2) a person with a mood disorder; (3) a person with a substance disorder; (4) a person with a head injury; or (5) a person with any combination of these disorders. Without knowledge of the background of the person taking the test, a computerized interpretation of this configuration may result in an invalid assessment, with all due respect to Meehl (1954). When assessing people, it is important to take into account quantitative *and* qualitative information, and sometimes the latter trumps the former (Wechsler, 1939).

The Wechsler Memory Scales I and II

Although the Wechsler Memory Scale-I was officially introduced to the profession in 1945, it has been in clinical use since 1940 (Wechsler, 1945). Since Wechsler reported that the WMS-I was the result of 10 years of experimentation, it can be assumed he began work on the scale in approximately 1930, about the same time he began work on the Wechsler Bellevue Intelligence Scale (Wechsler, 1939).

The Wechsler Memory Scale has been officially revised three times (Wechsler, 1987, 1997, 2009a). The original scale and all official revisions have remained in research and clinical use well into the second decade of the 21st century, although the first three versions of the test are not officially available from the publisher. Regardless of what one thinks about the original instrument and its revisions, this is a remarkable achievement and points to the perspicacity of Wechsler in identifying many of the fundamental elements needed to conduct a valid clinical assessment of memory.

Although the Wechsler Memory Scale-I (WMS-I) formally appeared in 1945, the origins of the scale can be traced back to 1917. In 1917, Wechsler published a paper based on his master's thesis at Columbia University titled "A Study of Retention in Korsakoff Psychosis." For this study, Wechsler developed a test battery to evaluate the nature of this disorder. According to Wasserman (2012), Wechsler patched together a clinical memory battery from existing published and unpublished tests, following a framework suggested by Whipple (1915). According to Boake (2002), some of the subtests were derived from the Cornell-Coxe Performance Ability Scale (Cornell & Coxe, 1934). The 1917 test battery contained (1) a screening questionnaire to assess personal and current information and orientation; (2) measures of auditory and visual-spatial attention; (3) a measure to assess the encoding and recall of easy and hard verbal word pairs; (4) a measure of the learning and recall of two lists of 10 unrelated words and two lists of 10 related words; and (5) measures of immediate and delayed recall ranging from 15 seconds to 10 minutes (Wechsler, 1917). Several components of this memory battery were incorporated into the WMS-I (Kent, 2013). Thus, as early as 1917, Wechsler realized the importance of screening for possible disorientation that would affect the validity of his assessment procedure; of assessing attention apart from learning; and of assessing immediate and delayed recall. It is significant to note that all versions of the WMS assess attention, learning (recall based on repeated trials), and memory (recall after a single presentation).

Some components of the WMS-I were also derived from a table that appeared in Wechsler's original book on the Wechsler Bellevue Intelligence Scale (Wechsler, 1939). In this book, he presented a review of the literature summarizing how various diagnostic groups had performed on standard psychological tests then in use. As a result, the scale's construction could be described as an early example of evidence-based practice.

The original publication describing the WMS-I (Wechsler, 1945) runs a scant nine pages and provides no information regarding the scale's reliability and validity, nor does it provide detailed instructions on how to clinically interpret the test results. The original scale contains questions derived from standard mental status exams of the day that screened people for suspected aphasia, dementia, and disorientation (the Personal and Current Information and Orientation subtests). In addition, it has measures of attention and working memory (the Mental Control and Memory Span subtests), and encoding (the Visual Reproduction, Logical Memory, and Associate Learning subtests). It does not assess delayed recall and has limited norms derived from "approximately" 200 adult males and females ranging in age from 25 to 50. Although Lichtenberger, Kaufman, and Lai (2002) and Drozdick, Holdnack, and Hilsabeck (2011) report that the standardization sample was hospitalized patients at Bellevue Hospital in New York, this is incorrect. Wechsler explicitly states in his 1945 paper that the subjects were not hospital patients. Norms for ages 20–24 and 51–64 were extrapolated from this sample.

Wechsler appropriated the terms Memory Quotient (MQ) from a publication by Wells and Martin (1923), and he noted that the memory quotient was analogous to an intelligence quotient (IQ). Like the IQ from the Wechsler Bellevue Intelligence Scale (WBIS) to which it psychometrically corresponded and was normed against, the MQ has a mean of 100 and standard deviation of 15. Wechsler developed the WMS-I to assess individuals with "specific organic brain injuries," including soldiers and sailors returning from war with head injuries. It was meant to be a quick and practical screening instrument. The WMS-I and II are presented in Table 2.1.

In terms of the origins of the WMS-I subtests, the six items of the Personal and Current Information subtest are similar in nature to those asked by Wells and Martin (1923) as part of their Memory Examination. The content of the Orientation and Mental Control subtests were derived from standard mental status exams of the day. For the Memory Span subtest, a Digit Span measure, Wechsler used the same series he employed in the Wechsler Bellevue Intelligence Scale, except that the maximum number of digits used in the WMS-I was limited to eight forward and seven backward. The Digit Span technique was introduced by Jacobs (1887) to investigate memory dimensions. In regard to the content of the WMS-I Visual Reproduction subtest, Cards A and B (Figures A and B) are from the Army Performance Scale (Government Printing Office, 1921), and the two figures comprising Card C come from the Stanford-Binet Intelligence Scale (Terman & Merrill, 1937). The Logical

Table 2.1 WMS-I (1945) and WMS-II (1946) Structure and Normative Data

Screening Subtests	Personal and Current Information
	Orientation
Attention and Working Memory	Memory Span
	Mental Control
Encoding	Visual Reproduction
	Logical Memory
	Associate Learning
Normative Group WMS-I	"About 200 normal adults"; Males and Females Ages 25–50
	Norms for ages 20–24 and 51–64 extrapolated
Normative Group WMS-II*	87 adults; 17 student nurses; 10 female "psychoneurotic" patients; 60 college students approximately three fourths female
Time to administer	15 minutes

*The test authors do not state the sex of the student nurses

Table 2.2 WMS-I and II Subtests and Domains Assessed

Subtests in Order of Presentation	*Domains Assessed*
Personal and Current Information	Long-term episodic memory; Screen for suspected aphasia and dementia
Orientation	Orientation to place and time
Mental Control	Verbal working memory and attention
Logical Memory	Encoding and immediate recall of two verbally presented paragraphs consisting of meaningful material
Memory Span	Digits forward: attention; Digits backwards: concentration or working memory
Visual Reproduction	Immediate recall of geometric designs
Associate Learning	Verbal paired associate learning; Encoding and immediate recall of easy and hard associates; Semantic memory

Memory subtest, Paragraphs A and B from the WMS-I, are modifications of Passages 5 and 1, respectively, of the Army Performance Scale (Government Printing Office, 1921). The content of the WMS-I Associate Learning subtest was derived from Wechsler's 1917 investigation into the retention deficit in Korsakoff psychosis.

Table 2.2 presents the WMS-I and II subtests in the order they are administered. As can be seen, they assess a variety of functions. As noted, Wechsler was aware of the need to screen for orientation and suspected language and cognitive problems when assessing memory. In order to accomplish this, the Personal and Current Information is administered first. This subtest assesses long-term episodic memory and is used to screen for suspected aphasia and dementia. It is followed by the Orientation subtest which evaluates one's orientation to place and time. Next, the Mental Control subtest is administered which assesses attention and verbal working memory. Assuming the subject passed these three subtests, the next four subtests were administered. Wechsler considered the Mental Control subtest to be harder than the Memory Span subtest and useful for identifying deficits not picked up the latter.

According to Arbit and Zagar (1979), Wechsler believed the first three subtests involved the retention of general information, while the latter four tapped memory functions. Their factor analysis of the performance of a group of 661 males and 589 females in the age groups of 13–39, 40–59, and 60–88 on the WMS-I revealed two factors (general retentiveness and memory), confirming Wechsler's belief.

In regard to the Logical Memory, Wechsler (1945) notes that the subtest consists of two memory passages similar to the memory selection on the 10th year of the Stanford-Binet Intelligence Scale, although as noted, they were derived from the Army Performance Scale. Wechsler believed this subtest assessed the immediate recall of logical material.

Although Digit Span (the Memory Span subtest) had historically been used by psychiatrists as a measure of retentiveness, Wechsler (1939) felt Digit Span Backwards correlated with difficulties with attention and concentration. As noted, the content of his subtest was derived from the WBIS.

The Visual Reproduction subtest requires the subject to draw two simple geometric figures, which were exposed for 10 seconds, from memory. Although the Visual Reproduction subtest was designed to assess short-term visual memory, the designs can be verbalized and the subtest is verbally and visually presented.

Wechsler designed the Associate Learning subtest to assess "easy and hard associates" or what currently would be considered levels of processing. An example of an easy associate is "Metal-Iron," and a hard associate "Obey-Inch." An easy associate was assumed to reflect a naturally occurring association or relationship between two words and is considered a measure of semantic memory. A hard associate reflected the pairing of two unassociated objects and presumably required a deeper level of processing. The use of easy and hard associates derived from Wechsler's study of patients with Korsakoff psychosis. Although Wechsler included both types of associates in the Associate Learning subtest, he provides no guidance on how to clinically interpret differences in performance on the two types of associates. The Associate Learning subtest contains a list of 10 paired-associates, five easy and five hard, which the subject is asked to learn over three trials. The test therefore measures verbal paired associate learning, encoding and immediate recall, and semantic memory.

By 1946, the WMS-I ranked 90th out of 100 tests in usage (Louttit & Browne, 1947), and its use by psychologists in an Army hospital was being described by Patterson (1946). By 1951, Robert Watson (1951) was already referencing the test in a standard clinical psychology text of the era. By 1984, despite having never been officially revised, it was the most frequently used formal test of memory (Lubin, Larsen, & Matarazzo, 1984). In 1989, it was rated as the 13th most used test in outpatient mental health facilities, and the most used memory test according to Piotrowski and Keller (1989). In a study of neuropsychological assessment in public psychiatric hospitals between 1979 and 1989, Slick and Craig (1991) found that the Wechsler Memory Scale was used by 28.1% of those surveyed in 1979 and 29.2% of those surveyed in 1989. In 1996, Lees-Haley, Smith, Williams, and Dunn reported that the WMS-I and WMS-II were the third most used forensic tests. In 2005, the Wechsler Memory Scales were rated as the most used memory tests by clinical neuropsychologists in the U.S. and Canada (Rabin, Barr, & Burton, 2005), a position they maintained 10 years later (Rabin, Paolillo, & Barr, 2016). The continued popularity of the WMS is also indicated by the fact that as of 2011, it was one of the 10 most popular tests taught in clinical psychology training programs in the U.S. and the most frequently taught memory battery (Ready & Veague, 2014). In addition, a recent survey by Russo (2018) of Veterans Affairs (VA) psychologists who provide neuropsychological assessments indicated that some version of the WMS was used on 46.7% of respondents.

Shortly after the original Wechsler Memory Scale was published, an alternate version, called the WMS-II, appeared in print (Stone, Girdner, & Albrecht, 1946). Although Stone, Girdner, and Albrecht are listed as the authors of the alternate version, Wechsler and Stone are also listed as authors in a reprint of the Wechsler Memory Scale manual, which includes both the WMS-I and II (Wechsler & Stone, 1973). It thus appears Wechsler was directly involved in the development of the WMS-II. At the time both versions of the WMS appeared in print, Wechsler was working at Bellevue Hospital in New York City and Stone was teaching at Stanford University. While the standardization of WMS-I involved "approximately 200 normal subjects, ages 25 to 50, both men and women" (Wechsler, 1945, p. 4), the standardization of the WMS-II involved only 17 student nurses and 10 female patients who were "diagnosed as psychoneurotics, whose ability to work on the tests of this kind was adjudged by the chief physician as unimpaired" (Wechsler & Stone, 1973, p. 21). The student nurses and patients were from Bellevue Hospital in New York City. The standardization of the WMS-II also included 60 college students, approximately "three-fourths female" who were enrolled in the elementary course in psychology at Stanford. Crook III, Youngjohn, and Larrabee (1992) report that the WMS-I and II have been shown to have different difficulty levels with respect to individual subtests (Bloom, 1959; Prigatano, 1978) and that Lezak (1983) does not consider them interchangeable.

The WMS-I and II have the same seven subtests, although the content of each subtest varies between versions. Each version is scored in the same manner. After the test battery is administered, a raw score is derived based on the seven subtests. A correction for age is then added to the raw score to derive a corrected score. The corrected score is used to derive a Mental Quotient, which corresponds to the FSIQ (Full Scale IQ) from the WBIS. A WMS MQ that is significantly lower than the WBIS IQ reportedly suggests a memory disturbance. Just how large the IQ-MQ difference had to be to be clinically significant was never specified in the manual for either test, but presumably was at least equal to or greater than one standard deviation. Milner (1975), Prigatano (1974), and Quadfasel and Pruyser (1955) have suggested that IQ scores 10–12 points greater than MQs suggest memory deficits.

One problem with making such comparisons today is that modern IQ tests, including the Wechsler Adult Intelligence Scale-IV (WAIS-IV), have been re-normed, and their scores are not directly compatible with the WMS-I or II, WMS-R, or WMS-III or with scores from prior versions of the WAIS. Prifitera and Barley (1985) observed that in making comparisons between the WAIS-R and the WMS, since one would anticipate lower WAIS-R scores compared to WAIS (and by implication WBIS) scores, any IQ-MQ discrepancies would theoretically be less pronounced.

The Flynn effect (Flynn, 2007) is the name attached to the finding that there have been massive gains in IQ from one generation to another, resulting in the inevitable obsolescence of norms. Flynn (2009) reported that between 1942 and 2008, an examination of IQ changes on the Raven's Progressive Mazes revealed a gain of 14 points for British schoolchildren ages 5–15. Trahan, Stuebing, Hiscock, and Fletcher (2014) completed a meta-analysis of the Flynn effect of 285 studies of changes in IQ scores on the Stanford-Binet and Wechsler intelligence scales and found that IQ scores on the Wechsler scales have increased about 2.93 points per decade, consistent with prior findings of about 3 points per decade. They also did not find evidence for the hypothesis that the Flynn effect is diminishing over time. From a practical standpoint, what this implies is that due to norm obsolescence, a Full Scale IQ of 100 on the WBIS (which was published in 1939 and against which the WMS-I was calibrated or normed) would be roughly equivalent to a Full Scale IQ of 80 on the WAIS-IV (which was published in 2008).

In other words, if a clinician today were evaluating a subject who obtained a WAIS-IV FSIQ of 80 and a WMS-I MQ of 100, these scores would be considered roughly equivalent and no memory dysfunction should be expected, nor would such scores imply superior memory functioning relative to IQ. If the same subject obtained a WAIS-IV FSIQ of 100 and a WMS-I MQ of 100, the clinician should suspect some sort of memory dysfunction, since the Flynn effect has been found to affect cognitive functions other than intelligence. These are some of the pitfalls of making IQ-MQ comparisons with the Wechsler intelligence tests. Making comparisons between other modern adult intelligence tests and the WMS is even more difficult, fraught with potential interpretive pitfalls, and is ill-advised.

For research purposes, the WMS-I appears to have been used far more than the WMS-II as judged by the number of research reports citing the use of the former (Kent, 2018). This has also likely been the case in clinical practice.

Critique

It appears the first report of the WMS failing to identify memory impairment in an individual who showed clinical memory loss as a result of psychosis with syphilitic meningo-encephalitis was made by Rosenzweig (1949). In a formal evaluation of a patient's neurocognitive functioning, Rosenzsweig reported that the patient obtained a Wechsler-Bellevue Scale IQ of 91 (with a close correspondence of his verbal and performance scales) and a Memory Quotient of 96 on the WMS (version unknown). Another early criticism of the WMS was by Cohen (1950), who used it to assess the performance of psychoneurotic, organic, and schizophrenic groups. After equating the groups for mean age and IQs, he found that there was no significant difference between the groups on this test in terms of their memory functioning. The same year, Howard (1950) also reported that the WMS failed to distinguish a group of 58 hospitalized "organic psychotics" from a control group consisting of an equal number of psychotics without organic pathology. In a later study of the instrument, Howard (1954) investigated the value of 11 patterns of signs from the WMS that purportedly had potential for differentiating "organic" from "non-organic" psychotics. He reported that only one of the 11 signs had a satisfactory degree of predictive efficiency, again calling into question the validity of the test battery. Krawiecki, Couper, and Walton (1957) published another study critical of the WMS. They found that the test failed to differentiate between 60 hospitalized patients, half of whom had recently acquired brain injury and half who displayed no evidence of neurological impairment. In addition, studies by Standlee (1953a, b) failed to find any effect on memory for patients undergoing electroconvulsive therapy (ECT) as assessed by the WMS.

Studies during the 1940s and 1950s that supported the validity of the WMS to assess memory dysfunction include Stone (1947), who investigated the effects of ECT on cognition and memory; Stieper, Williams, and Duncan (1951), who investigated the effects of ECT on 12 individuals with paranoid schizophrenia; and reports of the effects of ECT on cognitive functioning by Kendall, Mills, and Thale (1956) and Quintart (1959). Quadfasel and Pruyser (1955) also found cognitive deficits in patients with epilepsy using the WMS, and Shontz (1957) found memory deficits in individuals with right hemiplegia using the WMS. In addition, Victor, Herman, and White (1959) found memory impairment using the WMS when investigating patients with Wernicke-Korsakoff syndrome, consistent with Wechsler's original report in 1917 using a memory battery from which the WMS was derived.

Early on, issues were raised about reliability of the WMS. As noted, the original publication introducing the scale (Wechsler, 1945) provided no information on the test's reliability, nor did the article introducing the alternate version (Stone et al., 1946). The authors of the alternate version stated that "not enough cases had yet been retested to provide stable reliability quotients for the Wechsler Memory Scales" (Stone et al., 1946, p. 15). Toal (1957), who was an early critic of the WMS, noted that as of the date of his research, no information was available regarding the scale's reliability and validity. He was one of the first researchers to report reliability (internal consistency) data for the WMS-I. Other writers also critical of the lack of information regarding the scale's reliability and validity include Arbit and Zagar (1979); Heilbronner, Buck, and Adams (1988); Hulicka (1966); and Loring and Papanicolaou (1987).

In regard to factor analytic studies, there has been an ongoing debate about the factor structure of the WMS (see Arbit & Zagar, 1979; Dujovne & Levy, 1971; Heilbronner et al., 1988; Prigatano, 1978). Although several studies have suggested the original scale measures (1) the learning and immediate recall of verbal and visual material, (2) attention and concentration, and (3) long-term autobiographical memory and orientation with regard to time and place, some writers (Butters, 1984; Erickson & Scott, 1977; Lawrence, 1984) questioned whether the original scale(s) measure memory at all, since the MQ tends to correlate highly with IQ.

The WMS has also been criticized for its standardization limitations and as being a test which did little more than establish norms for a mental status exam (Erickson & Scott, 1977). Other criticisms of the WMS were that Wechsler failed to report norms when introducing the test to the professional community and that the test lacked contemporary norms for a large representative sample of people, especially those 65 and older (Crosson, Hughes, Roth, & Monkowski, 1984; D'Elia, Satz, & Schretlen, 1989; Hulicka, 1966; Ivison, 1977). In addition, various writers have complained that the manual did not provide subtest norms and standard scores (Ivison, 1977; Osborne & David, 1978; Prigatano, 1978; Watson, 1951). As might be expected, the WMS scoring procedures have been criticized for being too subjective (Crosson et al., 1984; Mack, 1986; Mitchell, 1987; Prigatano, 1978). Perhaps the most biting criticisms of the WMS were complaints that it does not assess delayed recall (see, for instance, Russell, 1975), and over-relies on assessing verbal memory to the exclusion of visual memory (Erickson & Scott, 1977; Lezak, 1983). Further information regarding the shortcomings of the WMS-I and II can be found in Butters (1992), Erickson and Scott (1977), Kent (1993, 2013, 2017), Lezak (1983), and Prigatano (1977, 1978).

Key Points

- The WMS-I and II were standardized on very small, unrepresentative samples (about 200 and 87 adults, respectively). In addition, the norms for those aged 20–24 and 51–64 were extrapolated.
- Individuals from ages 20–64 could be assessed.
- The WMS-I and II test manuals provide no information regarding the tests' reliability and validity or any explicit guidelines on how to interpret IQ-MQ differences.
- The WMS assesses three factors: (1) the learning and immediate recall of verbal and visual material, (2) attention and concentration, and

(3) long-term autobiographical memory and orientation with regard to time and place.

- Although the WMS does not assess delayed recall, it does include limited measures of long-term episodic and semantic memory.
- It is important to remember the Flynn effect in interpreting IQ-MQ differences. WMS MQ's are not directly applicable to the scores from any IQ test other than the Wechsler Bellevue Intelligence Scale, which was published in 1939. In addition, there is little research on the significance of IQ-MQ differences using adult intelligence tests other than those devised by Wechsler.
- The WMS-I and II do not appear to be interchangeable.

Case Study 1: George was a 37-year-old white single male who was involuntarily committed to a state hospital in the late 1970s as mentally ill and an inebriate. He was diagnosed by the admitting psychiatrist as suffering from schizophrenia, paranoid type, and alcohol abuse. He was referred for a psychological evaluation to determine if he had suffered any cognitive deterioration due to his mental illness and alcoholism. He was evaluated after having been abstinent from alcohol for 30 days. Testing included but was not limited to the Bender Gestalt Test (BGT), Wechsler Adult Intelligence Scale (WAIS), and Wechsler Memory Scale-II (WMS-II). The results of the BGT were strongly suggestive of an organic component to George's illness, as were his gross motor tremors and perseverative tendencies. The WAIS yielded a Verbal Scale IQ of 85, Performance Scale IQ of 91, and Full Scale IQ of 86, consistent with premorbid estimates of his native intellectual functioning (he had an eighth-grade education, was a poor student, and had a limited work history). The results of the WMS-II yielded a Memory Quotient of 64. An analysis of his subtest performance suggested problems with working memory, the immediate recall of visually presented information independent of motor dysfunction, learning and immediate recall on a paired associate task, and a deterioration in his semantic memory. He was unable to say the alphabet correctly from A to Z. Comparing his MQ of 64 to his Verbal IQ of 85 and Full Scale IQ of 86, the test results were consistent with a memory disorder and clinical observations of his behavior.

The Wechsler Memory Scale-Revised (WMS-R)

When the WMS was developed, the assessment of memory dysfunction was in its relative infancy, as were the fields of clinical psychology and neuropsychology. During the first half of the 20th century, much research had been undertaken to determine the constituents of intelligent behavior (see, for instance, Cattell, 1941; Hebb, 1949; Spearman, 1904; Thurstone, 1936), and the underlying brain functions associated with such conditions as aphasia (Benton, 2000). During this period, brain damage or dysfunction was often referred to as "organicity," and it was assumed there were universal indicators of such. Tests like the Bender Gestalt Test (Bender, 1938) and the Shipley Institute of Living Scale (Shipley, 1940) were introduced as single tests that purported to assess "organicity." It was not until the late 1940s that Halstead (1947) introduced the first modern comprehensive standardized neuropsychological test battery.

Prior to the WMS, other tests were published to assess memory dysfunction, such as the battery introduced by Wells and Martin in 1923 and the Babcock Story Recall Test (Babcock & Levy, 1940). The battery by Wells and Martin was not widely used because it was cumbersome to administer and score (Erickson & Scott, 1977). Wechsler's memory scale was likely well received because of its brevity, ease of administration and scoring, and face validity.

In 1953 William Scoville discovered the role the hippocampus played in episodic memory after performing a bilateral medial-temporal lobe resection on Henry Molaison (H. M.), who suffered from intractable seizures (Scoville & Milner, 1957). Following Scoville and Milner's report of the surgery, the search for the anatomical bases of other forms of memory and various neurocognitive functions accelerated. The invention of CT scans and the emergence of magnetic resonance imaging in the 1970s, along with other sophisticated neurological tools, provided new windows into the structure and function of the brain and resulted in an avalanche of studies of brain functioning across a variety of fields, including neurology, psychiatry, and neuropsychology.

By the time the WMS-R was published, the original scale had been in clinical use for nearly half a century. Prior to the first official revision, it is estimated that there had been over 50 other "revisions" or adaptations of the WMS (Kent, 1993), the most famous of which is Russell's adaptation (Russell, 1975). Clearly, the WMS was popular with researchers and clinicians despite its many theoretical and clinical shortcomings and multiple critics.

When the first official revision was published, David Wechsler had been dead for six years. According to the test manual (Wechsler, 1987), Wechsler began work on the revision in the late 1970s, and he was able to complete the major changes in the test before his death. By the time the WMS-R was published, the field of clinical neuropsychology had come into its own. Lezak's 1976 text on neuropsychological assessment was marketed as the first comprehensive sourcebook on adult neuropsychology. According to Kolb and Whishaw (2015), when the first edition of their classic *Fundamentals of Human Neuropsychology* (Kolb & Whishaw, 1980) appeared, human neuropsychology did not exist as a unified body of knowledge.

Just prior to the publication of the WMS-R, Cunningham (1986) estimated there were between 15 and 40 competing theories and models of memory, with no one model or theory dominating the field. Although there continues to be active debate about the nature and structure of memory (Baddely, Eysenck, & Anderson, 2009, 2015), clinicians today typically assess explicit or declarative episodic verbal and visual memory, or the conscious, intentional recollection of previous experiences (Kolb & Whishaw, 2008), because patients often complain about their difficulty recalling prior experiences (O'Connor & Lafleche, 2006). Unfortunately, procedural memory is rarely assessed because patients do not usually complain of such. Likewise, semantic memory is not often formally assessed. The clinical assessment of memory and learning ideally includes a paradigm exemplified by the structure of the California Verbal Learning Test (CVLT). The CVLT assesses the encoding of information across multiple trials, using voluntary and cued recall and recognition paradigms (Delis, Kramer, Kaplan, & Ober, 1987). Ideally, simple and complex information is presented in verbal and visual modalities, and immediate and delayed recall is assessed, along with measures of attention and working memory (Maruff & Darby, 2006). Recognition recall procedures are useful to determine if recall failures are due to encoding or retrieval problems. Furthermore, personal orientation, possible sensory impairment, and personal autobiographical memory are also customarily assessed (Lezak, Howieson, Bigler, & Tranel, 2012). In addition to assessing learning and memory using a paradigm exemplified by the CVLT, clinicians typically assess the recall of verbally presented meaningful information as typified by the WMS Logical Memory subtest. Attention and working memory evaluations are also usually part of the typical clinical assessment.

The publication of the WMS-R was clearly an attempt to respond to the WMS's critics. Despite being published a bit over three decades ago, the rationale for the development of the revision was presented in a scant 1.5 pages, and as was the case for the original scale, Wechsler did not provide a theory of memory upon which his revision was based in his manual (Kent, 1993, 2013). In addition, the scale was not explicitly anchored in what was known regarding the neuroanatomical underpinnings of memory (Kent, 2013). Although the WMS is one of the best-known memory batteries in the U.S., Wechsler did not publish much about memory. His main publications in this area were a study of retention in Korsakoff psychosis (Wechsler, 1917), some minor references to memory in his first major work on assessing adult intelligence (Wechsler, 1939), and two papers published in the early 1960s (Wechsler, 1961, 1963).

The major goals of the revision were as follows: (1) assess memory for verbal and figural stimuli, meaningful and abstract material, and immediate and delayed recall; (2) provide measures of different types of memory; (3) provide norms stratified at nine age levels; and (4) revise the scoring procedures to improve scoring accuracy. For the interested reader, Powel (1988) provides a succinct summary of the differences in subtests between the WMS-I and II and the WMS-R.

The WMS-R was designed to be clinician and patient friendly. It could be completed in 30 minutes when administering all subtests except the delayed versions, or 60 minutes when the whole battery was administered. The test manual (Wechsler, 1987) notes that the instrument is not suitable for making fine discriminations at high levels of memory functioning and is of limited use for persons falling outside the WMS-R norms for 16- to 74-year-olds and non-native English speakers. Unlike the manual for the WMS-I, the WMS-R manual provided some information regarding the use of the WMS-R scores with selected clinical groups, although the sample sizes for each clinical group are small.

Critique

The WMS-R consists of 13 subtests, 12 of which were used to derive index scores. The Information and Orientation subtest was used to screen for intact sensory functioning, disorientation, and handedness. The General Memory Index is somewhat comparable to the Memory Quotient from the WMS-I, since it is an index of the immediate recall of auditorily and visually presented material. From a clinical standpoint, assuming one was evaluating a subject who had been previously tested on either the WMS-I or II, one might be tempted to ascertain if there is a significant difference between the Memory Quotient (MQ) and General Memory Index (GMI). A strict comparison cannot be made, however, because the MQ and GMI do not contain the same subtests. The MQ is based on seven subtests, which include questions designed to assess orientation, attention and concentration, and the immediate recall of verbally and visually presented information; the GMI is comprised of five subtests that assess the immediate recall of verbally and visually presented material. In addition, the GMI has only three subtests in common with the MQ (Logical Memory I, Visual Reproduction I, and Verbal Paired Associates I). It should be noted that the Associate Learning subtest of the WMS was renamed Verbal Paired Associates for the WMS-R.

The GMI is comprised of two components: the Verbal Memory Index, which consists of two subtests (Logical Memory I and Verbal Paired Associates I), and the Visual Memory Index, which is comprised of three subtests (Figural Memory, Visual Paired Associates I, and Visual Reproduction I). The Figural Memory subtest was designed to assess the recall of abstract visual patterns via a recognition paradigm. The Visual Paired Associates subtest reportedly is a visual analog of the Verbal Paired Associates subtest. It was designed to assess the recall of six abstract line drawings paired with a different color via a recognition paradigm. The Figural Memory and Visual Paired Associates I and II subtests are new subtests. The Visual Memory Index is a composite that assesses immediate recall via free call and recognition procedures. As a result, it is a difficult index to interpret, because poor performance on this index can represent problems with encoding, voluntary recall, or storage or a combination of the three.

The Attention/Concentration Index (ACI) is comprised of three subtests. One assesses verbal working memory and attention (Mental Control); one assesses attentiveness and concentration (Digit Span, formerly known as Memory Span); and one assesses visual working memory (Visual Memory Span). Visual Memory Span is a new subtest.

The Delayed Recall Index (DRI) is comprised of four subtests. Two (Logical Memory II and Verbal Paired Associates II) assess the delayed recall of verbally presented information, and two (Visual Paired Associates II and Visual Reproduction II) assess the delayed recall of verbally and visually presented information. Although the DRI is a composite measure of the delayed recall of verbally or verbally and visually presented information, it is not directly comparable to the GMI, because the GMI consists of one additional subtest: Figural Memory. It is not clear from the manual why the test publisher designed the WMS-R in such a fashion. For clinical purposes, it would have been useful if the Figural Memory subtest was presented as a standalone measure of the immediate recall of visually presented information via a recognition paradigm, and not be part of the Visual Memory Index. That way the GMI index could have been directly compared to the DRI. Both would contain the same subtests, with the GMI assessing immediate recall and the DRI assessing delayed recall. Had the authors of the WMS-R chosen this path, the clinical interpretation of the GMI and DRI would have been more straightforward.

In looking at the manifest structure of the WMS-R, it is apparent that the test publisher provided subtests to assess personal information, orientation, and possible sensory impairment; working memory and concentration; and the immediate recall of visually and verbally presented material much like the WMS-I. In addition, an attempt was made to assess the delayed recall of verbally and visually presented information. To address the criticism that the Memory Quotient of the WMS-I was a global measure of diverse abilities, the WMS-R has several new indexes with each presumably representing a different process or ability.

The administration time for the entire test was estimated to be 45–55 minutes, according to the publisher. However, this estimate was based on a normal sample. Research has suggested that the actual time with clinical samples is more in the range of an hour for the entire battery (Axelrod, 1999). The content of the WMS-R is presented in Table 2.3.

Despite its many shortcomings, the WMS-R was a decided improvement over its predecessor, and the major goals of the revision were achieved. On the surface, the new instrument assessed memory in verbal and figural (visual) modalities. It seemingly assessed delayed recall. The norms were improved by including a larger and more representative sample size than the WMS-I. Subject selection was derived from a normal population of the United States. The sample was stratified based on age, sex, race (white versus non-white), geographic region, and education consistent with the 1980 Census. The scoring procedures were revised to be clearer and more objective.

The WMS-R was developed in such a manner that scores from it could be compared to scores from the Wechsler Adult Intelligence Scale-Revised.

Table 2.3 WMS-R Indexes, Related Subtests, and Normative Data

Major Index	Subtests	Domains Assessed
Verbal Memory Index	Logical Memory I	Encoding and immediate recall of two verbally presented paragraphs consisting of meaningful material
	Verbal Paired Associates I	Verbal paired associate learning; Encoding & immediate recall of easy and hard associates; Semantic memory
Visual Memory Index	Figural Memory	Encoding and immediate recall of abstract visual patterns via a recognition paradigm
	Visual Paired Associates I	Visual paired associate learning; Encoding and immediate recall of six abstract line drawings paired with a different color via a recognition paradigm; Visual memory
	Visual Reproduction I	Encoding and immediate recall of geometric designs; Visual memory; Motor functioning
General Memory Index*	Logical Memory I	Encoding and immediate recall of two verbally presented paragraphs consisting of meaningful material
	Verbal Paired Associates I	Verbal paired associate learning; Encoding & immediate recall of easy and hard associates; Semantic memory
	Figural Memory	Encoding and immediate recall of abstract visual patterns via a recognition paradigm
	Visual Paired Associates I	Visual paired associate learning; Encoding and immediate recall of six abstract line drawings paired with a different color via a recognition paradigm; Visual memory
	Visual Reproduction I	Encoding and immediate recall of geometric designs; Visual memory; Motor functioning
Attention/ Concentration Index	Mental Control	Verbal working memory and attention
	Digit Span	Digits forward: attention (verbal alertness); Digits backwards: concentration or working memory
	Visual Memory Span	Visual short-term memory; Procedural learning; Motor functioning
Delayed Recall Index	Logical Memory II	Delayed recall of two verbally presented paragraphs consisting of meaningful material
	Verbal Paired Associates II	Verbal paired associate learning; Delayed recall of easy and hard associates
	Visual Paired Associates II	Visual paired associate learning; Delayed recall of six abstract line drawings paired with a different color via a recognition paradigm; Visual memory
	Visual Reproduction II	Delayed recall of simple geometric designs; Visual memory; Motor functioning
Screening subtest**	Information and Orientation	Long-term episodic memory; Screen for suspected aphasia & dementia; Orientation to place and time; Hand preference; Sensory problems
Normative Information		Nine age groups ranging in age from 16 to 74; Norms for ages 18–19, 25–34, and 45–54 interpolated; Co-normed with the WAIS-R; Approximately equal numbers male/female; Sample size: 316
Time to Administer		From manual (Wechsler, 1997) for entire test: 45–55 minutes; Research estimates for all subtests: Short Form: 30 minutes; Long Form: 45–60 minutes; Times Between Immediate and Delayed Subtests: 30 minutes

*As noted earlier, the General Memory Index is derived from combining the weighted raw scores from all subtests comprising the Verbal Memory Index and Visual Memory Index
**Information and Orientation is a screening subtest and not used in the calculation of index scores

Some information was presented in the manual concerning how various clinical groups performed on the WMS-R. The whole test could be administered in about an hour. The test manual also presented information regarding the reliability and validity of the new instrument. Yet, for all its improvements, it still suffered from numerous shortcomings. Some of these shortcomings will be detailed.

Normative Sample: While the WMS-I was "normed" on an unrepresentative sample of about 200 people ages 25–50, the WMS-R was normed on only 316 people, a rather small sample in light of the year the revision was published and the stratification variables of the sample. In addition, the norms for ages 18–19, 25–34, and 45–54 were interpolated . The small sample sizes for each age group appear to have been a shortcut on the part of publisher. This shortcoming is remarkable since the WMS was the most used test of memory in the U.S., the test publisher was one of the largest in the U.S., and those aged 18–19 and 24–34 are high-risk groups for head injury.

Structural Peculiarities and Shortcomings: The WMS-I was heavily criticized for being biased toward assessing verbal memory. Only one of the seven subtests, Visual Reproduction, assessed the recall of visually presented material. Because of the way the WMS-R is structured, it is manifestly biased toward assessing the immediate recall of visually presented material. Of the five subtests which comprise the General Memory Index, on the surface, three of them (Figural Memory, Visual Paired Associates I, and Visual Reproduction I) are purported measures of the immediate recall of primarily visually presented material.

It is noteworthy that the Verbal Memory Index is essentially a measure of the immediate recall of verbally presented information (Logical Memory I and Verbal Paired Associates I), and the Visual Memory Index is purportedly a measure of the immediate *recall* and *recognition* of figural (visual) information (Figural Memory, Visual Paired Associates I, and Visual Reproduction I). So while the Verbal Memory Index involves subtests using a free recall methodology, the Visual Memory Index involves subtests using both free recall and recognition methodologies.

Another oddity of the WMS-R is the Delayed Recall Index, which is based on four subtests, two of which measure the delayed recall of verbally presented material (Logical Memory II and Verbal Paired Associates II), and two measure the delayed recall of (primarily) visually presented figural material (Visual Paired Associates II and Visual Reproduction II). It is not clear why the test's author chose to combine these four subtests into one index, instead of splitting them into a Verbal Memory Delayed Index and Visual Memory Delayed Index. If that had been done, the WMS-R Verbal Memory Index and proposed Verbal Memory Delayed Recall Index would have been comparable. In addition, if the WMS-R Visual Memory Index was based just on the Figural Paired Associates I and Visual Reproduction I subtests, as well as a delayed version of Figural Memory, then that index would be directly comparable to the proposed Visual Memory Delayed Recall Index. Why Figural Memory was not included in delayed recall testing is not addressed in the manual.

Another shortcoming of the WMS-R is that it incompletely assesses recall through a recognition paradigm. Recognition procedures are only used for purported measures of visual memory. Since none of the ostensibly verbal subtests assess immediate or delayed recall through a recognition paradigm, the clinician is unable to determine if memory failures are due to problems with incomplete encoding, retrieval problems, or storage issues.

Reliability and Validity: In regard to reliability, for five of the subtests, test-retest (stability) coefficients were used as reliability estimates, and internal consistency estimates are presented for the remaining seven subtests (Wechsler, 1987, p. 59). According to the test manual, the average reliability coefficients across age groups for subtests and composites range from .41 to .90, with a median value of .74. In regard to validity, the test manual summarizes factor analytic studies of the WMS-I. The manual reports that factor analytic studies of the WMS-I have generally revealed that it has three factors. As noted, the first factor consists of the learning and immediate recall of verbal and visual material (Logical Memory, Visual Reproduction, and Associate Learning subtests). The second factor assesses attention and concentration (Mental Control and Digit Span subtests). The third factor assesses long-term autobiographical memory and orientation with regard to time and place (Personal and Current Information and Orientation subtests).

In regard to the WMS-R, it will be recalled that an explicit goal of the test revision was to provide measures of delayed recall. Although such writers as Golden (2000, p. 241) reported that over 400 published studies and articles ". . . have supported the use of the WMS-R as a general test of memory and delayed memory . . . ." factor analytic research does not support such an assertion. Wechsler (1987) reports that principal components analyses were performed on the entire standardization sample using age-corrected raw scores with the effects of age partialled out on eight subtests, none of which included purported measures of delayed recall. The orthogonally rotated factor matrix yielded a two-factor solution. Factor I assesses general memory and learning and Factor II attention and concentration, factors which are similar to what were found in prior studies of the WMS-I. A principal components analysis on a mixed clinical sample yielded similar results. It should be noted that later research, which will be discussed in Chapter 4 of this book, has suggested that the WMS-R assesses three factors: (1) the learning and immediate recall of verbal and visual material; (2) attention and concentration; and (3) long-term autobiographical memory and orientation with regard to time and place.

The results of the factor analytic studies reported by Wechsler (1987) were taken as support for the two major composite scores of the WMS-R: the General Memory Index and the Attention/Concentration Index. What is most remarkable about the results of factor analytic studies reported in the manual is that Wechsler reports each delayed recall subtest loaded on the same factor as its immediate recall counterpart, indicating that the test failed to assess delayed recall. Since factor analytic studies failed to support the validity of the Delayed Recall Index, by extension, they do not support the validity of the Logical Memory II, Visual Reproduction II, Verbal Paired Associates II, and Visual Paired Associates II subtests as measures of delayed recall.

According to professional ethical guidelines, tests users are supposed to be familiar with the reliability and validity of the tests they use (Eignor, 2013). To do so, a responsible test user, minimally, needs to read the test manual and be familiar with available published critiques of the test. Such a practice is consistent with sound evidence-based practice as advocated by Bowden (2017b) and others. Assuming one followed such guidelines, then when administering the WMS-R, no "delayed recall" tests would be given, or if given, such test results would not be reported because there is no research evidence that they are valid measures of delayed recall. Yet this clearly has not been common clinical practice, to which most readers of reports describing WMS-R test results can attest. Based on this writer's experience of having practiced in the field for over 40 years, during which he supervised numerous psychologists, worked as a consultant evaluating vocational rehabilitation clients, completed hundreds of social security disability evaluations, and read an untold number of consultant reports, it has been observed when the WMS-R has been administered, the summary report nearly always describes any differences between measures of immediate versus delayed recall when they occurred. It would thus appear that the lack of validity of the WMS-R Delayed Memory Index has generally been unknown among clinicians, or, if known, ignored for clinical purposes. The lack of factor analytic support for the Delayed Recall Index of the WMS-R and the shortcomings in the standardization of the instrument in terms of small normative groups are two major shortcomings of the instrument. The interested reader can find more information regarding the reliability and validity of the WMS-R by consulting Kent (2013, 2017), Prigatano (1977, 1978), and the test manual (Wechsler, 1987).

Key Points

- The WMS-R is a significant improvement over the WMS in terms of the size of the standardization group, improved scoring, the purported assessment of delayed recall, and information regarding the scale's reliability and validity. Despite the above improvements, the standardization sample is small ($N = 316$), and norms for those aged 18–19, 24–34, and 45–54 are interpolated.
- Individuals from ages 16 to 74 can be assessed.
- Where previously, from a structural standpoint, the WMS-I was biased towards assessing verbal memory, the WMS-R is biased towards assessing visual memory.
- The WMS-R appears to assess three factors: (1) the learning and immediate recall of verbal and visual material; (2) attention and concentration; and

(3) long-term autobiographical memory and orientation with regard to time and place. These factors are similar to the factors comprising the original scale.

- Contrary to the publisher's original assertion (Wechsler, 1987), the WMS-R does not measure delayed recall.
- The WMS-R does not assess memory via a recognition paradigm except for some measures of visual memory. As a result, the examiner will have trouble determining if recall difficulties on measures of verbal memory are due to problems with encoding, storage, or retrieval or a combination of these.
- Caveat: In one printing of the WMS-R Figural Memory manual, for Item 1, on the second card with three figures, the middle is incorrectly reproduced.

Case Study 2: George was a 47-year-old white single male who was recommitted as mentally ill to a state psychiatric hospital, due to his inability to curb his excessive water intake. He was referred for psychological evaluation to assess his memory and capacity to learn from experience. He had been evaluated by the present writer a decade earlier, and had a 30-year history of paranoid schizophrenia and alcohol dependence. He was evaluated after he had been abstinent from alcohol for over 30 days. Testing included but was not limited to the Luria-Nebraska Neuropsychological Battery-Form I (LNNB), the Wechsler Adult Intelligence Scale-Revised (WAIS-R), and the Wechsler Memory Scale-Revised (WMS-R). The results of the LNNB indicated George was impaired on 7 of the 11 clinical scales. The results further suggested problems with spatially based movement, motor slowing, difficulty with spatial orientation, perseveration, and problems with attention and concentration. His impairments were considered chronic in nature. Testing on the WAIS-R yielded a Verbal Scale IQ of 76, Performance Scale IQ of 75, and a Full Scale IQ of 75. Test scores on the WAIS a decade earlier yielded IQs of 84, 91, and 86, respectfully. The differences between past and current IQ test scores were interpreted as indicative of a mild decline in intellectual functioning. The results of the WMS-R yielded a Verbal Memory Index score of 68, Visual Memory Index score of 51, General Memory Index Score of 52, Attention/Concentration Index score of 88, and Delayed Index score of 53. Prior testing on the WMS-II yielded a Memory Quotient of 64. The WMS-R test results were suggestive of a decline in George's memory functioning over the past decade, consistent with a downward trajectory in his psychosocial functioning. The overall results of the examination were consistent with the diagnoses of dementia, chronic paranoid schizophrenia, and alcohol dependence syndrome. In comparing the results of the current evaluation with the evaluation a decade earlier, it is significant to note that in each instance the WMS revealed significant memory impairment. The WMS-R, however, was better able to pinpoint the nature of George's memory impairment.

The Wechsler Memory Scale-III (WMS-III)

A mere decade went by before the WMS was revised again. Like before, David Wechsler was listed as the author. According to the publisher, the test was developed by a panel of experts employed by or consulting with the Psychological Corporation, and the revision was based on an extensive literature review (Psychological Corporation, 1997; Tulsky, Zhu, & Ledbetter, 2002). Like with the WMS-R, the WMS-III was co-developed with a new version of the WAIS, using similar research methodologies, normative samples, and clinical classification procedures to allow for meaningful comparisons between intellectual ability and memory functioning.

The goals of the revision fell into two broad categories, based on numerous criticisms of the WMS-R. First, the revision attempted to address normative and psychometric issues (standardization sample size, age range, representativeness, interpolated norms, and scale reliability). Second, the revision attempted to address issues related to content and configuration issues (specifically, concerns about the reliability and validity of the visual memory subtests, internal reliability, and the lack of recognition memory measures to identify specific retrieval issues). The structure of the WMS-III is presented in Table 2.4.

As can be seen from Table 2.4, the 1997 revision of the WMS resulted in several changes. Eight new subtests were added (Faces I and II, Family Pictures I and II, Letter-Number Sequencing, Spatial Span, Word List I and II). Four subtests were eliminated (Figural Memory, Visual Paired Associates I and II, and Visual Memory Span), suggesting that they had not been sufficiently researched when introduced into the WMS-R.

The WMS-III has 10 primary subtests (Logical Memory I and II, Verbal Paired Associates I and II, Letter-Number Sequencing, Faces I and II, Family Pictures I and II, and Spatial Span), and 7 optional subtests (Information and Orientation, Mental Control, Word Lists I and II, Digit Span, Visual Reproduction I and II). As previously noted, in the WMS-R, the Information and Orientation subtest was part of the standard battery and used as a screening measure to assess for disorientation and sensory impairment. Scores from this subtest were not used, however, to calculate any index scores. The WMS-R Mental Control and Digit Span subtests were also part of the standard battery, and along with the Visual Memory Span subtest, were used to calculate the Attention/Concentration Index. For the WMS-III, the Information and Orientation, Mental Control, Digit Span, and Visual Reproduction I and II subtests became optional, along with the newly developed Word Lists I and II subtests. Although the reader may wonder why one would *not* want to administer the Information and Orientation, Mental Control, and Digit Span subtests since they represent "best practices" and are customarily part of standard memory assessment, these tests were deemed optional if the examiner was pressed for time or had already obtained the information these subtests yield in another manner.

Table 2.4 WMS-III Indexes, Related Subtests, and Normative Data

Major Indexes	Components	Subtests*	Domains Assessed
Immediate Memory	Visual Immediate Index	Faces I	Encoding and immediate recall of visually presented faces via a recognition paradigm; Motor-free visual memory
		Family Pictures I	Encoding and immediate recall of visually presented complex meaningful material and spatial memory
	Auditory Immediate Index	Logical Memory I	Encoding and immediate recall of two verbally presented paragraphs consisting of meaningful material
		Verbal Paired Associates I	Verbal paired associate learning; Encoding and immediate recall of easy and hard associates; Semantic memory
General Memory	Visual Delayed Index	Faces II	Delayed recall of the encoding of visually presented faces via a recognition paradigm; Motor-free visual memory
		Family Pictures II	Delayed recall of the encoding of visually presented complex meaningful information and spatial memory
	Auditory Delayed Index	Logical Memory II	Delayed recall of the encoding two verbally presented paragraphs consisting of meaningful material
		Verbal Paired Associates II	Verbal paired associate learning; Delayed recall of the encoding of easy and hard associates
	Auditory Recognition Delayed Index	Logical Memory II**	Delayed recall of the encoding of two verbally presented paragraphs consisting of meaningful material via a recognition paradigm
		Verbal Paired Associates II**	Verbal paired associate learning; Delayed recall of the encoding of easy and hard associates via a recognition paradigm
Working Memory Index		Letter-Number Sequencing	Immediate recall of verbally presented information; Working memory
		Spatial Span	Visual working memory and procedural learning

(Continued)

Table 2.4 (Continued)

Major Indexes	Components	Subtests*	Domains Assessed
	Optional Subtests	Information and Orientation	Long-term episodic memory; Aphasia and dementia screen; Orientation to place and time; Handedness; Sensory problems
		Mental Control	Verbal working memory and attention
		Word Lists I	Immediate recall of the encoding of a verbally presented list after an interference task; Temporal recall of verbally presented information
		Word List II	Delayed recall of the encoding a verbally presented list and delayed recognition of a verbally presented task after an interference task
		Digit Span	Digits forward: attention (verbal alertness); Digits backwards: concentration or working memory
		Visual Reproduction I	Immediate recall of the encoding of simple geometric designs; Visual memory; Motor functioning
		Visual Reproduction II	Delayed recall and recognition of the encoding of simple geometric designs; Visual memory; Motor functioning
	Normative Information		Sample size 1,032 increased to 1,250 with weighting; Based on 1995 U.S. Census stratified on age, sex, race/ethnicity, educational level, geographical region; Co-normed with WAIS-III; Age range 16 to 89
	Time to Administer		100 minutes; 25–35 minutes between Immediate and Delayed subtests

*10 Primary Subtests: LM I & II, Verbal PA I & II, LNS, Faces I & II, Fam Pic I & II, and Spatial Span; 7 Optional Subtests: Infor & Orien, Mental Control, Word Lists I & II, Digit Span, Vis Rep I & II;

**Recognition scores from LM II and Ver PA II contribute to the Auditory Recognition Delayed Index

Critique

The WMS-III was clearly intended to be used in conjunction with the WAIS-III, just as the WMS-R was intended to be used with the WAIS-R and the WMS-I was intended to be used with the WBIS. The WMS-III was co-normed with the WAIS-III, making direct comparisons between the two tests possible. As Skeel, Sitzer, Fogal, Wells, and Johnstone (2004) have noted, making comparisons between IQ and memory tests which have not been co-normed introduces error into the interpretation process. Having memory and IQ tests which are co-normed allows the clinician to compare the subject's memory complaints or impairment with his or her loss in other intellectual functions (Babcock, Shipley, Weider, Hunt, & Eisenson, 1953).

Although "memory" may be compromised in apparent isolation from other cognitive abilities (Banich & Compton, 2018), the relationship between intelligence and memory functioning is complex. With dementia, for instance, there is usually a decline in intellectual and memory functioning. With certain types of head injury, intelligence as measured by traditional IQ tests may be relatively preserved but accompanied by one or more memory deficits. One can also have superior memory in light of modest intellectual functioning (Luria, 1987), or very high intellectual ability and average memory functioning.

In the process of revising the WMS, the publisher was aware of this complex relationship, as evident from Hawkins and Tulsky (2001, p. 875), who wrote:

> Since memory performance expectations may be IQ-based, unidirectional base rate data for IQ-Memory Score discrepancies are provided in the WAIS-III/WMS-III Technical Manual. The utility of these data partially rests on the assumption that discrepancy base rates do not vary across ability levels. . . . FSIQ stratified base rate data generated from the standardization sample (weighted $N = 1,250$, aged 16–89) demonstrate substantial variability across the IQ spectrum. A superiority of memory score over FSIQ is typical at lower IQ levels, whereas the converse is true at higher IQ levels. These data indicate that the use of IQ-memory score unstratified "simple difference" tables could lead to erroneous conclusions for clients with low or high IQ. IQ stratified standardization base rate data are provided as a complement to the "predicted difference" method detailed in the Technical Manual.

The clinical practice of determining memory dysfunction based on computing IQ and memory test score differences is fraught with pitfalls. Unfortunately, the publisher of the WMS-III implicitly encourages this practice since clinicians using the test likely use computer scoring, which will compute the differences between WMS-III and WAIS-III scores if the latter are entered into the scoring program. One problem with computerized scoring, which makes the calculation of the statistical significance of multiple score differences easy, is that statistical significance is often confused with clinical significance. Although computerized scoring is a time saver, especially with a lengthy and complex test like the WMS-III, the use of computerized scoring can be dangerous in the hands of novices, as computer-generated test results and interpretation are potentially prone to misinterpretation. Computerized scoring and interpretation creates the illusion of validity that the test may not merit. For instance, if computerized scoring yields statistically significant differences between immediate and delayed recall indexes, with the latter being lower than the former, the clinician might be prone to describing the subject at hand as having difficulty with delayed recall or long-term memory. Such an interpretation is questionable, because factor analytic studies have not supported the validity of the WMS-III delayed recall indexes, nor are WMS-III measures of delayed recall measures of long-term memory or long-term retention in the usual sense.

In regard to computerized scoring, the Psychological Corporation (2002) published the WAIS-III WMS-III WIAT-II Writer to assist in computerized scoring of the WMS-III. The program can be used to generate score comparisons among the three tests. In addition to the computerized program which was available through the Psychological Corporation, not many researchers or clinicians are likely aware that Tanner (2009) made available a no-cost Windows-based computer program for the WMS-III that can be used to facilitate reporting of WMS-III test results.

Unlike its immediate predecessor, the technical manuals for the WMS-III provide a general discussion of some basic theories of memory and the neuroanatomy of memory, although the test is not anchored in an explicit theory of memory. Not many clinicians or researchers are likely aware that the Psychological Corporation actually published two technical manuals for the WAIS-III and WMS-III (Psychological Corporation, 1997; Tulsky et al., 2002). The first was published when the test originally came on the market, and a revised technical manual came out in 2002. It is not likely persons who adopted the WMS-III for clinical or research use prior to 2002 are aware of the revised manual, or even if they are have purchased and read it. Perhaps the most fascinating "update" in the revised manual is the publisher's acknowledgment that while the results of confirmatory factor analytic studies of the WMS-III reported in the original (1997) technical manual provided support for a five-factor model (working memory, auditory immediate memory, auditory delayed memory, visual immediate memory, and visual delayed memory) and thus the explicit structure of the test, more recent factor analytic studies failed to find these factors. Studies since the publication of the original technical manual indicated that WMS-III subtests load on only three factors: auditory memory, visual memory, and working memory. The more recent factor analytic studies also failed to provide support for the distinction between immediate and delayed recall. While acknowledging the failure to find a delayed factor, the publisher took the curious position of recommending the continued use of the immediate and delayed indexes on the basis of clinical and theoretical considerations (Tulsky et al., 2002). Unfortunately, although factor analytic studies inform us about the underlying structure of the WMS-III, they fail to inform us regarding how the WMS-III relates to the known neuroanatomy of memory (Kent, 2013).

As noted previously, eight new subtests were added to the WMS-III, and four subtests from the WMS-R were deleted. As a result of the addition of the new subtests, there was a significant increase in time needed to administer the complete battery. The original WMS took 15 minutes to administer. This increased to 30 minutes for the short form and 45–60 minutes for the long form of the WMS-R. For the WMS-III, the administration time increased to 100 minutes if all subtests are given. As the time to administer each revision of the WMS has increased, so has the time to score each revision, especially if the test is hand-scored. Due to the complexity of the WMS-III, computer assisted scoring is almost mandatory, especially if one wishes to compute the statistical significance of various combinations of score differences, such as the differences between the subject's performance on the WAIS-III, the WIAT-II, and the WMS-III.

Scoring of the WMS-III yields 51 separate scores, including 11 primary subtest scores and 8 primary indexes (Ryan, Arb, & Ament, 2000), making clinical interpretation time consuming and needlessly difficult. Transitioning from the WMS-R to the WMS-III is also complicated by the change in the names of the various indexes and their constituents. The major changes will be mentioned.

Previously, the WMS-R had a General Memory Index, which consisted of the immediate recall of two verbally presented subtests and the immediate recall of three visually presented subtests (two via a recognition format and one via a fee recall format). The WMS-III General Memory Index, despite having the same name, is not comparable to the WMS-R General Memory Index. First, it is a measure of *delayed recall*, not immediate recall. Second, it contains a Visual Delayed Index comprised of two subtests, one purportedly assessing the delayed recall of visually presented faces using a recognition procedure, and the second purportedly assessing the delayed recall of the encoding of visually presented complex meaningful information and spatial memory. In addition, the WMS-III contains an Auditory Delayed Index consisting of two subtests that assess the delayed recall of the encoding of two verbally presented paragraphs of meaningful material, and the encoding and delayed recall of a verbal paired associate task. It also includes an Auditory Recognition Delayed Index, which is based on scoring the Logical Memory II subtest via a recognition paradigm by asking the subject a series of yes or no questions about each paragraph, and scoring Verbal Paired Associates II via a recognition paradigm.

The Verbal Memory Index of the WMS-R is basically comparable to the Auditory Immediate Index of the WMS-III. The same subtests comprised each index, except that the subtests for the WMS-III had been slightly updated.

The Visual Memory Index from the WMS-R, which one might assume is similar to the Visual Immediate Index on the WMS-III, is entirely different. The two indexes have no subtests in common.

The Delayed Recall Index on the WMS-R consists of four subtests (Logical Memory II, Verbal Paired Associates II, Visual Paired Associates II, and Visual Reproduction II). The roughly comparable WMS-III index, General Memory, has three sub-indexes, each of which consists of two subtests. Of the six subtests making up General Memory Index, only the Logical Memory II and Verbal Paired Associates II are directly comparable to the subtests contained in the WMS-R Delayed Recall Index. As a result, one cannot make direct comparisons between the WMS-R Delayed Recall Index and the WMS-III General Memory Index.

The Working Memory Index from the WMS-III has no comparable index on the WMS-R. It is comprised of the Letter-Number Sequencing subtest, which is a new subtest. A series of letters and numbers are verbally presented, and the subject is asked to repeat back the series, starting with the numbers first (in order from lowest to highest), and then the letters in order. In addition, it is comprised of another new subtest, Spatial Span. For this subtest, the subject is asked to reproduce a series of tapping sequences on an array of blocks that were first demonstrated by the examiner. It thus appears to be a measure of working memory and procedural learning. Conceptually, one might think that the closest thing to the WMS-III Working Memory Index on the WMS-R is the Attention / Concentration Index. However, the WMS-R Attention/Concentration Index is comprised of the Mental Control, Digit Span, and Visual Memory Span subtests. None of these subtests overlap with the subtests comprising the WMS-III Working Memory Index.

The WMS-III also introduced two new additional subtests: Word List I and II. These subtests are a list-learning task similar in nature to the California Verbal Learning Test. For Word List I, the subject is read List A, which consists of 12 unrelated words, and then asked to recall as many as possible. Four learning trials are presented. The subject is then read List B, which consists of 12 new unrelated words and asked to recall as many as possible. The subject is then asked to recall as many words as possible from List A. This subtest thus measures the recall of a word list after an interference task, or the temporal recall of verbally presented information. Word List II is administered 25–35 minutes after the administration of Word List II, using free recall and recognition paradigms.

Although the names for several of the WMS-III subtests are identical to their WMS-R counterparts, as was the case with the WMS-R and the WMS-I, the publishers of the WMS-III tweaked the content and scoring of several subtests. For specifics regarding these changes, the interested reader can consult the technical manual. Another good reference for researchers and clinicians wishing to use the WMS-III is Tulsky and Ledbetter (2000).

According to Lezak, Howieson, Loring, and Hannay (2004), most WMS-III summary score reliability coefficients run from .82–.93, with the exception of the Auditory Recognition Delay Index, which is .74, and the individual test reliabilities run a bit lower. Compared to the WMS-R, the test appears to be significantly improved in terms of reliability.

According to the test manual, the WMS-III distinguishes between auditory and visual memory based on *the modality of presentation of the subtests*. However, all purported measures of visual memory (such as Faces I and II and Family Pictures II and II) are administered auditorily and visually. Thus, all subtests contain a verbal component, despite the finding of a visual memory factor in factor analytic studies. In other words, the WMS-III contains no pure measures of visual or spatial memory.

The publisher published a variant of the WMS-III called the WMS-III Edition Abbreviated. It was designed to be a fast and reliable survey of auditory and visual memory ability and to provide an estimate of general memory ability when extended memory testing is not appropriate (*The Wechsler Memory Scale-Third Edition-Abbreviated*, n.d.). Information regarding this test can be found in Drozdick et al. (2011). Since this test variant appears to have been little used, as indicted by the few articles in the research literature discussing the scale, it will not be discussed.

Key Points

* Like the WMS-R, the WMS-III is a significant improvement over its predecessor. Many subtests have improved scoring guidelines. The technical manual provides much more information regarding the test's development and some basic information regarding research into memory, working memory, and the neuroanatomy of memory.
* The norming and standardization of the test is greatly improved. The standardization sample ($N = 1,032$, increased to 1,250 with weighting) is based on 1995 U.S. census data and stratified for age, sex, race/ethnicity, educational level, and geographic region.
* People from 16 to 89 years of age are able to be assessed.
* The test manual provides some preliminary information for the use of the test with various clinical groups.
* Compared to the WMS-R, the WMS-III provides more measures based on a recognition paradigm to assist the clinician or researcher in determining if memory failures are due to encoding, consolidation, or retrieval problems.
* As a result of a significant test restructuring, moving from interpreting the WMS-R to interpreting the WMS-III is not easy. Eight new subtests were added to the WMS-III, and four subtests from the WMS-R were eliminated. While the General Memory Index of the WMS-R assesses the immediate recall of verbally and visually presented material, the General Memory Index of the WMS-III purportedly assesses the delayed recall of verbally and visually presented material. The Visual Memory Indexes of the WMS-R and WMS-III contain no identical subtests, making it impossible to compare the two. Although the Attention/Concentration Index from the WMS-R theoretically corresponds to the WMS-III Working Memory

Index, they contain no overlapping subtests, making direct comparisons impossible.

- Factor analytic studies indicate that the WMS-III subtests load on only *three* factors: auditory memory, visual memory, and working memory, and fail to provide support for the distinction between immediate and delayed recall. Like the WMS-R, the WMS-III does not validly assess delayed recall.
- Compared to the WMS-R, the complete WMS-III battery takes much longer to administer and score.

The Wechsler Memory Scale-IV (WMS-IV)

Twelve years elapsed between the publication of the WMS-III and the WMS-IV. During this period, there was an explosion of investigations into the nature of memory and its neuroanatomical substrates, due to the increasing use of imaging procedures like MRIs, SPECT scans, and the like. Neuropsychological investigations of memory functioning also proliferated.

By the time the WMS-IV was published, there had been many critiques of the WMS-III. The factor structure of the WMS-III continued to be debated. Drozdick et al. (2011) reported that factor analytic studies failed to provide support for the Visual Memory Index, calling into question whether the WMS-III measured anything other than immediate verbal memory and working memory. Researchers and clinicians had complained about several of the new WMS-III subtests, like the Faces and Family Pictures subtests (Pearson, n.d.a). The former was not felt to be sensitive to brain damage or dementia, and the latter was not considered to be a measure of visual memory. As a result of concerns about the validity and sensitivity of many of the WMS-III subtests, when the WMS-IV was developed, several WMS-III subtests were either revised or eliminated to better meet clinical needs. For detailed information regarding the rationale underlying the WMS-IV revision, the interested reader may wish to consult Pearson (n.d.a).

Clinicians also complained about the length of time it took to administer the WMS-III. While the complete WMS-R took 45–60 minutes to administer, the complete WMS-III took 100 minutes, almost twice as long. Given the nature of the populations being assessed, the WMS-III was not a patient-friendly instrument. Nor was it clinician friendly, for as the time to administer the WMS-III increased, so did the time it took to score and interpret the battery. In the new era of managed care, spending so much time administering and scoring one instrument was not seen as cost effective by some.

In a response to complaints that the administration time was too long, and noting the WMS-IV had many "optional procedures that are used to answer specific questions," Pearson (n.d.a) indicated that the WMS-IV recognition trials were optional and should only be used where there was a clinical question regarding encoding versus retrieval deficits. The curious reader might wonder: under which situations would one *not* want to know an answer to this critical question? Perhaps for research purposes such testing would not be necessary, but for routine clinical testing, being able to identify the reason underlying memory failures is valuable information for intervention efforts, and such information could impact medication recommendations. Pearson (n.d.a) also took the position of stating that the administration of all WMS-IV subtests would only be needed "for unusual" cases. Thus, a brief WMS-IV can be administered in situations where one only wants to obtain enough information to decide, at a gross level, if the subject at hand is suffering from memory dysfunction or for research purposes where only some subtests or indexes are used as research variables.

Pearson (2011) developed six versions of the WMS-IV. The first is the WMS-IV Adult Battery for ages 16–69, which includes 10 core subtests (Logical Memory I and II, Verbal Paired Associates I and II, Visual Reproduction I and II, Designs I and II, Symbol Span, and Spatial Addition) and an optional Brief Cognitive Status Exam (BCSE). The BCSE is quantifiable and has measures of Orientation, Time Estimation, Mental Control, Clock Drawing, Incidental Recall, Inhibition, and Verbal Production. The BCSE is a significant improvement over the WMS-III Information and Orientation and Mental Control subtests. It provides additional information in a cost-effective manner regarding the subject's functioning that is clinically useful. The Adult Battery takes about 60–80 minutes to administer. The five indexes which can be derived from the battery are the Auditory Memory Index, Visual Memory Index, Visual Working Memory Index, Immediate Memory Index, and the Delayed Memory Index.

The second version of the WMS-IV is the Older Adult Battery for individuals 65–90. It supposedly takes about 30 minutes to administer. It has seven core subtests (Logical Memory I and II, Verbal Paired Associates I and II, Visual Reproduction I and II, Symbol Span), as well as the BCSE, which is optional. Four indexes can be derived from the battery: Auditory Memory, Visual Memory, Immediate Memory, and Delayed Memory. For individuals 65–69, either of the first two batteries can be administered, depending upon the purpose of the exam.

The third version of the WMS-IV is the Logical Memory/Visual Reproduction Battery. It has four subtests: Logical Memory I and II and Visual Reproduction I and II.

The fourth version of the WMS-IV is the Logical Memory/Designs Battery. It also has four subtests: Logical Memory I and II and Designs I and II.

The fifth version of the WMS-IV is the Visual Reproduction/Logos Battery. It contains subtests that make up the Visual Memory, Visual Immediate Memory, and Visual Delayed Memory Indexes.

The sixth version of the WMS-IV is the Logos/Names Battery. According to the publisher, the Logos and Names subtests were developed as possible replacements for the WMS-III Family Pictures subtest (Wechsler, 2009b). It consists of subtests from which the Auditory-Visual Memory, Auditory-Visual Immediate Memory, and Auditory-Visual Delayed Indexes are derived.

These six versions are marketed as the WMS-IV Flexible Approach. According to Pearson (2011), they ". . . enable clinicians to identify memory difficulties by using alternate indexes derived from new subtests configurations." Discussion of the last four batteries is beyond the scope of this book, and the interested reader who wishes more information regarding them is encouraged to contact Pearson. Based on the literature review procedure described in Chapter 1, as of early 2020, there does not appear to be a lot of published research regarding the validity and utility of the last four batteries.

As was the case with its predecessors, nearly all aspects of the WMS-III had been criticized. For instance, some scoring procedures were felt to be too long or too complex, and so, with the WMS-IV, Pearson once again tried to improve the scoring process. The WMS-III normative data were criticized for a lack of screening during the standardization cases for possible cognitive impairment or suboptimal performance by participants in the normative groups, and as a result, malingering detection procedures were developed for the WMS-IV (Pearson, n.d.a). Because of criticisms of WMS-III visual memory subtests, Pearson developed subtests that were believed to assess the functioning of the dorsal and ventral streams of visual processing (the so-called what and where streams). In addition, because the WMS-III had only one visual working memory subtest, an effort was made to remedy this problem.

According to the publisher's website, the four major revision goals of the WMS-IV were (1) to improve its clinical utility; (2) to enhance its user friendliness; (3) to improve the test's psychometric properties; and (4) to update the test structure (Pearson, n.d.b). The WMS-IV technical and interpretive manual also indicates that the test was designed specifically to assess three underlying cognitive constructs: Auditory Memory, Visual Memory, and Visual Working Memory (Wechsler, 2009b). If the complete WMS-IV Adult Battery is administered, one can derive Auditory Memory Index, Visual Memory Index, and Visual Working Memory Index scores, in addition to Immediate Memory Index and Delayed Memory Index scores. It is significant to note, however, that the publisher reports that the latter two indexes are not supported by factor analysis due to the high correlations between immediate and delayed memory. It is likely many users of the WMS-IV are not aware of the lack of validity of these latter two indexes. The Older Adult Battery, being shorter, only has four indexes (see Table 2.5).

The process of preparing for the new revision appears to have followed basically the same path as was used for the development of the WMS-III. The content of the subtests was reviewed to evaluate cultural and gender bias, reliability and validity, score range, floor and ceiling issues, and clinical utility (Drozdick et al., 2011). A survey of the literature on the WMS-III was completed, and customer service data was reviewed. A panel of researchers and experts on memory and assessment were consulted to guide the revision, which was the most radical of all revisions. If clinicians found transitioning from the WMS-R to the WMS-III difficult, the transition from the WMS-III to the WMS-IV was even more challenging. For the WMS-IV, 11 subtests from the WMS-III were eliminated (Information and Orientation, Spatial Span, Mental Control, Faces I and II, Digit Span, Family Pictures I and II, Letter Number Sequencing, and Word List I and II), and four new subtests were developed (Spatial Addition, Symbol Span, Designs I and II). The Brief Cognitive Status Exam was updated. The Logical Memory I and II, Verbal Paired Associates I and II, and Visual Reproduction I and II subtests were retained with modifications.

Tables 2.5 and 2.6 provide information regarding the structure and content of the Older Adult and Adult batteries and the domains assessed. Although the two major versions purport to assess auditory and visual memory, the publisher acknowledges that just as there are no pure measures of verbal memory, there likewise is no pure measure of visual memory (Pearson, n.d.a). Thus, all purported tests of memory measure more than one cognitive function, consistent with what one would expect from our current knowledge regarding brain networks (Anderson, 2014; Banich & Compton, 2018). All cognitive tasks are multiply determined at a neuroanatomical level. The fact that each unique cognitive task draws on multiple brain networks probably helps explain why factor analytic studies of the WMS fail to show "pure" measures of any memory function. It should be noted that that the WMS is not unique in this regard (see Carroll, 1993).

Critique

Clearly the WMS-IV is the most radical and comprehensive revision to date. The publisher developed a multiplicity of battery variations to meet diverse clinical and research needs. The specialty battery for older adults was devised to meet the assessment challenges posed by the graying of America. With the expected increase in the incidence of Alzheimer's and other dementias in the coming years (World Health Center, 2012), the need to evaluate older adults for memory and cognitive problems in a timely and patient-friendly manner is a pressing health care concern.

Many of the structural problems introduced by the WMS-III were corrected. However, in the process of restructuring the WMS-IV, new challenges for clinical interpretation once again were created for the clinician wishing to transition from the WMS-III to the WMS-IV, or comparing WMS-III results with WMS-IV results. For instance, the WMS-III and WMS-IV Immediate Memory Indexes are not identical. While each index consists of four subtests, assuming the Adult Battery is administered, only Logical Memory I and Verbal Paired Associates I are common to each, and these two subtests were slightly revised for the WMS-IV. Thus, although both contain subtests assessing the immediate recall of verbally and visually presented material, they do so in a different manner, so one cannot directly compare the results of the WMS-III Immediate Index with the WMS-IV Immediate Index.

The WMS-III General Memory Index, which is purportedly a measure of the *delayed* recall of verbally and visually presented information through free

Table 2.5 WMS-IV Older Adult Battery (Ages 65–90) Indexes, Related Subtests, and Normative Data

Index	Subtests	Domains Assessed
Auditory Memory (AMI)	Logical Memory I	Encoding and immediate recall of two verbally presented paragraphs consisting of meaningful material
	Logical Memory II	Delayed recall of two verbally presented paragraphs consisting of meaningful material
	Verbal Paired Associates I	Verbal paired associate learning; Encoding and immediate recall of easy and hard associates; Semantic memory
	Verbal Paired Associates II	Verbal paired associate learning; Delayed recall of easy and hard associates; Semantic memory
Visual Memory (VMI)	Visual Reproduction I	Encoding and immediate recall of simple geometric designs; Visual memory; Motor functioning
	Visual Reproduction II	Delayed recall and recognition of simple geometric designs; Visual memory; Motor functioning
	Symbol Span	Visual working memory and procedural learning
Immediate Memory (IMI)	Logical Memory I	Encoding and immediate recall of two verbally presented paragraphs consisting of meaningful material
	Verbal Paired Associates I	Verbal paired associate learning; Encoding and immediate recall of easy and hard associates
	Visual Reproduction I	Encoding and immediate recall of simple geometric designs; Visual memory; Motor functioning
Delayed Memory (DMI)	Logical Memory II	Delayed recall of two verbally presented paragraphs consisting of meaningful material
	Verbal Paired Associates II	Verbal paired associate learning; Delayed recall of easy and hard associates
	Visual Reproduction II	Delayed recall and recognition of simple geometric designs; Visual memory; Motor functioning
Optional Subtests	Brief Cognitive Status Exam	Assesses orientation, time estimation, mental control, clock drawing, incidental recall, inhibition, verbal production
Normative Information	1,400 representative sample based on 2005 Census; Co-normed with WAIS-IV	
Time to Administer	30 minutes	

Source: CVLT-II Trials 1–5 T score can be substituted for Verbal Paired Associates I subtest score; CVLT-2 Long-Delay T-score can be substituted for Verbal Paired Associates II score

Table 2.6 WMS-IV Adult Battery (Ages 16–69) Indexes, Subtests, and Normative Data

Index	Subtests	Domains Assessed
Auditory Memory Index (AMI)	Logical Memory I	Encoding and immediate recall of two verbally presented paragraphs consisting of meaningful material
	Logical Memory II	Delayed recall of two verbally presented paragraphs consisting of meaningful material
	Verbal Paired Associates I	Verbal paired associate learning; Encoding and immediate recall of easy and hard associates; Semantic memory
	Verbal Paired Associates II	Verbal paired associate learning; Delayed recall of easy and hard associates; Semantic memory
Visual Memory Index (VMI)	Designs I	Encoding and immediate recall of visual details and visuospatial locations of geometric designs; Visual memory
	Designs II	Delayed recall and recognition of visual details and visuospatial locations of geometric designs; Visual memory
	Visual Reproduction I	Encoding and immediate recall of simple geometric designs; Visual memory; Motor functioning
	Visual Reproduction II	Delayed recall and recognition of simple geometric designs; Visual memory; Motor functioning
Visual Working Memory Index (VWMI)	Spatial Addition	Visual and spatial working memory
	Symbol Span	Visual working memory and manipulation of visual details
Immediate Memory Index (IMI)	Logical Memory I	Encoding and immediate recall of two verbally presented paragraphs consisting of meaningful material
	Verbal Paired Associates I	Verbal paired associate learning; Encoding and immediate recall of easy and hard associates; Semantic memory
	Designs I	Encoding and immediate recall of visual details and visuospatial locations of geometric designs; Visual memory
	Visual Reproduction I	Encoding and immediate recall of simple geometric designs; Visual memory; Motor functioning
Delayed Memory Index (DMI)	Logical Memory II	Delayed recall of two verbally presented paragraphs consisting of meaningful material
	Verbal Paired Associates II	Verbal paired associate learning; Delayed recall of easy and hard associates
	Designs II	Delayed recall and recognition of visual details and visuospatial locations of geometric designs; Visual memory
	Visual Reproduction II	Delayed recall and recognition of simple geometric designs; Visual memory; Motor functioning
Optional	Brief Cognitive Status Exam	Orientation; Time estimation; Verbal working memory; Incidental recall; Inhibition; Verbal production
Normative Information	1,400 representative sample based on 2005 Census; Co-normed with WAIS-IV	
Time to Administer	65–80 Minutes; 20–30 minutes between immediate and delayed recall	

Source: CVLT-II Trials 1-5 T score can be substituted for Verbal Paired Associates I score; CVLT-II Long-Delay T-score can be substituted for Verbal Paired Associates II score

recall and recognition paradigms, theoretically might correspond to the WMS-IV Delayed Memory Index. However, the former consists of six subtests and the latter of four, and of these subtests, the only overlaps are the Logical Memory II and Verbal Paired Associates II subtests using the free recall paradigm. Therefore, these two indexes are not comparable.

The WMS-III Working Memory Index is comprised of two subtests, one measuring verbal working memory and the other visual working memory. The WMS-IV has only a Visual Working Memory Index, which is comprised of two new subtests (Spatial Addition and Spatial Span). The WMS-IV does not assess verbal working memory, as it was assumed this construct would be assessed through the WAIS-IV or another procedure. For clinicians not administering the WAIS-IV or other measures of verbal working memory or only administering the WMS-IV, the omission of a measure of verbal working memory might be considered by many as a flaw in the instrument, since verbal working memory problems are common in head-injured people, people who have suffered some sort of neurological insult, and people complaining of mild cognitive impairment (Banich & Compton, 2018; Lezak et al., 2012). As a result of the new structure of the WMS-IV, one cannot make direct comparisons between the WMS-III Working Memory Index and the WMS-IV Visual Working Memory Index.

Although the time to administer the complete WMS-IV Adult Battery was decreased to 65–80 minutes compared to 100 minutes for the WMS-III battery, this amount of time is still a challenge for adults who have attention issues, significant cognitive difficulties, and various physical challenges, like chronic pain conditions. Add to this that a significant amount of time must be spent for scoring and test interpretation, the result is a battery that once again is not particularly patient or clinician friendly. The length of time it takes to administer, score, and interpret the complete Adult Battery likely were powerful drivers for Pearson to develop shorter, alternative batteries.

For clinicians having test data from prior versions of the WMS to compare to results from the WMS-IV, making clinical judgments about any "changes" in memory functioning for the subject at hand is hardly straightforward, as noted previously. For clinicians who are new to the field and who have little or no experience with or knowledge of prior versions of the test, making judgments about changes is not only fraught with difficulty but also a potential malpractice landmine. Many new clinicians are not likely aware of how the scoring and content of the core WMS subtests have evolved, and many might naively assume that the Logical Memory subtests contained in the WMS-I, WMS-R, WMS-III, and WMS-IV are directly comparable, when they are not.

As the WMS has evolved, it is remarkable that six of the seven subtests making up the original WMS-I appear in all three revisions, albeit in revised form (see Table 2.7). The persistence of the core subtests validates Wechsler's original beliefs about how memory should be assessed and what should be assessed. Wechsler recognized the importance of screening for disorientation

Table 2.7 The Evolution of the WMS Across Time

WMS-I and II	WMS-R	WMS-III	WMS-IV-Adult Battery
Personal and Current Information Orientation	Information and Orientation	Information and Orientation	Brief Cognitive Status Exam (Includes measures of Orientation and Mental Control)
Mental Control	Mental Control	Mental Control	
Logical Memory	Logical Memory I and II	Logical Memory I and II	Logical Memory I and II
Memory Span	Digit Span	Digit Span	
Visual Reproduction	Visual Reproduction I and II	Visual Reproduction I and II	Visual Reproduction I and II
Associate Learning	Verbal Paired Associates I and II	Verbal Paired Associates I and II	Verbal Paired Associates I and II
		Subtests Unique to Each Revision	
	Visual Memory Span	Spatial Span	Symbol Span
	Visual Paired Associates I and II	Faces I and II	Spatial Addition
	Figural Memory	Family Pictures I and II	Designs I and II
		Letter-Number Sequencing	
		Word Lists I and II	

Source: Shaded subtests represent subtests appearing in all versions, albeit in revised form.

and sensory and cognitive dysfunction that could invalidate the assessment results, and he selected measures to assess for these conditions. He recognized the need to screen for attention and concentration problems, which also could result in invalid conclusions. And he recognized the importance of assessing learning and memory. All versions of the WMS tap these important variables. In addition, all versions of the WMS validate Wechsler's belief about which forms of memory to assess, namely working memory (although he did not call it by that name when the original WMS was developed) and the recall of verbal and visual information. All revisions have attempted to refine many of Wechsler's fundamental beliefs while at the same time incorporate new advances in our knowledge of the nature and structure of memory and the science of psychological assessment. The seven core subtests of the WMS-I can be seen as the "conceptual core" of the WMS. These core subtests align with the findings of Carroll (1993) regarding the structure of learning and memory, as will be discussed in Chapter 5.

Like prior revisions, the WMS-IV is significantly improved in terms of the content and scope of the administration and technical manuals. With each successive revision, scoring guidelines have improved, the standardization and norming procedures have advanced, and efforts have been made to link each revision with advances in our understanding of memory processes. In addition, the last two revisions have made an effort to assess incomplete effort and possible malingering, consistent with current best practice guidelines (Bowden, 2017a; Chafetz et al., 2015). Unfortunately, effort subtests or embedded effort measures are not included in the standard WMS-IV battery, although they are available through Advanced Clinical Solutions (Pearson, 2009a, 2019). Not including such materials as a standard part of the WMS-IV test kit is an added cost to test consumers and a shortcoming of the Adult and Older Adult Batteries.

The WMS-IV Adult Battery introduces new indexes. The *Auditory Memory Index* is comprised of four subtests and is a measure of the immediate *and* delayed recall of verbally presented material consisting of paragraphs and easy and hard associates. The *Visual Memory Index* is comprised of four subtests and is a measure of the immediate recall and delayed recall and recognition of visually presented information. The *Visual Working Memory Index* is comprised on two new subtests (Spatial Span and Symbol Span) and assesses visual working memory. The *Immediate Memory Index* is comprised of four subtests, two of which measure the immediate recall of verbally presented material and two of which measure the immediate recall of visually presented material. The *Delayed Memory Index* is also comprised of four subtests. One assesses the delayed recall of two verbally presented paragraphs of meaningful material. The second assesses the delayed recall of easy and hard associates. The third assesses the delayed recall and recognition of visual details and visuospatial locations of geometric designs. The fourth assesses the delayed recall and recognition of simple geometric designs, visual memory, and motor functioning. As noted earlier, the WMS-IV also has an optional Brief Cognitive Status Exam, which is a quantifiable mental status exam.

Although one can compare the Immediate Memory Index with the Delayed Memory Index, since they contain the same four subtests in immediate and delayed forms, each index is a mixture of verbally and visually presented material. If there is a significant difference between the two, unfortunately it could be due to problems with the recall of verbally or visually presented information, a combination of these two, or difficulties with consolidation, attention, or other issues. Although most users of the WMS-IV likely use the computer assisted scoring and interpretive program, a review of the sample interpretative report provided by Pearson on their website (Pearson, 2009b) indicates that even with this assistance, interpretation is not straightforward or easy. As with the WMS-III scoring assistant, the WMS-IV scoring assistant allows the user to compute a variety of scores and an almost overwhelming number of statistical comparisons, depending on how much information from various tests are entered into the program. Many examiners will find the process of clinically interpreting significant differences between various subtests and indexes tiring and time-consuming. A good guide to test and score interpretation is provided by Drozdick et al. (2011). All in all, however, the WMS-IV technical and interpretive manual (Wechsler, 2009a) is greatly improved compared to manuals and guides accompanying the WMS-III.

Like the two prior revisions of the WMS, the WMS-IV was designed to assess delayed recall. And like its predecessors, it failed. The WMS-IV technical manual (Wechsler, 2009b) presents a confirmatory factor analysis of the WMS-IV that supports an a priori theoretical model of Visual Memory (Designs II and Visual Reproduction II subtests), Visual Working Memory (Symbol Span and Spatial Addition subtests), and Auditory Memory (Logical Memory II and Verbal Paired Associates II subtests). In addition, a two-factor model of Visual Memory (Designs II, Visual Reproduction II, Symbol Span, and Spatial Addition subtests) and Auditory Memory (Logical Memory II and Verbal Paired Associates II subtests) was also supported. A later study by Hoelzle, Nelson, and Smith (2011), which compared the dimensional structures of the WMS-III and WMS-IV, using a methodology similar to that which was applied to the normative data presented in the WMS-IV technical manual, found an invariant two-factor model consisting of auditory learning/memory and visual attention/memory. Hoelzle et al.'s (2011) results did not support the three-factor solution described by Wechsler (2009b). A study by Pauls, Petermann, and Lepach (2013) examined the factor structure and measurement invariance of the WMS-IV in a group of clinically depressed individuals and matched controls. Using confirmatory factor analysis, the authors found a three-factor solution consisting of auditory memory, visual memory, and visual working memory. It should be noted that once again no immediate versus delayed factors were identified. The authors concluded that despite the finding of visual working memory as a separate factor, possible differences in visual working memory functions between healthy and depressed individuals could restrict comparisons of the WMS-IV Working Memory Index. Surprisingly, at the time this book was being written (mid-2018 through late 2019), an updated literature search via the APA PsychNet revealed very few studies of the factor structure of the WMS-IV, and the few that were reported, like Holdnack, Zhou, Larrabee, Millis, and Salthouse (2011), also appear to support a two- or three-factor solution with separate immediate and delayed factors failing to emerge in the analysis. It is likely that the debate regarding the factor structure of the WMS-IV and prior revisions will continue for some time. In regard to the upcoming WMS-V, assuming the new revision attempts to assess delayed recall, unless it uses a significantly longer time delay between the administration of the immediate and delayed subtests than was used in prior revisions, assuming the past is a predictor of the future, efforts to validly assess delayed recall appear doomed.

It is significant to note that the WMS-IV (Wechsler, 2009b) does not appear to directly define the meaning of delayed recall as it pertains to the Immediate and Delayed Indexes. Rather, the concept of delayed recall is described operationally as the time between the administration of the immediate and delayed recall subtests. Other than noting that factor analytic studies fail to find psychometric support for the Delayed Recall Index, it is unclear what this index measures, if anything, although Kent (2017) has suggested delayed recall may actually be assessing a form of intermediate memory. The inclusion of delayed recall scores in the WMS-IV appears to have occurred because it was felt by the publisher (Wechsler, 2009b, p. 20) that "the differentiation of immediate versus delayed memory is an important clinical tool." In the section of the interpretive manual that describes the performance of various clinical groups on the WMS-IV, Wechsler cites several studies where this differentiation was clinically useful. In regard to the composition of the Delayed Recall Index, the publisher also notes that Tulsky, Chelune, and Price (2004) had reported that the usefulness of the WMS-III General Memory Index was reduced by the inclusion of recognition tasks. As a result, the publisher developed a delayed memory index that only uses free recall conditions.

One of the innovations of the WMS-IV was to present the use of contrast scores. According to the publisher, a contrast score adjusts a particular score based on the performance on another relevant measure. The publisher (Wechsler, 2009b, p. 41) further states, "In the WMS-IV, contrast scores determine the examinee's relative ability to perform a task, controlling for the examinee's ability on a component skill that is required to perform the task." Concerning the comparison between Immediate Memory Index (IMI) and Delayed Memory Index (DMI) scores, the Delayed Memory Index Contrast Scaled Score is provided to determine if the DMI score is higher or lower than expected based on an examinee's performance on the IMI. According to the publisher, low scores indicate the examinee's delayed memory performance is low compared to their immediate memory performance, and high scores indicate better than expected delayed memory. In this particular situation, the examinee's performance on immediate measures is used to evaluate the examinee's performance on delayed measures. In other words, the contrast scaled score represents how good the delayed memory score is when compared to individuals with a similar level of immediate memory or initial encoding (Wechsler, 2009b). The contrast score is, in other words, an overall indicator of forgetting and consolidation.

Although the standardization of the WMS-IV appears quite good, one oddity deserves to be mentioned. The publisher reports that the normative sample was stratified according to five educational levels: 0–8 years of education (never attended high school); 9–11 years (attended but did not graduate from high school); 12 years (high school graduate or equivalent); 13–15 years (some college); and 16 or more years (college degree or further education). The publisher also notes that for 16- to 19-year-olds, information on parent education was obtained using a question on the consent form that asked the parent or examinee to specify the highest grade completed by each parent living in the home, and for examinees residing with both parents, the average of the two education levels was used. It is not clear why the average of the examinee's parental education was used, and not the amount of education completed by 16- to 19-year-olds.

Key Points

- The primary goals of the new revision were to expand the clinical utility of the test, enhance its user friendliness, improve its psychometric properties, and update the test structure (Pearson, n.d.a, b). By most reasonable standards, Pearson accomplished these goals. The test is better normed, and during the standardization process, the publisher took steps to screen for cognitive impairment and suboptimal performance. In addition, no weighting procedures are used, as was the case for the WMS-III. Several subtests have been revised and scoring procedures improved.
- As with all prior revisions, the manifest structure of the WMS-IV changed significantly, making it very difficult to compare WMS-IV test results with prior revisions of the WMS.
- The publisher developed six different batteries, each designed for a different purpose. Two batteries were specifically designed to assess older adults, and four special batteries were developed to address specific clinical and research needs. Unfortunately, there appears to be little published research regarding the reliability and validity of the four special batteries.
- The publisher did a reasonably good job of providing information regarding how various clinical groups performed on the instrument.
- The psychometric properties of the basic battery are improved, and information is presented on the scale's reliability and validity.
- The publisher made improvements in assessing memory functions using a recognition paradigm, so clinicians and researchers can determine whether retrieval issues are due to encoding or retrieval problems.
- The publisher introduced the use of contrast scores, which are clinically useful.
- The WMS-IV does not assess verbal working memory.
- Like all revisions of the WMS, the WMS-IV does not validly assess delayed recall. In addition, the publisher does not appear to objectively define what "delayed recall" measures. Clinicians and researchers might naively assume WMS-IV measures of delayed recall are measures of long-term retention or long-term memory. The WMS-IV only assesses delayed recall after a 20–30-minute period.
- Current research suggests the WMS-IV assesses three factors: auditory memory, visual memory, and visual working memory. Factor analytic studies do not support all of the manifest structure of the WMS-IV.
- The basic adult test battery takes approximately 80 minutes to administer. While taking less time to administer than its predecessor, it still is not user or clinician friendly.
- The "core subtests" of the WMS have persisted for three quarters of a century.

It has been said that the more things change, the more they stay the same. One could say that this is certainly true of the core of the WMS. Although the WMS has evolved in the past 75 years, not all changes have been improvements. Critiques of the present revision are eerily similar to the major critiques of the original version of the test, namely that the content was too focused on assessing verbal memory and the test did not assess delayed recall.

In the next chapter, we will describe the evolution of the core subtests as presented in Table 2.7. It should come as little surprise to the seasoned clinician that three of these subtests have been used repeatedly to assess the memory function of several clinical groups.

Chapter 3

The Evolution of the Core Subtests

In Chapter 2, it was noted that there has been a core of subtests that appear in (nearly) all versions of the WMS. These core subtests, which consist of the original seven subtests comprising the WMS-I and WMS-II, were referred to as the "conceptual core." As noted in Chapter 2, in some instances, a particular subtest was part of the standard battery; in others, the subtest was deemed "optional." For example, the Visual Reproduction subtest was a standard subtest in the WMS-I and II and the WMS-R, was designated as "optional" for the WMS-III, and once again became a standard subtest in the WMS-IV Adult and Older Adult Batteries. The purpose of this chapter is to briefly describe how the core subtests have evolved in content and administration across time. For specifics regarding changes in the scoring procedures, please consult the pertinent administration and technical manuals.

The Personal and Current Information and Orientation Subtests

Table 3.1 provides information on the Personal and Current Information and Orientation subtests across all WMS versions.

It may seem odd to the experienced assessor that the WMS-I contains questions typically asked as part of the traditional mental status exam. When the WMS was published, the field of clinical psychology was still emerging and the profession of clinical neuropsychology nonexistent. There were few clinical psychologists in the U.S., and state licensing laws were in their infancy. Psychologists often performed psychological testing under the direction of a psychiatrist, especially in hospital settings. The independent practice of psychology was a rarity.

Prior to developing the WMS, David Wechsler had considerable experience with psychological testing. In addition to conducting testing for his master's thesis, Wechsler worked with the U.S. Army during World War I to develop tests for new draftees, which may explain why the WMS was mentioned in a 1946 article describing the role of the psychologist in the Army (Patterson, 1946).

Table 3.1 The Personal and Current Information and Orientation subtests

Version	Subtest Name	Content and Administration
I	Personal and Current Information	Subject asked age, birthdate, to name the president, prior presidents, their governor, and city's mayor
	Orientation	Subject asked date, name of the place they live in, and city
Rev	Information and Orientation	Content of WMS-I Personal and Current Information and Orientation subtests merged; additional questions asked about handedness, hearing difficulty, visual acuity, color-blindness
III	Information and Orientation	Nearly identical content to above, mild rewording of questions
IV	Brief Cognitive Status Exam (BCSE)	Subject evaluated regarding Orientation, Time Estimation, Clock Drawing, Incidental Recall, and Verbal Production; The BCSE results are quantifiable with norms provided for interpretation

As a result of his vast clinical experience and research of retention in Korsakoff psychosis, Wechsler was aware of the need to assess the examinee's orientation for person, place, and time and the value of screening for language, sensory, and cognitive problems. By providing specific mental status questions about the person's history, awareness of surroundings and orientation, and sensory functioning, Wechsler was standardizing the assessment process to ensure the validity of the assessment. It is important to remember that Wechsler specifically designed the WMS to be a brief screening instrument for military personnel who may have sustained some sort of head trauma. While the content of the WMS-I Personal and Current Information and Orientation subtests looks crude by today's standards, in the late 30s and early 40s, it reflected the state of the art. Over the course of revising the instrument, these subtests have become increasingly sophisticated. The most recent version of the original tests, the Brief Cognitive Status Exam, allows the examiner to quantify the results of the exam and interpret them based on age and education norms, which is a major improvement over previous versions of this subtest.

The Personal and Current Information and Orientation subtests (and their variants) have rarely been used by themselves in research studies to assess the impact of open or closed head injury on memory, probably because they were designed to be screening subtests. Nonetheless, Howard (1950) found the Personal and Current Information subtest discriminated between a group of people with paresis and controls, and Altepeter, Adams, Buchanan, and Buck (1990) reported that the Personal and Current Information subtest successfully discriminated between patients with and without closed head injury. Impairment on the former subtest can be due to disorientation to person and impairment in recent and long-term episodic memory. Impairment on the latter may be due to disorientation to time and place.

The Memory Span/Digit Span Subtest

As can be seen from Table 3.2, the content of Memory Span/Digit Span slightly changed with each revision. The administration, however, remained the same. The Digit Span subtest was eliminated from the WMS-IV after a decision was made to only assess visual working memory for that revision.

Digit Span remained part of the WAIS-IV, however, and it was assumed that many psychologists administered this test to allow for the calculation of IQ and memory score differences using the computer assisted scoring program. So even though the Digit Span subtest did not appear in the WMS-IV, the publishers of the WMS-IV and WAIS-IV were aware of the value of the Digit Span subtest.

In this writer's opinion, it is unfortunate that Digit Span is not part of the WMS-IV. If the WAIS-IV is not administered, and Digit Span measures are obtained from tests other than the WAIS-IV, a problem arises in comparing the test results with the Visual Memory Span Index because these measures

Table 3.2 The Evolution of the Memory Span Subtests

Version	Subtest Name	Content and Administration
I	Memory Span	Examiner reads a series of digits and asks subject to say digits in same order; Next examiner reads a series of digits and asks subject to repeat them in reverse order; Maximum 8 digits forward, 7 digits backwards; MS-F begins with 4 digits; MS-B begins with 3 digits; Discontinue after 2 failures of both trials of any item
Rev	Digit Span	Examiner reads a series of digits and asks subject to say digits in same order; Next examiner reads a series of digits and asks subject to repeat them in reverse order; Maximum 8 digits forward, 7 digits backwards; DS-F begins with 3 digits; DS-B begins with 2 digits; Discontinue after 2 failures of both trials of any item
III	Digit Span Note: Subtest optional	Examiner reads a series of 7 digits and asks subject to say digits in same order; Next examiner reads a series of 7 digits and asks subject to repeat them in reverse order. Maximum 9 digits forward, 8 digits backwards; DS-F begins with 2 digits; DS-B begins with 2 digits; Discontinue after 2 failures of both trials of any item
IV	Digit Span not present	

were not co-normed. If the WMS-IV was the only test of memory administered, then the examiner did not have this information to assess the nature of
the patient's complaints. Verbal short-term and working memory problems are
characteristic of a number of clinical conditions and very common clinical
complaints in individuals suffering from a variety of neurological disorders,
including head trauma, various dementing conditions, and the like.

The Mental Control Subtest

As noted earlier, the original Mental Control subtest was devised as a screening
measure. Wechsler and Stone (1973, pp. 5–6) specifically stated its primary
value was "in cases of organic brain disease that are not too far gone but show
deficits which would not be made evident by simple rote memory tests." By
"simple rote memory tests," Wechsler and Stone were specifically referring
to the WMS Memory Span test, which was a briefer version of the Digit Span
test developed for the WBIS. Wechsler (1939) noted that Digit Span tests had
long been used by psychiatrists as a test of retentiveness. He also observed
that Digit Span tests, whether digits forward or backward, generally correlated
poorly with intelligence tests, and that Digit Span was a poor measure of Spearman's "g." Based on his studies of intellectual functioning, Wechsler found low
scores on Digit Span Backwards were good measures of intelligence at lower
levels, however, and often a sign of being intellectually challenged. While noting that Digit Span test results are frequently associated with attention deficits,
he considered low Digit Span Backwards scores as indicative of problems with
what we currently call verbal working memory. Table 3.3 presents information
on how the Mental Control subtest has evolved across revisions.

Table 3.3 The Mental Control Subtests

Version	Subtest Name	Content and Administration
I	Mental Control	Subject asked to count backward from 20 to 1, 10-second time limit; Subject asked to say alphabet as fast as s/he can, 30-second time limit; Subject asked to count by threes beginning with 1, as quickly as s/he can, is stopped when reaches 40, 45-second time limit
Rev	Mental Control	Same as above, except counting backwards has 30-second time limit
III	Mental Control	Subject asked to count from 1 to 20; say the alphabet, say the months of year, count from 20 to 1; say days of week backwards, say months of year backwards, say days of week
IV	In Brief Cognitive Status Exam	Subject asked to count backwards from 20 to1; Subject asked to say the months of the year backwards

The Logical Memory Subtest

The Logical Memory subtest has been a constant in all versions of the WMS. Like other "core" WMS tests, it has undergone constant refinement. In terms of content, versions of Story A have appeared in all revisions. The WMS-R introduced a delayed recall version of this subtest, and the scoring was made more objective. As can be seen from Table 3.4, the content of the two paragraphs has changed for each revision, and the way the Logical Memory I and II subtests are administered has changed across revisions. The WMS-III introduced cuing procedures if the subject could not voluntarily recall the paragraphs, and recognition trials. In addition, the WMS-III introduced thematic scoring procedures for Logical Memory I and II.

Table 3.4 The Logical Memory Subtests

Version	Subtest	Content	Administration
I	Logical Memory	Story A and B	After reading each story to subject, subject asked to recall content
Rev	Logical Memory I	Story A slightly revised; New Story B	After reading each story to subject, subject asked to recall content
	Logical Memory II	Same as LM I	After 30 minutes, subject asked to recall Stories A and B
III	Logical Memory I	Story A of WMS-Rev slightly revised; Story B from WMS-Rev replaced with new story	After reading each story, subject asked to recall content
	Logical Memory II	Same as LM I	Recall trial: After 25–35 minutes, subject asked to recall Story A and B; If subject can't remember stories, a cue is given; Recognition trial: Subject asked 15 yes or no questions about Story A, then 15 yes or no questions about Story B
IV	Logical Memory I	New Story A of WMS-III replaced with new story; Story B is revision of WMS-III Story A	Subject read Story A twice and asked to recall story; Subject read Story B once and asked to recall story
	Logical Memory II	Same as LM I	Recall trial: After 20–30 minutes, subject asked to recall Story A, then Story B; cue given if subject can't remember either story; Recognition trial: Subject asked 8 yes or no questions regarding Story A, and 15 yes or no questions regarding story B

The Logical Memory subtests are among the most researched WMS core components. They have been the focus of factor analytic studies and used to investigate neurological disorders like brain lesions (Cooper, Numan, Crosson, & Velozo, 1989); temporal lobe epilepsy (Barr, 1997; Soble et al., 2016; Wilde et al., 2003); and the lateralization of brain function. Good performance on Logical Memory subtests correlates with verbal comprehension, healthy aging, and a variety of other psychological factors that will be discussed later in this book. Impairment on this subtest has been observed in people with bipolar disorder (Cankorur, Demirel, & Atbasoglu, 2017) and other psychiatric conditions. Performance on Logical Memory has also been shown to have good ecological validity, as demonstrated by studies of older people with memory problems (Crook, Youngjohn, Larrabee, & Salama, 1992). The Logical Memory subtest has been popular with clinicians and researchers alike over the years, and it is expected to appear in the next WMS revision, due to the large amount of research about this subtest.

The Visual Reproduction Subtest

Table 3.5 presents the evolution of the Visual Reproduction subtest. The WMS-R introduced a delayed recall version of Visual Reproduction and a new administration procedure. The WMS-III introduced recognition procedures into the Visual Reproduction subtest. The WMS-IV introduced a copy procedure to assess for dysgraphia. With each revision of the WMS have come new and refined scoring procedures. Compared to the scoring procedures included with the WMS-I, the current procedures are far more objective and clinically useful. The WMS-IV administration manual has excellent guidelines that help the clinician learn to score the Visual Reproduction subtests in a reliable and valid manner.

Table 3.5 The Visual Reproduction Subtests

Version	Subtest	Content	Administration
I	Visual Reproduction	3 cards: Cards A and B each have I design Card C has 2 designs	Cards A and B: Subject shown each card for 10 seconds, design removed, subject asked to draw it from memory Card C: Subject told card has 2 designs on it and is harder, shown card for 10 seconds, card removed, subject asked to draw from memory

Version	Subtest	Content	Administration
Rev	Visual Reproduction I	4 cards; Card A same as WMS-I Card A; Card B new design; Card C same as WMS-I Card B; Card D new design	Cards A, B, C presented one at a time, for 10 seconds, subject asked to draw each design from memory; Subject told Card D has 2 designs, to look at each design carefully, card removed after 10 seconds and subject asked to draw each design from memory
	Visual Reproduction II	See above	45–55 minutes after Visual Reproduction I, subject asked to draw the designs on Cards A-D from memory
III	Visual Reproduction I	5 designs: Card A new design; Cards B–D same designs as WMS-R Cards A–C respectively; Card E modification of designs from WMS-I	Series of 5 designs shown, one at a time, for 10 seconds each, and subject asked to draw design from memory
	Visual Reproduction II	See above	1st recall: Subject asked to draw 5 designs presented in Visual Reproduction I from memory 2nd recognition: Subject shown a series of 48 designs, one at a time, and asked to identify designs from Visual Reproduction I 3rd copy: Subject asked to copy designs while looking at them 4th discrimination: Subject asked to choose which of 6 designs on page matches the target design at the top of the page
IV	Visual Reproduction I	5 designs; Items 1–3 contain 1 design; Items 4–5 contain 2 designs, same designs as WMS-III	Series of 5 designs shown, one at a time, for 10 seconds each, and subject asked to draw design from memory
	Visual Reproduction II	See above	For recall trial: Subject asked to draw 5 designs presented in Visual Reproduction I from memory; For recognition trial: Subject asked to choose which of 6 designs on a page match the original design; For copy trial: Subject asked to draw designs while looking at them

Table 3.6 The Associate Learning/Verbal Paired Associates Subtests

Version	Subtest	Content	Administration
WMS-I and II	Associate Learning	10 word pairs 6 easy; 4 hard	3 trials; 1st trial subject read 10 word pairs, then first word of pair read, and subject asked to recall correct "associate"; 2nd and 3rd trials same as 1st
WMS-R	Verbal Paired Associates I	8 word pairs from WMS; 4 easy; 4 hard; Note: 2 easy word pairs from WMS eliminated	Up to 6 recall trials given to learn to criterion of 1 perfect repetition; examiner reads group of 8 word pairs, then reads the 1st word of each pair, and subject asked to recall 2nd word from memory
	Verbal Paired Associates II	8 words (1st word of 8 pairs presented in Verbal Paired Associates I)	1 recall trial after 30-minute delay; examiner reads 1st word pair, subject is to respond with correct associate
WMS-III	Verbal Paired Associates I	8 entirely new word pairs, all high imagery, unrelated (hard) words	4 trials; Examiner reads 8 word pairs, then reads 1st word of each pair, and subject is to recall 2nd word from memory
	Verbal Paired Associates II	8 words (1st word of 8 pairs presented in Verbal Paired Associates I) for free recall trial 24 word pairs for recognition trial	1 recall trial after 25–35 minute delay: Examiner reads 1st word pair, subject is to respond with correct associate 1 recognition trial: Examiner reads 24 word pairs, one pair at a time; subject asked to respond yes if the word pair is one s/he was asked to remember
WMS-IV	Verbal Paired Associates I	10 entirely new word pairs; 4 easy; 6 hard	4 recall trials; examiner reads 10 word pairs, then reads 1st word of each pair, and subject is to recall 2nd word from memory
	Verbal Paired Associates II	10 words (1st word of each 10 pairs presented in Verbal Paired Associates I) Recognition trial: 30 word pairs	1 recall trial after 25–35 minute delay: Examiner reads 1st word pair, subject is to respond with correct associate 1 recognition trial: Examiner reads 24 word pairs, 1 pair at a time, and subject to respond yes if the word pair is one s/he was asked to remember

The Associate Learning/Verbal Paired Associates Subtest

As can be seen from Table 3.6, the Associate Learning/Verbal Associates subtests have also been refined over time. Delayed recall procedures were added with the WMS-R. The WMS-III introduced recognition procedures. In addition, the number of trials and content of the subtests have slightly changed with each revision.

Summary

In summary, six of the seven subtests which comprised the WMS-I and II have appeared in all revisions, sometimes as standard subtests, and sometimes as optional subtests. And Digit Span is part of the WMS-I and II, WMS-R and WMS-III. Although the Digit Span subtest is not a core subtest of the WMS-IV because the publisher chose to assess only visual working memory, it was assumed by Pearson that many clinicians would be administering the WAIS-IV, thus gaining access to the Digit Span subtest for assessment purposes. Since the WMS-IV computer scoring program allows for the entering of data from the WAIS-IV, clinicians have access to the information derived from Digit Span for assessment purposes.

In terms of frequency of usage, the Logical Memory, Visual Reproduction, and Verbal Paired Associates have been the most used WMS subtests for clinical and research purposes. The popularity of these subtests was recognized by the Pearson in the most recent revision of the WMS. Several special purpose batteries were devised that used various combinations of these subtests. In addition, they are part of the standard Adult and Older Adult Batteries.

Chapter 4

Selected Factor Analytic Studies of the Wechsler Memory Scales

Recurrent Themes

In this chapter, we will review some factor analytic studies of each version of the WMS. Consistent with the intent of this book, the review will be selective in nature, although representative of the major studies that have been completed.

Studies of the WMS

Kear-Colwell (1973) factor analyzed the WMS using 250 patients referred for testing for organicity. The results of the study yielded three primary factors: learning and recall of fairly complex novel material (Logical Memory, Visual Reproduction, and Associate Learning), attention and concentration (Mental Control and Memory Span), and orientation and information (Personal and Current Information and Orientation).

In a review of the literature, Arbit and Zagar (1979) reported that a factor analytic study of 622 patients ranging from 15 to 87 by Davis and Swenson (1970) yielded two factors: memory and freedom from distractibility. They also noted that in a sample of persons aged 16 to 72, Dujovne and Levy (1971) found three factors: general retentiveness, simple learning, and associational flexibility. Observing that prior factor analytic studies of the WMS had found contradictory results because of the confounding of subject age and sex, Arbit and Zagar (1979) studied the effects of age structure and sex on the factor structure of the WMS. Examining males and females in three age groups (13–39, 40–59, and 60–88), the authors found a two-factor structure of general retentiveness and memory for the total male and female samples. Although males and females had the same factor structure at the 13–39 and 40–59 age groupings, the two-factor structure did not emerge for females or males in the 60–88 age range, suggesting the structure of memory as assessed by the WMS changed with aging.

Noting that memory functioning commonly declines with age, Zagar, Arbit, Stuckey, and Wengel (1984) investigated changes in memory functioning with age as assessed by the WMS-I. Examining data from 1,264 males and 1,141 females ranging in age from 20 to 79 using theoretical, psychometric, and statistical criteria, the authors found a one-factor solution across all age groups, which they called "memory."

In a paper discussing the clinical assessment of memory, Lawrence (1984) presented a critique of the WMS. She noted that past studies of the WMS that looked at both normal and neurologically impaired individuals had yielded only two or three factors. Lawrence cautioned that a potentially severe problem in the interpretation of results from most memory tests, including the WMS, is that they are highly correlated with IQ in both normal and brain-damaged subjects. Lawrence also discussed the results of a factor analytic study by Larrabee, Kane, and Schuck (1983), which evaluated the performance of patients with suspected neurological impairment on the WMS and WAIS. The authors found a substantial overlap between the two scales. Larrabee et al. (1983) additionally found that Visual Reproduction loaded on the visuospatial components of the WAIS, and that only the Associate Learning and Logical Memory subtests appeared to be "pure memory" items.

Ernst et al. (1986) reported the results of a factor analysis of the WMS with 30-minute delayed recall measures of the Logical Memory, Visual Reproduction, and the Associate Learning subtests. The authors noted that Prigatano (1978) and Skillbeck and Woods (1980) had concluded that the general pattern of results from the factor analysis of the WMS yielded a three-factor solution (learning/recall, attention/concentration, and information/orientation), and that the factor structure found depended upon the particular variables included in the analysis. The results of the Ernst et al. (1986) analysis yielded a four-factor solution; two of the major factors were attention/concentration and repetition learning; the other two factors were considered minor and of trivial importance. Their findings were consistent with the findings of Larrabee et al. (1983), who found that delayed recall was a better measure of memory than immediate recall in the Visual Reproduction subtest. The results of their analysis also revealed that the "easy" and "hard" associates on the Associate Learning subtest loaded on the same factor, and suggested that the Associate Learning subtest may be a better measure of verbal learning/recall than Logical Memory, because the latter appears to be related to attention and concentration abilities.

DesRosiers and Ivison (1988) also examined the nature of the Associate Learning subtest from the WMS-I and II by reviewing the performance of 500 general medical patients across five 10-year age groups (ranging from 20 to 69) on the WMS-I and 600 general medical patients across six 10-year age groups (ranging from 20 to 79) on the WMS-II. The general medical patients were hospitalized for other than neuropsychiatric reasons. The results of their study revealed strong age effects on both versions of the Associate Learning and more marked sex effects on the WMS-II Associate Learning subtest. In addition, the authors found that while the WMS-I Associate Learning subtest yielded a three-factor solution, which fell on a continuum from easy to hard, the WMS-II Associate Learning subtest yielded a dichotomous two-factor (easy-hard) solution.

Heilbronner, Buck, and Adams (1989) conducted two factor analytic studies of several verbal and nonverbal clinical memory tests, including Russell's (1975) version of the WMS, the WMS-I MQ, and the Associate Learning subtest. One factor analytic study included immediate recall measures, and the second included delayed recall measures. Using a sample of 119 patients referred for evaluation, they found the Visual Reproduction I and II subtests loaded on a factor of nonverbal memory tests. In regard to Logical Memory I and II and Associate Learning subtests, all loaded on a verbal learning and memory factor. The authors observed that Logical Memory II appeared to be a purer measure of verbal memory than Logical Memory I.

Larrabee, Trahan, and Curtiss (1992) examined the construct validity of the Continuous Visual Memory Test by comparing the performance of 92 healthy adults aged 18 to 61 on this test with other attention and memory measures, including the WMS-I Visual Reproduction test along with a 30 minute delayed recall version of the subtest. The Visual Reproduction immediate recall subtest was found to load on verbal intellectual ability and visual/nonverbal cognitive ability and verbal memory. The Visual Reproduction delayed recall subtest also loaded verbal intellectual ability and a visual/nonverbal cognitive dimension, as well as visual memory.

Compton, Sherer, and Adams (1992) completed a factor analysis of subtests from the WMS-I (Digit Span, the Associate Learning four hard word pairs), Russell's (1975) revision, and the Warrington Recognition Memory Test. These tests were completed by 156 persons referred to the University of Oklahoma Health Science Neuropsychology Laboratory for psychological or neuropsychological assessment. The WMS Associate Learning and Logical Memory I and II subtests loaded on a verbal memory factor. Visual Reproduction I and II loaded on a visual memory factor, and the Digit Span subtest loaded on an attention factor.

Boone, Pontón, Gorsuch, González, and Miller (1998) completed a factor analysis of four measures of prefrontal lobe functioning: 250 subjects completed a two-hour test battery that included the WMS-I Logical Memory and Visual Reproduction subtests. Neither WMS subtest loaded on any measure of frontal lobe functioning in this study.

Summary

As can be seen from the previous section, various studies have suggested the original WMS assesses either two (general retentiveness and learning) or three factors (learning and immediate recall, attention and concentration, and verbal recall), depending on the variables analyzed. None of these findings, except Compton et al. (1992), indicates that the Visual Reproduction subtest reliably assesses visual memory. Based on a review of the literature, Erickson and Scott (1977) have suggested the WMS-I should be scored on the basis of the factors suggested by Kear-Colwell (1973). Presumably, test interpretation should also be based on those factors. There is a hint from these studies that the delayed version of any given subtest appears to be a better measure of the domain of interest (e.g., Logical Memory, Verbal Paired Associates, etc.) than the immediate version. The results of the research cited also suggest that immediate versions might be tapping attentional or short-term memory factors rather than "memory" per se.

Studies of the WMS-R

When the WMS was revised, two of the major goals of the revision were to assess delayed recall and visual memory. As noted previously, the WMS had been criticized for primarily being a measure of the immediate recall of verbally presented information. The revision had norms stratified at nine age levels; improved scoring; new index scores in place of a global MQ; subtests purportedly assessing visual and spatial recall; and new purported measures of delayed recall. As noted earlier, however, Wechsler (1987) reported that a factor analysis of the WMS-R yielded only two factors: general memory and learning, and attention and concentration.

Bornstein and Chelune (1989) examined the factor structure of the WMS-R in relation to age and educational level in a large group ($N = 434$) of patients referred for examination at two large medical centers. The authors subjected the subtest scores to a series of principal components analysis of variance. A separate set of analyses were performed that included WAIS-R Verbal IQ and Performance IQ scores. The authors found that the inclusion of IQ scores influenced the factor structure across age groups. With the inclusion of IQ scores, a three-factor solution was obtained for all age groups (less than 39 years of age, 40–55 years of age, and greater than or equal to 56 years of age). For the study, the subjects were assigned to three groups based on level of education (less than 12 years, 12 years, and more than 12 years). For subjects with less than 12 years of education, a two-factor solution accounted for 60.4% of the variance. An additional weak factor was also found. For subjects with 12 years of education, a two-factor solution was also found, which accounted for 63.4% of the variance. For subjects with more than 12 years of education, a three-factor solution was found that accounted for 77% of the variance. The three factors were verbal memory, nonverbal memory, and attention. The authors failed to find a delayed recall factor.

Leonberger, Nicks, Larrabee, and Goldfader (1992) examined the factor structure of the WMS-R along with the Halstead-Reitan Neuropsychological Test Battery of 237 patients evaluated at a large Midwestern medical center. The immediate and delayed recall subtest scores were analyzed separately to avoid the clustering of variables due to the similarity of methods. The results of the analysis using immediate recall scores yielded five factors: nonverbal and spatial reasoning, verbal comprehension and expression, memory, attention and concentration, and psychomotor speed. The results of the analysis using the delayed recall measures also yielded the same five factors. The authors reported that their analysis supported the validity of the Verbal Memory, Delayed Recall, and Attention/Concentration Indexes of the WMS-R but not the Visual Memory Index.

In a similar, related study, Nicks, Leonberger, Munz, and Goldfader (1992) reported the results of a factor analysis of the WMS-R and the WAIS of 133 patients referred for neuropsychological assessment at a university medical center. The authors found six factors that accounted for 76% of the variance. These factors were described as (1) perceptual organization; (2) verbal comprehension; (3) attention/concentration; (4) complex verbal memory; (5) a factor which was comprised of the immediate and delayed recall Verbal Paired Associates subtests; and (6) a factor with loadings from the immediate and delayed recall Visual Paired Associates subtests.

Smith et al. (1992) examined the factor structure of a core battery from Mayo's Older Americans Normative Studies (MOANS), which included the WMS-R. They report that a two-factor model of the WMS-R involving attention and general memory was supported for 526 community-dwelling persons ages 55–97.

Smith, Ivnik, Malec, and Tangalos (1993) examined the factor structure of the core battery from the MOANS project, which included the WMS-R in a clinical sample of 417 patients. In this study, they found that the WMS-R loaded on five factors: verbal comprehension, perceptual organization, attention, learning, and retention.

In a related study, Smith et al. (1994) used the full factor scores generated by the five-factor model reported by Smith et al. (1992, 1993) as criterion variables for the development of a short assessment battery. Using the WMS-R Mental Control, Visual Reproduction, Verbal Paired Associates (with slightly modified administration), Visual Paired Associates, and Logical Memory subtests, the authors reported that Mental Control loaded on an attention/concentration factor, the Verbal and Visual Paired Associates subtests loaded on a learning factor, Visual Reproduction loaded on a perceptual organization factor, and the Logical Memory and Visual Reproduction percent retention scores loaded on a retention factor.

Burton, Mittenberg, and Burton (1993) completed a confirmatory factor analysis of the WMS-R on the standardization sample ($N = 316$). They found that a three-factor model consisting of attention/concentration, immediate memory, and delayed memory accounted for 91% of the score variance. The authors noted that previous studies supporting a verbal/nonverbal index distinction might not be a viable one.

Schmidt, Trueblood, Merwin, and Durham (1994) performed a factor analysis of 12 commonly used measures of attention in a sample of 120 outpatients. Among the measures examined were the Attention Index of the WMS-R and its subtests (Digit Span, Visual Memory Span, and Mental Control). While their investigation yielded a clear one-factor solution, it was unclear as to whether this factor assessed a global attentional domain, a specific aspect of attention, or general neuropsychological impairment. The authors cautioned clinicians and researchers that many commonly used measures of attention are not based on any particular model of attention, such as the model suggested by Mirskey (1989), so it is unclear when "attention" emerges as a factor, what exactly this factor represents.

Franzen, Wilhelm, and Haut (1995) examined the factor structure of the WMS-R using the indices and scales scores as variables in a population of substance abusers. Tested within one week of the termination of the detoxification period were 352 substance abusers engaged in inpatient treatment. The subjects were administered several tests, including the WMS-R. The General Memory, Delayed Memory, Verbal Memory, and Visual Memory indexes loaded on a general memory factor and the Attention/Concentration Index loaded on an attention factor.

Gass (1996) reported the results of a study that investigated Minnesota Multiphasic Personality Inventory-2 variables in attention and memory test performance of 48 male patients with closed head injuries and 80 patients with psychiatric disorders. The subjects were administered the Logical Memory I and II and Visual Reproduction I and II subtests, along with other neurocognitive and personality measures. The Logical Memory subtests were found to load on a verbal memory factor and the Visual Reproduction subtests on a visuographic memory factor.

Jurden, Franzen, Callahan, and Ledbetter (1996) looked at the factorial equivalence of the WMS-R across standardization and clinical samples. The authors concluded, based on their study and prior research that a three-factor model consisting of attention/concentration, verbal memory, and visual memory were plausible representations of the WMS-R, and that the factor structure of the WMS-R was essentially the same in the standardization and clinical groups studied.

Berger (1998) examined the usefulness and construct validity in neuropsychological assessments. One hundred twelve patients were administered the WAIS-R, the WMS-R Logical Memory I and II and Visual Reproduction I and II subtests, and the Halstead-Reitan Neuropsychological Test. Berger reported that the Logical Memory and Visual Reproduction subtests loaded on a verbal comprehension factor, suggesting that the latter contained verbal components. In addition, the Logical Memory I and Visual Reproduction I subtests loaded on a freedom from distractibility factor.

Bowden, Carstairs, and Shores (1999) conducted a confirmatory factor analysis of the WAIS-R and WMS-R in a community sample of 399 healthy young adults in Australia. They noted that exploratory factor analytic studies of the original WMS suggest that it is essentially a measure of verbal learning and recall (Larrabee et al., 1983; Ryan, Rosenberg, & Heilbronner, 1984), and that only confirmatory factor analytic studies (Smith et al., 1992, 1993) of the WMS-R and WAIS-R provide support for a version of the immediate versus delayed recall distinction. The purpose of the Bowden et al. (1999) study was to test alternative models of cognition, focusing in particular on models of memory. The results of their study revealed that Mental Control and Visual Memory Span subtests loaded on an attention/concentration factor; Logical Memory I and II and Verbal Paired Associates I and II loaded on a verbal memory factor; and Figural Memory, Visual Paired Associates I and II, and Visual Reproduction I and II loaded on a visual memory factor. It should be noted that in their article, the authors appear to equate measures of delayed recall with long-term memory.

Johnstone, Vieth, Johnson, and Shaw (2000) presented the results of a study that investigated whether recall based on multiple presentations of material (i.e., learning) is statistically distinct from recall based on a single presentation (i.e., memory). The authors used raw standard scores from the WMS-R Logical Memory (a measure of verbal learning) and Visual Reproduction (a measure of visual memory) subtests, and a variety of other memory tests, to evaluate 291 participants referred for suspected cognitive dysfunction. A promax factor analysis of the 291 participants test results revealed four factors (verbal memory, spatial memory, verbal learning, and tactile-motor learning) supporting the distinction between learning and memory constructs.

Noting that little is known about the factor structure of the WMS-R for patients aged over 75 years of age and its neurological significance, Kinno et al. (2017) examined the differential effects of the factor structure of the WMS-R on cortical thickness and complexity in a Japanese sample of 50 elderly patients. The authors found that four factors (recognition memory, paired associate memory, visual-and-working memory, and attention) can be crucial factors for interpreting WMS-R results in the population studied.

Summary

While the studies cited in the previous section are not all the studies that have examined the factor structure of the WMS-R, they are, in this writer's opinion, representative of most of those published. What conclusions can be drawn from them?

1. In the manual describing the structure of the WMS-R (Wechsler, 1987), the publisher notes that a factor analysis of the instrument revealed only two factors: general memory and learning and attention and concentration. In other words, there was no empirical evidence that the delayed recall subtests actually assessed delayed recall.
2. Other than Leonberger, Nicks, Larrabee, and Goldfader (1992) and the Burton et al. (1993) study, most of the studies reviewed have not provided empirical support for purported measures of delayed recall.
3. Most commonly, it appears various factor analytic factors have suggested the WMS-R assesses either two or three factors. The two-factor solutions

appear to be verbal memory and attention; the three-factor solutions verbal memory, visual memory, and attention. Purported measures of visual memory fairly consistently loaded on a verbal memory factor, because the way each of these tests is administered recruits verbal language functions. Purer tests of verbal memory, like Logical Memory and Verbal Paired Associates, however, do not load on visual memory factors.

4.   Although various factor analytic studies do appear to validate the measures that comprise the Attention/Concentration Index, as Schmidt et al. (1994) have cautioned, it is unclear what attention functions this index measures. As Mirskey (1989) has observed, attention is a complex phenomenon.

5.   Some studies suggest that the immediate versions of several WMS subtests load on measures of attention and concentration.

6.   It would appear the factor structure of the WMS-R is not substantially different from the factor structure of the WMS.

7.   The factor structure of the WMS-R appears to vary depending upon age and the nature of neurological insult (i.e., disease process, head injury, cognitive changes associated with aging).

Studies of the WMS-III

As previously noted, although results of the initial confirmatory factor analytic studies of the WMS-III reported in the original (Psychological Corporation, 1997) technical manual provided support for a five-factor model (working memory, auditory immediate memory, auditory delayed memory, visual immediate memory, and visual delayed memory), the publisher (Tulsky et al., 2002) in the revised technical manual acknowledged that later factor analytic studies failed to find these factors. Later studies indicated that WMS-III subtests load on only three factors: auditory memory, visual memory, and working memory, and they failed to provide support for the distinction between immediate and delayed recall.

Burton, Ryan, Axelrod, Schellenberger, and Richards (2003) reported on the results of a confirmatory factor analysis of the WMS-III in a clinical sample with cross-validation in the standardization sample (combined $N = 1,250$). The results of their analysis yielded four factors: auditory memory, visual memory, working memory, and learning. Consistent with prior research, they also were unable to find empirical support for the validity of the delayed memory indices.

Price, Tulsky, Millis, and Weiss (2002) also presented the results of a confirmatory factor analysis of the WMS-III with cross-validation. The authors noted that Millis, Malina, Bowers, and Ricker (1999) had attempted to replicate the factor analysis presented in the technical manual (Wechsler, 1997) using the correlation matrices presented in the manual. Because the analysis conducted by Millis et al. (1999) used similar but not identical combinations of subtests as those used in the original confirmatory factor analysis of the WMS-III, the results of their study did not exactly replicate the results originally reported in

Wechsler (1997). The Millis et al. (1999) study also failed to find support for delayed recall measures. The purpose of the Price et al. (2002) study was to extend the work of Millis et al. using a refined methodology to yield clearer results. The results of their study yielded a three-factor model consisting of verbal (immediate and delayed), visual (immediate and delayed), and working memory factors. Their analysis did not find empirical support for purported measures of delayed recall.

Tulsky and Price (2003) reported the results of a joint WAIS-III and WMS-III factor analytic study. The authors noted that their study was the first to simultaneously factor analyze these tests. The purpose of their study was to investigate the underlying structure of the subtests contained in the WAIS-III and WMS-III so that an expanded model of cognitive functioning could be advanced for clinical use. The authors studied several different factor models that varied in composition from two to ten factors. The results of their study produced a six-factor model for both tests consisting of verbal, perceptual, processing speed, working memory, auditory memory, and visual memory. In regard to the WMS-III, the Letter-Number Sequencing, Digit Span, and Spatial Span subtests loaded on the working memory factor; Logical Memory I and II, Verbal Paired Associates I and II, and Word List I and II subtests loaded on the auditory memory factor; and Faces I and II, Family Pictures I and II, and Visual Reproduction I and II subtests loaded on the visual memory factor.

Hoelzle et al. (2011) compared the dimensional structures of the WMS-III and WMS-IV to determine if the latter had a more coherent and clinically relevant factor structure. Data was obtained from the WMS-III and WMS-IV technical manuals (Wechsler, 1997, 2009b). The results of their study suggested that for the WMS-III, only a three-factor model consisting of verbal, visual, and working memory dimensions was consistent across all age groups. In regard to the WMS-IV, the authors found an invariant two-dimensional factor structure consisting of auditory learning/memory and visual attention/ memory. Bosnes, Troland, and Torsheim (2016) completed a confirmatory factor analysis of the WMS-III in an elderly Norwegian sample. Their sample consisted of 122 healthy individuals. The results of their study indicated that a three-factor model best fit their data. The three factors were working memory, visual memory, and auditory memory.

Summary

Although initially indicating that factor analytic studies of the WMS-III supported a five-factor model (Wechsler, 1997), the publisher later reported that further research supported a three-factor model consisting of auditory memory, visual memory, and working memory. Subsequent studies have largely supported this finding, although Burton et al. (2003) found a fourth factor, which they called learning. None of the studies cited, other than the original factor analytic study cited in Wechsler (1997), found support for measures of delayed recall. Based on the evidence available, the WMS-III appears to reliably assess visual memory. This was not true of its predecessors.

Studies of the WMS-IV

As noted previously, the WMS-IV technical manual (Wechsler, 2009b) presented a confirmatory factor analysis of the WMS-IV that supports an a priori theoretical model of visual memory (Designs II and Visual Reproduction II subtests), visual working memory (Symbol Span and Spatial Addition subtests), and auditory memory (Logical Memory II and Verbal Paired Associates II subtests). It will be recalled that the WMS-IV was explicitly designed to assess these factors (Wechsler, 2009b). The authors also cited support for a two-factor model of visual memory (Designs II, Visual Reproduction II, Symbol Span, and Spatial Addition subtests) and auditory memory (Logical Memory II and Verbal Paired Associates II subtests).

As indicated earlier, Hoelzle et al. (2011) found an invariant two-dimensional factor structure for the WMS-IV consisting of auditory learning/memory and visual attention/memory. No support was found for measures or indices of delayed recall. The authors suggested that the WMS-IV, compared to the WMS-III, might have greater utility in identifying lateralized memory dysfunction.

Noting that between-group comparisons are permissible and meaningfully interpretable only if diagnostic instruments are proved to measure the same latent dimensions across different groups, Pauls et al. (2013) conducted a rigorous test of measurement invariance using confirmatory factor analysis to evaluate which model solution would best explain memory performance as measured by the WMS-IV across a clinical depression group and matched controls. The result of their study yielded a three-factor model consisting of auditory memory, visual memory, and visual working memory. They also reported differences in visual working memory functions between healthy controls and depressed individuals, which restricts comparisons of the WMS-IV working memory index.

Bouman, Hendriks, Kerkmeer, Kessels, and Aldenkamp (2015) published a report of a confirmatory factor analysis of the Dutch version of the WMS-IV. Noting that several studies of the factor structure of the WMS, WMS-R, and WMS-III in healthy controls and various clinical groups had yielded inconsistent results for the underlying factor structure, the authors examined the latent factor structure of the Dutch WMS-IV via a series of confirmatory factor analyses. The authors investigated the factor structure of both the Adult Battery and the Older Adult Battery. The results of their investigation yielded three factors for the Adult Battery (auditory memory, visual memory, and visual working memory) and two factors for the Older Adult Battery (auditory memory and visual memory).

Frisby and Beaujean (2015) tested Spearman's hypothesis, which posits that the size of black-white mean differences across a group of diverse mental tests is a positive function of each test's loading onto the general (g) factor, using a bi-factor model with the WAIS-IV/WMS-IV standardization data. The authors found support for the weak form of the Spearman hypothesis which suggests that both g and non-g factors were involved in the observed mean score differences between Black and White adults.

Park and Jon (2018) investigated whether working memory can be clearly subdivided according to auditory and visual modalities. 115 Korean patients with a variety of psychiatric conditions were administered the Letter-Number Sequencing and Digit Span subtests from the Korean version of the WAIS-IV, and the Symbol Span and Spatial Addition subtests from the Korean version of the WMS-IV. Confirmatory factor analysis was used to determine whether the working memory measures better fit a one-factor or two-factor model. The results of the study supported a two-factor model, or the existence of a modality-specific working memory system. It thus provided support for the visual working memory subtests of the WMS-IV.

Granite (2018) examined the construct validity of the Visual Working Memory Index (VWMI). Two single factor confirmatory factor analysis models were used to test whether the VWMI is a valid measure of visuospatial working memory. The findings suggested that the VWMI is a valid measurement for assessing visuospatial working memory.

Summary

Based on studies by the publisher (Wechsler, 2009b) and additional confirmatory factor analyses studies, it appears that the WMS-IV Adult Battery reliably measures auditory and visual memory, like the WMS-III. Unlike the WMS-III, due to the way the WMS-IV is constructed, it only assesses visual working memory. As noted previously, the Working Memory Index of the WMS-III is comprised of the Letter-Number Sequencing and Spatial Span subtests. Neither of these subtests is part of the WMS-IV. The Visual Working Memory Index of the WMS-IV is comprised of the Spatial Addition and Symbol Span subtests. Although the Symbol Span subtest is part of the Older Adult Battery, the battery does not have a working memory index.

It bears repeating that although the WMS-IV has purported tests of delayed recall, and a Delayed Recall Index, and various delayed recall scores, factor analytic studies of the WMS-IV suggest it does not validly assess delayed recall. Nonetheless, the technical manual does cite several studies where several clinical groups differ in their performance on immediate versus delayed recall versions of some subtests.

It is significant to note that an APA PsychNet Gold literature search for factor analysis studies of the WMS-IV for the years 2015–2020 conducted in early 2020 turned up very few studies during this time period. Although the reason for this relative lack of studies is unclear, it may reflect the improvement in the psychometric properties of the WMS-IV compared to its predecessors, thus resulting in less debate about its factor structure.

Chapter 5

Clinical and Research Uses of the Wechsler Memory Scales

The Wechsler Memory Scales are the best known and most used standardized tests of memory in the United States, and have been for a number of years. Their popularity is not just a result of continuous clever marketing by the publisher. Since the late 1980s, they have undergone constant refinement, with each revision designed to address the major shortcomings of the previous version. For instance, the three major criticisms of the original WMS were its poor standardization, the fact that it did not assess delayed recall, and that it was essentially a measure of verbal memory. On the surface, the WMS-R addressed these concerns.

In many ways, the WMS-III and WMS-IV have not significantly improved upon the manifest structural improvements of the WMS-R. The third and fourth revisions both continued to unsuccessfully assess delayed recall, which was a major shortcoming of the WMS-R. Both also attempted to better measure visual memory, with varying degrees of success, and the WMS-IV appears to have finally achieved that goal. The standardization of each successive revision was significantly better than its immediate predecessor, and there have been continual improvements in scoring and the quality of the normative data. In addition, the WMS-III and WMS-IV have recognition procedures to tease out encoding versus retrieval problems.

Despite all the improvements in the scale, the general failure of the WMS revisions to assess delayed recall is disappointing. However, as Hoelzle et al. (2011) have noted, the WMS is not unique in this regard, as numerous factor analytic studies of various measures of memory have failed to differentiate between immediate and delayed memory constructs. For example, Carroll's (1993) massive survey of factor analytic studies of the structure of cognition did not yield clear results that supported immediate and delayed constructs.

In investigating measures of learning and memory, Carroll (1993) reports evidence that supports the following conclusions. First, individuals differ in a *general memory ability* that affects their performance across a variety of tasks and behaviors involving memory. Second, there is evidence for more specific factors of memory. The specific factors include *memory span* (the amount of information the individual can immediately recall after one exposure);

associative memory (the ability to form arbitrary associations in stimulus material such as that on testing, and the individual can recall what stimulus is paired with another); *free recall memory* (an ability to register in memory a supraspan collection of materials and then retrieve all or most of the materials in any order, in a recall phase); *meaningful memory* (after a study phase, the ability to recall, reproduce, or recognize more material from the study phase than others); and *visual memory* (the ability in a study phase to create a mental representation, or possibly an image of visual material that is presented, where the visual image is not readily codable in some modality other than visual, and to use that representation in responding in a test phase by recognition or recall). Carroll also notes that there is a *general learning factor* that correlates with fluid and crystallized intelligence (Cattell, 1971), and evidence of *unique factors of learning ability* specific to particular kinds of learning situations. In regard to the unique factors of learning, this conclusion is consistent with what we know about brain networks and cognition. Different tasks recruit different brain networks (Anderson, 2014).

Due to the failure of factor analytic studies to differentiate immediate and delayed constructs, Hoelzle et al. (2011) note some researchers have suggested that factor analysis not be used to evaluate memory instruments. The failure of such studies to differentiate immediate from delayed recall is related to the significant shared variance between immediate and delayed constructs. With significant shared variance between immediate and delayed recall, it is logical to expect that performance on measures of immediate recall would predict performance on measures of delayed recall. Although, in general, immediate recall test performance predicts delayed recall test performance, the two are not identical. If such were the case, the correlation between measures of each would be perfect, and it is not.

There is not a great difference in how immediate and delayed recall are assessed on the WMS-R, WMS-III, or WMS-IV. The time between immediate and delayed recall tests ranges from 20 to 35 minutes depending on the revision. Since factor analytic studies did not support a distinction between these constructs in the WMS-R, it would not be logical to expect that factor analytic studies would support a distinction between these constructs in later revisions due to the minimal difference in the time intervals involved. And, as noted previously, they have not.

Some clinicians and researchers appear to assume measures of delayed recall are measures of long-term retention or memory. For instance, Logue and Wyrick (1979), in discussing the development of Russell's (1975) revision of the WMS, state the test measures short-term and long-term retention. In other words, they equate long-term retention with a test that assesses delayed recall after only 30 minutes. Bowden et al. (1999) make a similar assumption.

Long-term memory is usually considered to be a product of memory consolidation that customarily takes place over several hours, days, and years. In regard to this, Kent (2017) has suggested that the delayed recall procedures used with the WMS-IV could be relabeled as measures of intermediate memory, which is a form of short-term memory. This form of memory may last from an hour to a couple of days, but it is not yet permanently consolidated (Lezak et al., 2012). The point is, current WMS tests of delayed recall are not measures of long-term retention, unless one defines long-term retention as a period of 35 minutes or less, nor are they measures of long-term memory. Some items on the Personal and Current Information and Orientation subtests (and their variations) do assess long-term memory in the form of semantic memory, as do the easy associates of the Associate Learning/Verbal Paired Associates subtests.

A possible reason past factor analytic studies have not found separate immediate and delayed recall factors may be due to the length of time between these measures. If the interval were increased to several hours, it is possible that separate factors would emerge. Very few studies have investigated delayed recall with the WMS at this interval, likely due to clinical, practical, and economic considerations. Ladowsky-Brooks (2016) examined accelerated forgetting by assessing delayed recall after four hours. In addition, Vakil, Arbell, Gozlan, Hoofien, and Blachstein (1992) assessed delayed recall after 40 minutes and 24 hours. These studies will be examined later in this book.

Returning to Carroll (1993) and his investigation of the factor structure of learning and memory, his findings overlap remarkably with the core subtests and manifest structure of most versions of the WMS. Carroll's general memory factor appears to correspond to the MQ of the WMS-I and various memory indexes of the revisions, since it is a composite score. The Memory Span factor is directly comparable to the Digit Span subtests. The Associate Learning factor is assessed by the Associate Learning/Verbal Paired Associate subtests. The Free Recall factor is the process used to assess learning and memory in all revisions. The Meaningful Memory factor is assessed by the Logical Memory subtests. The Visual Memory factor is assessed by the Visual Reproduction subtest. The General Learning Ability factor would presumably correspond to one's overall level of performance on the WMS and performance on the Associate Learning/Verbal Paired Associates subtests. Assuming this mapping of the structure and content of the core WMS onto Carroll's model is fundamentally accurate, it should come as no surprise why the WMS has survived while other tests of memory have faded away from the clinical landscape. The core of the WMS, as originally conceived by David Wechsler, appears eerily prescient of the later findings by Carroll (1993) in regard to the factor structure of learning and memory. *The WMS scales endure, despite their many flaws, because they assess the factors of learning and memory described by Carroll. In other words, they have clinical utility because they have theoretical validity.*

In the remainder of this chapter, the author will summarize some of the ways the WMS has been used to investigate different clinical populations.

Investigations of Head Injury, Including Brain Damage and Dysfunction

As might be expected, shortly after publication of the WMS-I, the test was used to investigate people with suspected memory impairment and brain damage or dysfunction. In the early days of the assessment of memory, the WMS was used as an indicator of what then was called "organicity." Based on the clinical work of individuals like Luria (1976) and Goldstein (1995), who evaluated and treated soldiers with traumatic head injuries in the early part of the 20th century, it became known that memory dysfunction was often a sign of brain injury. One of the primary reasons Wechsler developed the WMS was to screen for suspected memory dysfunction among soldiers returning from war who had sustained head injuries. At the time Wechsler (1945) published his scale, there was no widely used formal test of memory (Erickson & Scott, 1977; Tulsky, Chiaravalloti, Palmer, & Chelune, 2003). As a result, the WMS met a pressing clinical need. Despite the fact the WMS-I was designed to assess the memory function of soldiers who had sustained head injuries, Wechsler presented no information in his manual on how this population typically performed on the WMS-I compared to normal controls.

The WMS-R test manual (Wechsler, 1987), however, provides some information regarding the performance of 20 patients with closed head injury on the WMS-R. This information is presented in Table 5.1. As can be seen from the table, this mixed group of patients with closed head injuries performed well below average on all WMS-R index scores. They performed especially poorly on the General Memory, Visual Memory, and Delayed Recall Indexes.

Table 5.2 provides information on 22 patients with traumatic brain injury (TBI) who were administered the WMS-III. The information comes from the WMS-III technical manual (Tulsky et al., 2002).

As can be seen from Table 5.2, patients with traumatic brain injury performed well below average on the WMS-III Visual Immediate, Immediate Memory, Visual Delayed, and General Memory Indexes as indicated by scores that fell at least one standard deviation below the mean. Their performance is not dissimilar from the performance of closed-head-injury patients on the WMS-R, as presented in Table 5.1.

Table 5.1 WMS-R Index Scores of Patients With Closed Head Injuries (N = 20)

Index	Mean	SD
General Memory Index	77.2	21.1
Attention/Concentration Index	82.5	16.3
Verbal Memory Index	83.5	20.5
Visual Memory Index	76.4	18.3
Delayed Recall Index	71.1	19.2
Information and Orientation	13.0	1.1

Source: Wechsler (1987)

Table 5.2 WMS-III Index Scores of 22 Patients With Traumatic Brain Injury

Index	Mean	SD
Auditory Immediate	89.3	19.3
Visual Immediate	74.9	13.9
Immediate Memory	78.9	17.7
Auditory Delayed	89.6	21.8
Visual Delayed	74.3	13.9
Auditory Recognition Delayed	93.6	16.6
General Memory	81.9	16.5
Working Memory	91.9	11.9

Table 5.3 WMS-IV Index Scores of 32 Persons With Moderate to Severe TBI

Index	TBI Group Mean and SD Scores	Matched Controls Mean and SD Scores
Auditory Memory	80.0 (18.5)	101.0 (14.0)
Visual Memory	82.5 (20.1)	101.2 (14.2)
Visual Working Memory	85.5 (17.4)	104.6 (12.4)
Immediate Memory	80.7 (19.0)	102.2 (15.4)
Delayed Memory	77.8 (21.1)	100.4 (14.9)

It is important to note that patients with discrete lesions in one quadrant or hemisphere of the brain might be expected to yield different profiles than the groups described by Wechsler (1987, 1997). The cognitive deficits displayed by people with TBI vary due to age, severity of injury, cause of injury, and time since injury. People with traumatic brain injury people represent a heterogeneous group.

Table 5.3 is adapted from Wechsler (2009a). It presents data from 32 individuals who sustained moderate to severe traumatic brain injury and who were tested with the WMS-IV Adult Battery within six months to three years post injury.

As can be seen, the TBI group scored significantly below matched controls on all index scores. It is significant to note that in the TBI group, there does not appear to be a significant difference between TBI Immediate Memory Index and Delayed Memory Index scores, or between the Auditory Memory Index and Visual Memory Index scores. Although the WMS-IV appears sensitive to the effects of TBI, in looking at Table 5.3, the impression is one of an across-the-board decline in memory functions assessed, suggesting that the patients assessed suffered from diffuse injuries.

The following studies are presented in roughly the order they appeared in the literature. As will be seen, while early studies seemed to focus primarily on the ability of the WMS to detect global brain injury or memory impairment, more recent studies began to investigate increasingly nuanced issues such as the ability of the WMS to assess lateralized brain impairment, modality-specific memory impairment, and predicting and assessing treatment outcome.

One of the earliest studies of the discriminatory power of the WMS was conducted by Cohen (1950), who investigated the difference in memory functions, as assessed by the WMS-I, in three groups. Cohen observed that most prior studies of memory appearing in the literature were confined to investigations of normal individuals. Cohen studied 144 white, male World War II veterans, ages 20–40, which were divided into three groups. The first group ($N = 81$) were diagnosed with anxiety and conversion disorders; the second group ($N = 45$) with traumatic brain injuries, tumors or cysts, or encephalitis; and the third group ($N = 15$) with schizophrenia. After equating the three groups for age and IQ, he found no significant difference between the groups in their performance on the WMS-I.

The same year, Howard (1950) published a study comparing the performance of 43 institutionalized patients with psychosis and organicity to 43 institutionalized patients with just psychosis, on the WMS-I. The first or "organic" group contained 20 patients with paresis, 10 with encephalitis, and 13 with epilepsy. While he found no significant differences between patients with encephalitis and epilepsy and the control group of institutionalized patients with psychosis, Howard (1950) reported that the control and paretic groups differed significantly in their MQ and performance on the Personal and Current Information, Orientation, Mental Control, Logical Memory, and Visual Reproduction subtests.

In a study investigating the validity of some tests of "organicity," Parker (1957) compared the performance on the WMS-I of a group of 30 adult male patients with a diagnosis of brain damage of recent origin (defined as within 6–10 months of the time of his study) to a control group of 30 psychiatric patients without brain damage. He found no significant difference between the groups.

A few years later, Carroll (1963) reported the results of an archival study that compared the performance of 15 "organic" to 15 patients with no organicity on the WMS. Although he found no significant difference in MQ between the groups, he noted that the two groups did differ in their performance on the Associate Learning and Visual Reproduction subtests.

Howard (1966) published the results of a 15-year follow-up of some of the patients he examined for his 1950 paper. He contrasted the performance of a convenience sample of 19 of the original patients with psychosis and organicity to a group of institutionalized controls on the WMS-I. He found no significant differences between the two groups, and concluded that that WMS scores decreased with age (as predicted by Wechsler) and length of institutionalization.

Brooks (1976) presented a study of the relationship between performance on the WMS-I and brain damage resulting from severe closed head injury. He compared 82 patients with severe head injury to 34 controls. Compared to normal controls, Brooks (1976) found the head injury group had significant differences in IQ and on the Mental Control, Digit Span, and Visual Reproduction subtests. He also noted that the group with brain damage performed poorer than did controls on Logical Memory during immediate and delayed recall trials, and they displayed a lower rate of learning on Associate Learning compared to controls.

Gronwall and Wrightson (1981) studied the relationship between the duration of post-traumatic amnesia (PTA) and performance on memory tests including the WMS-I in two samples of young adults with closed head injuries. Seventy-one patients were grouped into three grades of severity based on their length of PTA (less than one hour; 1–24 hours; greater than one day). The authors found that the MQ of the third group (i.e., greater than one day) was significantly lower than that of the first two groups. The mean MQ for group 1 ($N = 20$) was 95.3; group 2 ($N = 38$) 96.79; and group 3 ($N = 13$) 78.64.

Torkelson, Jellinek, Malec, and Harvey (1983) studied the relationship of medical and psychological factors (as assessed by the WMS-I and WAIS) to adaptive physical functioning (APF) at discharge and length of rehabilitation stay following traumatic brain injury (TBI). He used a sample of 32 individuals who had sustained TBI within a year of admission to a rehabilitation program. They found that their MQ was unrelated to their APF at discharge.

Squire and Butters (1992) observed that verbal memory is affected more by damage to the left hemisphere than damage to the right hemisphere, and that figural or nonverbal visual memory is affected more by damage to the right hemisphere than damage to the left hemisphere. Snow and Sheese (1985) compared the performance of males and females with lateralized cerebral infarcts and found those with left hemisphere damage performed more poorly on the Logical Memory and Associate Learning subtests (using an unspecified version of the WMS), and those with right hemisphere infarcts more poorly on Visual Reproduction. No sex differences were found.

Gass and Russell (1986) studied the impact of depression and brain damage on memory test performance of 135 brain-damaged patients and found significant impairments in the WMS-R Logical Memory I and II and WAIS-R Digit Span tests. They noted that performance on these measures was more affected by brain injury than depression.

Blair and Lanyon (1987) investigated the effectiveness of an intensive brain injury rehabilitation program on social and adaptive skills and the relationship of cognitive functioning to those skills. Ten severely head-injured adults who were treated in the program were matched against 10 waiting-list controls. Cognitive improvement was assessed by a variety of measures including the WMS Logical Memory and Visual Reproduction subtests. The authors found no significant difference between the two groups on WMS measures following treatment.

In an archival study, Bigler and Alfano (1988) examined the effects of anoxic brain injury in 12 patients. In order to provide a clinical assessment of the effects of anoxic brain damage, the 12 cases were closely matched on the severity and degree of diffuse atrophy. All subjects had completed neuroimaging studies and a battery of neuropsychological tests. The test performance of the 12 subjects with anoxia was compared to a carefully matched closed-head-injury group. All subjects had completed a variety of tests including the WMS. The anoxic group performed more poorly than the closed-head-injury group on all WMS subtests and the MQ, with the exception of the Visual Reproduction subtest.

In a study that attempted to standardize and validate a 30-minute delayed recall version of WMS-I Visual Reproduction subtest, Trahan, Quintana, Willingham, and Goethe (1988) examined the performance of four different clinical groups (severe head trauma, left hemisphere cerebrovascular accident (CVA), right hemisphere CVA, and Alzheimer's) on this measure. They also investigated the relationship between the WMS Visual Reproduction and WAIS-R Block Design subtests. Their investigation found significant differences between Visual Reproduction immediate and delayed recall measures in all four clinical groups, and that the Visual Reproduction immediate recall score correlated significantly with the Block Design scores in all four groups. Like Howard (1966), they reported that Visual Reproduction scores declined with age. In addition, the authors reported that patients in all four clinical groups performed below age-matched control subjects. They failed to find differences between left and right cerebral infarct patients in performance on the Visual Reproduction subtests and explained this finding by noting Visual Reproduction performance correlated positively with measures of verbal memory, indicating the Visual Reproduction is not a pure measure of visual memory.

Using an unknown version of the original WMS and other psychological tests, Acker and Davis (1989) investigated psychological test scores associated with late outcome in head injury. They studied whether psychometric data could predict post-acute head injury outcome. The authors found that WMS MQ significantly correlated with outcome as assessed by the Social Status Outcome measure.

Cooper et al. (1989), in noting that memory disorders are common deficits after closed head injuries, investigated whether verbal memory was a unitary function. Assuming verbal memory to be a unitary function, the authors posited that there would be no differences between the performance of subjects with brain damage on the California Verbal Learning Test (CVLT), a measure of list recall involving singe units or words, and the Russell (1975) version of the WMS. In their study, the authors retrieved archival records of 48 blunt head injury patients who were, on average, 42 months post injury. All subjects were veterans and had suffered coma and/or posttraumatic amnesia. As expected, all subjects performed substantially below the reported performances of normal samples on the WMS and the CVLT. In addition, the authors found that although the WMS Logical Memory and CVLT tests shared substantial common variance in terms of general and verbal memory, there was a proportion of variance in Logical Memory recall that could not be accounted for by the

CVLT, and vice versa. The authors concluded that verbal memory is not a unitary function. Their study suggests that successful performance on Visual Reproduction is partially a function of verbal memory.

Chlopan, Hagen, and Russell (1990) investigated the impact of lateralized anterior and posterior lesions on the WAIS Digit Span subtest and Russell's (1975) version of the WMS with a 30-minute delay. They predicted subjects with lesions in the left posterior quadrant would be most impaired on Logical Memory, and their research supported this prediction for both immediate and delayed recall trials. They also predicted subjects with lesions in the right posterior quadrant would be most impaired on Visual Reproduction. This prediction was only partially supported. All four (right anterior, right posterior, left anterior, and left posterior) lesion groups were found to be impaired on Visual Reproduction immediate and delayed recall. On delayed testing, however, the right posterior group was found to be significantly more impaired than the right anterior group.

Gass, Russell, and Hamilton (1990) investigated the validity of MMPI scores and MMPI-based cognitive complaints as indicators of memory and concentration disturbances in a group of 70 closed head trauma patients using the WAIS-R Digit Span test and Russell's (1975) version of the WMS. The results suggested a lack of relationship between any MMPI variables and test performance.

Altepeter et al. (1990) looked at the utility of the Luria Memory Words Test and Russell's (1975) version of the WMS plus the Personal and Current Information and Associate Learning subtests in discriminating 60 brain-damaged from 60 non-brain-damaged patients. The former correctly classified 76% of the brain-damaged subjects, and the latter 72%. Of the five WMS subtests used, the Personal and Current Information, Logical Memory delayed recall, and Associate Learning subtests were most useful in making the discrimination.

Cooley and Stringer (1991) used selected measures from the WMS-I to examine the ability of 23 brain-damaged patients and outside observers, like close friends or relatives, to predict the patients' performance on standard clinical tests of memory. The authors found significant correlations between observers' and patients' predictions of patients' performance on Logical Memory I and II and Trials 1 and 3 of the Associate Learning subtest, suggesting brain-damaged patients have some ability to make accurate self-assessments.

Powell, Cripe, and Dodrill (1991) studied the effectiveness of the Rey Auditory-Verbal Learning Test at assessing patients with mixed brain impairment compared to other neuropsychological measures, including the WMS-I Logical Memory and Visual Reproduction subtests. The subjects included 50 patients with a mixture of medically confirmed neuropathologies and 50 controls with no evidence of neurological impairment. The Logical Memory subtest was found to discriminate between the two groups.

Mutchnick, Ross, and Long (1991) examined the contribution of tests comprising the Impairment Index devised by Halstead (1947) with regard to their ability to predict brain impairment. The subjects for this study consisted of 491 patients who had been selected from a larger pool of 2,500 patients who were primarily medical patients referred for neuropsychological evaluation. The Impairment Index is comprised of scores from a number of measures including the WMS-I MQ and Delayed Memory Total Percent score (which is the percentage of material recalled from the Logical Memory, Visual Reproduction, and Associate Learning subtests after one hour). The authors found the Impairment Index was sensitive to brain impairment.

Vakil et al. (1992) investigated the relative importance of informational units and the role they played in the recall of 40 closed-head-injury (CHI) patients who were, on the average, four years post injury compared to a group of 40 controls. They used the WMS-I Logical Memory subtest and assessed recall at 40 minutes and 24 hours. In addition, they developed a scoring system that measured depth of processing. They found the control group significantly outperformed the CHI group; that immediate recall was better than delayed recall; and more important ideas were better recalled overall than less important ones. The investigators also found that the rate of forgetting for less important ideas was steeper than the rate of forgetting for more important ideas for both groups. In other words, both groups forgot less important informational units quicker than more important informational units.

Sherer et al. (1992) investigated the sensitivity of the WMS-I and the Russell (1975) revision of the WMS to the effects of IQ and brain damage in matched groups of 64 brain-damaged (BD) and non-brain-damaged (NBD) patients. The investigators found that the WMS MQ, and Mental Control, Logical Memory I, Memory Span, and Visual Reproduction 1 subtests were affected by IQ, while only the Logical Memory II and Visual Reproduction II subtests were affected by brain damage when the BD and NBD groups were equated on IQ.

Vakil, Hoofien, and Blachstein (1992) compared the performance of 20 individuals with left brain damage (LBD) to 20 individuals with right brain damage (RBD). It was hypothesized that the former would show impairments on verbal learning, as assessed by the WMS Associate Learning subtest, and the latter would show impairments in visual learning, as assessed by the Gollin Incomplete Figures, a task which is easy to verbalize and considered to be a measure of figural memory, and the Stylus Maze, which was considered more of a spatial learning task. The RBD group performed better than the LBD group on the verbal learning task, while the LBD group performed better on the spatial learning task. No significant difference was found in the performance on the Gollin Incomplete Figures, suggesting that a task using visually and verbally codable stimuli is not useful in discriminating between LBD and RBD groups.

Gass and Ansley (1994), in an investigation of the MMPI correlates of post-stroke neurobehavioral deficits using Russell's (1975) version of the WMS, performed a factor analysis on age- and education-corrected scores of 14 commonly used neuropsychological tests. They found the Visual Reproduction delayed recall subtest loaded on a visuospatial factor, and the Logical Memory delayed recall subtest loaded on a verbal factor.

Bigler and Snyder (1995) reported a case history of four individuals with well-documented mild traumatic brain injury in whom pre- and post-injury neuroimaging studies were available. All patients received a battery of neuropsychological tests, which included the WMS-R, between 5 and 12 months post-injury. Three out of four participants obtained intact scores on the WMS-R.

Guilmette and Rasile (1995) investigated the sensitivity, specificity, and diagnostic accuracy of three verbal measures used to assess 16 adults with mild traumatic brain injury. The measures included the Rey Auditory-Verbal Learning Test (RAVLT), WMS-R Logical Memory I and II subtests, and the Expanded Paired Associates Test. The Logical Memory I and II subtests significantly discriminated between the brain-injured group and controls.

Farmer and Eakman (1995) examined the ecological validity of neuropsychological tests (including the WMS-R) relative to instrumental activities of daily living (IADL) among 55 participants in a post-acute brain injury rehabilitation program. The authors found that higher Visual Memory and Delayed Memory Index scores were significantly associated with success on IADL tasks.

Wilhelm and Johnstone (1995) evaluated the use of the WMS-R indexes to provide valuable information about the memory abilities of individuals who had sustained traumatic brain injury. They administered the WMS-R to 36 individuals with moderate to severe TBI and 18 normal controls, and found that while TBI patients scored significantly lower on all indexes compared to controls, the indexes did not accurately represent the performance on all tests making up the index. They recommended interpreting individual subtest scores, rather than index scores, when engaging in rehabilitation planning.

Noting that verbal memory may be mediated by the left hippocampus and visual memory by the right hippocampus, Bigler et al. (1996) investigated the relationship between hippocampal volume and memory performance of TBI patients on several selected tests, including WMS-R Logical Memory and Visual Reproduction subtests by dividing immediate recall into delayed recall to derive saving scores. It was felt that saving scores might be a better indicator of retention of information compared to the regular subtest scores. The authors found that the absolute volume of the left hippocampus was significantly related to saving scores on both the Visual Reproduction and Logical Memory subtests. Bigler et al. (1997) had previously found that hippocampal atrophy did not systematically relate to any WMS-R indexes. The failure to find any significant relationships was thought to be due to the global nature of the indexes. The 1997 study was completed before Bigler et al. (1996), but published later.

In a study investigating the performance of African American subjects with unilateral brain lesions on Russell's (1975) version of the WMS,

Lewis-Jack et al. (1997) found their subjects were more impaired than were controls on the Visual Reproduction and Logical Memory measures except for the Logical Memory Percentage Retained score. None of the four lesion groups (left anterior, left posterior, right anterior, right posterior) differed systematically on the Russell subtests.

Tremont, Hoffman, Scott, Adams, and Nadolne (1997) noted that comparisons have been proposed between WMS-R indexes and WAIS-R scores to identify the severity of memory disorder and distinguish different neurological disorders, on the basis that IQ scores tend to "hold" better than memory scores in brain-injured patients (Bornstein, Chelune, & Prifitera, 1989). Tremont et al. (1997) note that one problem with making IQ-memory score comparisons is that both are sometimes reduced in some neurological conditions. The researchers compared WMS-R index scores and premorbid IQ, using a premorbid index based on demographic factors and current test performance across two severity levels of patients who had suffered closed head injuries. They also investigated whether WMS-R index score comparisons were helpful in determining head trauma severity. Patients were assigned to two head injury groups: mild head injury and moderate/severe head injury matched on age and level of education. The Oklahoma Premorbid Intelligence Examination (OPIE) (Scott, Krull, Williamson, Adams, & Iverson, 1997) was used to determine premorbid intelligence. The researchers found that moderate/severe head-injured patients displayed significantly larger discrepancies between OPIE scores and the WMS-R Delayed Recall Indexes than did mild head-injured patients. The former group showed a discrepancy of 19 points versus 10 points for the latter group. The authors also concluded that comparing current memory functioning to estimates of premorbid intellectual functioning appeared to be a sensitive indicator of the presence and degree of intellectual and memory dysfunction in head-injured patients.

Noting that decreased self-awareness often accompanies brain damage, Trudel, Tryon, and Purdum (1998) quantified the degree of long-term impairment in disability awareness in 63 adults with closed head injuries and assessed its relationship to a variety of measures, including the WMS-R. They found impaired awareness was associated with decreased General Memory Index scores.

Bell, Primeau, Sweet, and Lofland (1999) examined the neuropsychological functioning of persons suffering from migraine headache, nonheadache chronic pain, and mild TBI patients. There were 20 patients in each group who did not differ in the number of prescribed medications, sex ratios, race, age, years of education, or intelligence. The subjects were administered several neuropsychological tests, including the WMS-R Logical Memory I and II, Verbal Paired Associates I and II, and Visual Reproduction I and II subtests. The authors reported that the mild TBI patients were most often impaired on Verbal Paired Associates I and II subtests.

Fisher, Ledbetter, Cohen, Marmor, and Tulsky (2000) used the WAIS-III and WMS-III to evaluate the cognitive functioning of patients with mild and moderate to severe brain injury. The goals of the study were to identify if the tests would reveal abnormal score patterns in patients with mild traumatic brain injury, and how those scores compared to individuals with moderate/severe brain trauma and normal controls. The results of their investigation revealed that individuals with moderate to severe brain injury scored significantly lower than did controls on all WMS-III indexes, except for the Auditory Recognition Delayed Index. Individuals with mild brain injury performed poorer than controls on the Auditory Immediate Index and the Auditory Delayed Index. The results also revealed that symptomatic mild brain-injured patients obtained some low scores comparable to those with more severe injuries.

Another study using MMPI indices of psychological disturbance and attention and memory test performance was conducted by Ross, Putnam, Gass, Bailey, and Adams (2003). The study used the Memory Assessment Scale (MAS); CVLT; WAIS-R Digit Span; and the Logical Memory I and II, Visual Reproduction I and II, and Visual Memory Span subtests from the WMS-R to investigate attention and memory in psychiatric and head-injured patients. The study found no correlation between WMS-R and CVLT indices of attention and memory and those derived from the MAS. Positive correlations were found between elevations on the basic MMPI clinical scales of Hypochondrias, Depression, Hysteria, Psychasthenia, and Schizophrenia and the WMS-R variables, however.

Walker, Batchelor, Shores, and Jones (2009) investigated whether the application of demographically corrected WAIS-III/WMS-III index scores would be associated with higher diagnostic efficacy statistics (sensitivity) than that obtained with age-corrected indices in evaluating patients with moderate to severe traumatic brain injury and 12 years or less of formal education. They found that for individuals with 7–12 years of education who had sustained moderate to severe brain trauma, the application of demographic corrections did not improve upon the diagnostic efficiency compared with that produced by age-corrected indices.

What can be concluded from the results of the aforementioned studies? The following observations are offered.

Key Points

- Although index scores may be useful in determining if a person has sustained suspected brain injury or memory impairment, exclusive use of index scores may be misleading. Composite scores may be insensitive to impairment. As Lezak (1988) has noted, composite scores are often made up of disparate measures. As a composite, they may obscure specific facets of a person's neuropsychological status or misrepresent it generally. Use index scores with caution when interpreting WMS results. Always look at individual subtest performance in light of the patient's clinical presentation and developmental, social, and medical history. Ask yourself, do the test scores make neuropsychological sense? Test findings that don't make neuropsychological sense should always be suspect.

- Of the many subtests that have been used over the years in the WMS, the tests that appear to be of greatest utility are the core subtests that have been present in the WMS since its introduction. Remember, none of the new subtests in the WMS-R were retained in the WMS-III. And none of the new subtests of the WMS-III were retained in the WMS-IV.

- The most studied core subtests are Associate Learning (Verbal Paired Associates), Memory Span (Digit Span), Visual Reproduction, and Logical Memory.

- In general, although persons suffering from left posterior damage perform more poorly on the Associate Learning/Verbal Paired Associates and Logical Memory subtests, those suffering from right posterior damage do not always perform more poorly on the Visual Reproduction subtests. As the literature review has revealed, the relationship between laterality and performance on these measures is complex, as might be expected from what we know about the interrelationship among various brain networks. It is important to familiarize yourself with the literature in this area in order to draw valid conclusions from your test results.

- Despite the failure of numerous factor analytic studies to find statistical support for separate immediate and delayed indexes, some research studies have found that the delayed indexes are, at times, sensitive to neuropsychological dysfunction and thus have clinical utility. It appears that comparing immediate and delayed recall measures are more useful in assessing individuals who suffer from a major neurocognitive disorder like moderate to severe traumatic brain injury than in evaluating persons with mild head injury.

- All versions of the WMS have proven clinically useful in assessing persons with brain damage.

- In comparing the test results between various versions, it is important to remember that indexes with similar names from different revisions do not measure the same constructs. Because the WMS has evolved over the years, even making comparisons with identically named subtests, such as Logical Memory, is fraught with difficulty since the content and scoring procedures for the subtests have changed over time. In other words, do not assume that the performance of an individual on the WMS-I Logical Memory subtest will be identical to his/her performance on the WMS-IV Logical Memory I subtest. With those limitations in mind, should a person score two standard deviations below average on the WMS-I or WMS-IV Logical Memory and Visual Reproduction subtests, one can be reasonably certain that both these scores suggest impaired functioning.

• Various versions of the WMS have proven useful is assessing outcome from traumatic brain injury.

Investigations of Mild Cognitive Impairment, Dementia, Parkinson's, and Amnesia

The WMS-R test manual (Wechsler, 1987) provides no information regarding the expected performance of individuals suffering from mild cognitive impairment or Parkinson's, and relatively little information regarding the expected performance on the test for individuals with Alzheimer's (AD) or other dementias and Korsakoff's. The information available is summarized in Table 5.4. As can be seen from the table, patients diagnosed with AD performed over two standard deviations below average on all WMS-R Index scores except the Attention/Concentration Index, where they fell about one standard deviation below average. The sample of those diagnosed with Dementia was somewhat less impaired, but they still performed well below average on all indexes. Those with Korsakoff's performed about two standard deviations below average on the General Memory and Verbal Memory Indexes, and they were especially impaired on the Delayed Recall Index. In addition, their performance on the Attention/Concentration Index was grossly within normal limits, and on the Information and Orientation subtest well below average.

Some information regarding the performance of persons with mild AD, Parkinson's, and Korsakoff's is provided in the WAIS-III/WMS-III Technical Manual (Wechsler, 1997). The information is summarized in Table 5.5. As can be seen from the table, persons diagnosed with Alzheimer's disease were globally impaired on all WMS-III indexes, with most scores over two standard deviations below average. Persons with Parkinson's scored about a standard deviation below average on most indexes except Auditory Recognition Delayed, suggesting a mild global decline in their memory functioning. Patients with Korsakoff's had Working Memory Index scores within normal

Table 5.4 WMS-R Performance of Persons Diagnosed With Alzheimer's (*N* = 24), Dementia (*N* = 18), and Korsakoff's (*N* = 8)

Index or Subtest	Alzheimer's Mean and SD	Dementia Mean and SD	Korsakoff's Mean and SD
General Memory Index	62.0 (14.7)	78.1 (17.9)	67.5 (13.8)
Attention/Concentration Index	81.0 (16.9)	80.6 (18.0)	90.8 (21.1)
Verbal Memory Index	68.2 (16.0)	84.6 (16.3)	70.0 (11.5)
Visual Memory Index	68.7 (14.3)	77.5 (14.4)	77.4 (19.0)
Delayed Recall Index	61.7 (12.4)	76.9 (15.0)	57.3 (6.2)
Information and Orientation subtest	10.2 (2.9)	12.6 (1.3)	7.9 (2.3)

Table 5.5 WMS-III Performance of Persons Diagnosed With Mild AD (*N* = 35), Parkinson's (*N* = 10), and Korsakoff's (*N* = 10)

Index	Mild AD Mean and SD	Parkinson's Mean and SD	Korsakoff's Mean and SD
Auditory Immediate	68.7 (11.0)	86.0 (17.4)	73.1 (7.8)
Visual Immediate	70.6 (10.9)	84.7 (15.1)	67.8 (6.8)
Immediate Memory	62.9 (11.4)	82.3 (17.8)	64.4 (8.2)
Auditory Delayed	66.1 (9.6)	85.8 (17.2)	63.5 (5.3)
Visual Delayed	67.5 (8.1)	80.9 (13.1)	65.4 (8.3)
Auditory Recognition Delayed	65.6 (8.6)	90.0 (14.1)	64.5 (8.0)
General Memory	60.4 (8.9)	81.8 (15.1)	57.8 (6.7)
Working Memory	80.4 (16.9)	85.6 (13.0)	97.8 (13.0)

Table 5.6 WMS-IV Performance of Persons Diagnosed With MCI (*N* = 5) and AD (*N* = 48)

Index	MCI Mean and SD	MCI Matched Controls Mean and SD	AD Mean and SD	AD Matched Controls Mean and SD
Auditory Memory	89.9 (14.9)	105.6 (14.8)	68.5 (18.2)	107.1 (16.2)
Visual Memory	89.3 (15.3)	102.1 (13.5)	69.7 18.8)	102.5 (13.6)
Visual Working Memory	91.6 (13.5)	107.2 (12.0)	NA	NA
Immediate Memory	90.8 (13.7)	105.8 (13.8	71.7 (17.4)	107.4 (15.6)
Delayed Memory	87.5 (17.2)	103.5 (14.2)	63.6 (18.7)	104.6 (15.5)

limits, but were quite impaired on all other indexes, with the General Memory Index being especially hard hit.

Table 5.6 presents information on the WMS-IV performance of persons diagnosed with mild cognitive impairment (MCI) and probable AD. The information was derived from the WMS-IV Technical and Interpretive Manual (Wechsler, 2009b). As can be seem from Table 5.6, persons diagnosed with MCI score approximately one standard deviation below matched controls on all indexes. Persons with probable AD scored two standard deviations or more below matched controls on all indexes.

One of the most difficult challenges the clinician faces when evaluating an older person with memory complaints is determining if the complaint is due to normal aging, mild cognitive impairment, dementia, an untreated medical condition like thyroid dysfunction, anxiety or depression, sensory impairment, or some combination thereof. Contrary to the stereotype that "all older people are alike," people over 65 represent a heterogeneous population. As many investigators have pointed out, assessing older individuals poses unique challenges. For a bit dated but still excellent reference on the assessment of older adults, the interested reader is encouraged to consult Poon et al. (1986).

Among the challenges the clinician faces in assessing older adults is the older person's fear of losing their independence and civil rights, as a result of being labelled with a mild cognitive disorder or dementia. In addition, significant others and family members may see them as incompetent to make major life decisions. It will be recalled that just because a person suffers from mild cognitive impairment or Alzheimer's disease doesn't mean they are incompetent to make decisions or even drive. The determination of competency is a legal matter, with social and psychological consequences.

Another challenge in assessing older persons is the fear of being labelled mentally ill. Older people, compared to younger people, are often not as receptive to mental health services. Combined with this, many therapists are biased against treating older adults, feeling they are unable to benefit from psychotherapy. And many older adults have difficulty relating to therapists who are significantly younger than they are or of a different cultural, ethnic, or racial group.

In addition, compared to younger people, older adults also do not have as much experience with standardized testing. This is especially true of assessment protocols that use computerized-based testing.

It is also not unusual for the novice assessor to fail to establish adequate rapport with the person being assessed, which can have a negative effect on the person's compliance. The failure to establish rapport is more likely in assessment clinics that attempt to collect background and complete memory screening in a short time frame, like two hours. As an example, about a decade ago the present writer was asked to perform a clinical interview and neurocognitive screening within a one-hour period at a neurologist's office. During the hour the patient was being assessed, the neurologist and a social worker interviewed family members and/or significant others regarding the patient's functioning and medical history. The second hour of the patient's appointment was devoted to providing tentative assessment findings to the patient and his or her family. As might be expected, several patients experienced this assessment process as threatening and dehumanizing, although the neurologist viewed the process as "time-efficient."

Clinicians who have not been specifically trained to work with older adults often fail to appreciate the emotional, cognitive, and physical demands placed on a frail older adult who is expected to undergo a two-hour exam, let alone three to six hours of testing, which is often completed during one marathon test period, especially in university settings. Marathon test sessions are often justified in terms of expediency. Such assessment procedures appear more geared towards meeting the needs of the assessment team than the patient. The competent assessment of older adults involves having basic knowledge in the areas of aging and human development, psychopharmacology, neurology, and neuropsychology, as well as knowledge of each test's reliability and validity, including ecological validity. In addition, it involves having good psychotherapeutic skills. The ability to establish rapport to the point where the older person feels comfortable sharing often extremely sensitive and at times painful personal information within a relatively short period of time is a skill not easily acquired or taught. The practice of assessment is not unlike the practice of individual psychotherapy—both involve science and art (Levy, 1963).

Unfortunately, in this writer's experience, many training programs these days give too much weight to what might be labelled quantitative assessment (an overemphasis on trying to determine the statistical significance between various test scores), computerized scoring and interpretations, and the like. Not enough emphasis is placed on teaching the more qualitative aspects of the assessment process, such as the clinician's role in assessment. Failure to take into consideration qualitative patient information, like the person's social, educational, and work history, can contribute to invalid assessments (Lezak, 1976; Matarazzo, 1990; Wechsler, 1939). An example of the value of examining qualitative information in assessment, such as the nature of a subject's errors in test performance, is exemplified by the Boston Process Approach to neuropsychological assessment (Libon, Swenson, Ashendorf, Bauer, & Bowers, 2013).

Case Study 3: William is a 72-year-old white married male, referred for assessment by his physician, due to William's concerns about his memory during the past 18 months. Approximately two years prior, he sustained a severe heart attack while traveling in a remote Chinese province. Due to a lack of available medical resources, he had to return to the U.S. for medical intervention and as a result, he did not receive timely and appropriate medical treatment until two weeks after his heart attack. He reports that since his heart attack, his memory is not as good. In regard to his health history, William was in relatively good health prior to his heart attack. He had been treated for mild hypertension for four years, and he had no history of psychiatric or substance abuse problems. He had always exercised regularly. In regard to his educational and work history, William received a PhD in history from a prestigious university, and he spoke three languages. He had a successful career teaching history at the university level prior to retirement at age 67 and had been published in numerous peer-reviewed journals. William underwent a complete neuropsychological assessment including evaluation of his intellectual, memory, and personality functioning. Personality testing and a clinical interview revealed no evidence of anxiety, depression, or personality dysfunction. The WAIS-IV yielded scores in the superior range with no evidence of deterioration. The WMS-IV yielded several index scores in the high borderline range. As a result, he was diagnosed with a minor neurocognitive disorder, in light of his documented premorbid educational and work history and subjective complaints.

As can be seen from the case study, knowledge of William's life and medical history was critical at arriving at an accurate assessment of his memory functioning. It is known that anoxia secondary to a severe heart attack can negatively impact the hippocampus resulting in memory complaints.

Studies of Mild Cognitive Impairment, Idiopathic Dementia, and Alzheimer's

The following is a review of the use of various versions of the WMS to assess mild cognitive impairment and various dementing conditions. Readers wishing to learn more about the potential neuropsychological sequelae of various neurological disorders are encouraged to consult such excellent references as Grant and Adams (2009) and Larner (2008).

Logue and Wyrick (1979), in a study which sought to validate Russell's (1975) version of the WMS, compared the performance of 29 normal aging individuals to a group of 29 persons aged 55–85 with dementia on the WMS. The groups were matched for age, education, and sex. The Russell version significantly discriminated between the groups. Both groups showed greater impairment in figural as opposed to semantic memory.

Weingartner et al. (1981) investigated memory failure in progressive idiopathic dementia (PID). They compared 14 patients with progressive idiopathic dementia (presumably Alzheimer's) to 14 normal controls on a variety of measures, including an unknown version of the original WMS. Patients with PID scored significantly lower than did controls on all seven subtests of the WMS. The mean MQ for the PID group was 82 compared to 113 for the control group.

Naugle, Cullum, Bigler, and Massman (1986) investigated some of the neuropsychological characteristics and atrophic brain changes in persons with presenile ($N = 41$) and senile dementia ($N = 97$) through an archival study. Subjects were administered the WAIS and WMS-I under standard conditions. Despite significantly greater age, the researchers found that the senile patients did not perform significantly more poorly on the neuropsychological measures (specifically MQ, Logical Memory, Visual Reproduction, and Associate Learning) when controlling for education. Nor was there a significant difference between the two groups in cortical atrophy.

Observing that several investigations had suggested that prior item intrusion errors may be diagnostic of the early stages of Alzheimer's, Jacobs, Salmon, Tröster, and Butters (1990) investigated the presence of such errors in the figural memory productions of patients with Alzheimer's and Huntington's disease. They compared the performance of 39 subjects with Alzheimer's to 23 persons with Huntington's and 29 controls on the Visual Reproduction subtest from the WMS-I. The found both the Alzheimer's and Huntington's patients made more intrusion errors than normal controls, and the Alzheimer's group made more intrusion errors than did the Huntington's group.

Christensen, Hadzi-Pavlovic, and Jacomb (1991) performed a meta-analysis to identify tests that were useful in differentiating demented patients from normal elderly persons. The WMS-R and WMS-I were found useful in this discrimination. Especially useful were the MQ, Logical Memory I and II, Associate Learning and Verbal Paired Associates, Visual Reproduction I, and Mental Control scores.

Hom (1992) investigated the effects of AD on neuropsychological functioning. One of the measures he used was Russell's (1975) version of the WMS. He compared 35 persons with probable Alzheimer's disease (AD) to 30 normal aging healthy controls. Hom (1992) found significant differences between the groups on all WMS measures.

Mittenberg, Malloy, Petrick, and Knee (1994) examined whether impaired depth perception discriminates AD from aging and major depression. He compared 20 persons with presumed AD to 20 gender-, age-, and education-matched healthy controls without AD. Study participants completed testing, which included the WMS-R Logical Memory I and II and Visual Reproduction I and II subtests. Stereopsis scores were impaired in AD versus control groups but not significantly related to any WMS-R measures. In a second study that investigated the differential diagnosis of AD versus depression, 27 patients were examined and completed the same medical workups and psychological testing (immediate subtests only) described earlier. After initial examination, 13 patients were assigned to the depressed group. At the time of the initial examination, stereopsis was found to be impaired in the AD group compared to the depression group. On testing completed as part of a 16-month follow-up, patients with AD were found to have significantly deteriorated on the Visual Reproduction subtest compared to depressed controls.

Tomer, Larrabee, and Crook (1994) studied the structure of everyday memory in 273 adults aged 50–79 with age-associated memory impairment. As a means of studying factorial invariance across age, the subjects were assigned to three groups: 50–58 years old, 59–67 years old, and 68–79 years old. The subjects were administered a variety of measures, including the WMS-I Logical Memory and Associate Learning (hard associates) subtests. An analysis revealed that Logical Memory and Associate Learning (hard associates) loaded on a Narrative Memory factor across all age groups.

Ardila et al. (2000) investigated the neuropsychological characteristics of a large kindred with familial Alzheimer's disease caused by the E280A single presinilin-1 mutation. They found that persons with the mutation who presented with memory complaints performed more poorly on WMS-I Logical Memory and Associate Learning subtests and total scores than did those without memory complaints and the mutation.

Johnson (1994) investigated the utility of the Episodic Memory Scale (EMS) for evaluating episodic memory through a concurrent validity study. The participants in this study were 17 subjects with AD living in the community and 17 individuals with central nervous system dysfunction. All participants were administered the EMS along with other tests, including the WMS-R Logical Memory and Verbal Paired Associates subtests, which together comprise the

Verbal Memory Index. The EMS positively correlated with the Verbal Memory Index at the $p < .001$ level and the Verbal Memory Index significantly differentiated between the two groups.

Building on the results of a prior study that found AD patients compared to those with ischemic vascular dementia were able to improve from command to copy conditions on a clock drawing test, Libon, Malamut, Swenson, Sands, and Cloud (1996) investigated the profile underlying the cognitive deficits responsible for this profile. Among the tests used to determine the cognitive deficits was the Boston Revision of the Mental Control subtest. The Mental Control scale was found useful in differentiating the performance of these two groups.

Marson, Dymek, Duke, and Harrell (1997) investigated the subscale validity of the Mattis Dementia Rating Scale by comparing the performance of 50 patients with probable AD on this instrument and a variety of other measures including the WMS-R Attention/Concentration and Verbal Memory Indexes. The authors found the corresponding Mattis scales correlated positively with the WMS-R measures.

White and Murphy (1998) investigated working memory for nonverbal auditory information (tones) in persons with AD using a variety of neuropsychological measures, including the WMS-I Memory Span subtest, a measure of auditory working memory. The authors found intact tone perception but a progressive decline in working memory for auditory nonverbal information with advancing AD.

Brown and Storandt (2000) investigated the sensitivity of category-cued recall to very mild AD using several measures, including the WMS-R Logical Memory subtest. The Logical Memory subtest was found to have utility is discriminating between normal controls and those with mild and very mild AD.

Giovannetti et al. (2001) investigated the nature of the different mechanisms for deficits in concept formation in persons with AD and ischemic vascular dementia (IVD). The Boston Revision of the Mental Control subtest was used as a measure of executive functioning. The Similarities subtest of the WAIS-R was used as a measure of concept formation. Patients with AD produced a greater proportion of in-set errors, while IVD patients produced a greater proportion of out-of-set errors. The IVD patients' impaired concept formation was found to be related to deficits in executive systems necessary to monitor responses and sustain a mental set.

Efklides et al. (2002) explored the relationship among a Greek version of the WMS-I, Rivermead Behavioral Memory Test (RBMT, a measure of prospective memory) and the Everyday Memory Questionnaire, and the differential effects of Alzheimer's disease on the previously mentioned tests. In regard to the WMS, a confirmatory factor analysis revealed that it loaded on verbal semantic memory, the formation of new associations, and orientation. The Visual Reproduction subtest did not load on the same visual memory processes as did the Pictures and Faces subtests of the RBMT, and the authors noted that performance on the Visual Reproduction subtest appeared to rely on verbal processes guiding performance. Patients with AD performed significantly lower than did healthy adults on the WMS-I and RBMT.

Johnstone, Hogg, Schopp, Kapila, and Edwards (2002) noted that while the main cognitive deficits associated with AD are known, the relative degree of impairment in each had yet to be adequately determined. The authors calculated indices of relative decline for 32 patients with probable AD by comparing estimates of premorbid intellectual functioning to concurrent neuropsychological scores, which included measures from the WMS-R. The study found intelligence as assessed by the WAIS-R Full Scale IQ declined least, followed by attention (as assessed by the WMS-R Attention/Concentration Index), memory (as assessed by the WMS-R General Memory and Delayed Memory indexes), speed of processing, and cognitive flexibility.

Johnson, Storandt, and Balota (2003) examined the nature of prose recall in dementia compared to normal aging. They examined the responses of 48 young adults, 47 nondemented older adults, and 70 people with mild AD on the Logical Memory subtest of the WMS-I under immediate and delayed recall conditions. Using a revised scoring system, the authors found that compared to young adults, healthy older adults showed good immediate recall but deficits in delayed recall. Persons with AD made errors of omission at immediate recall, which the authors attributed to attentional rather than memory dysfunction.

Hopkins and Libon (2005) examined the neuropsychological functioning of 24 dementia patients with psychosis to 24 outpatients without psychosis diagnosed with either probable Alzheimer's disease or ischemic vascular dementia on the Boston Revision of the Wechsler Memory Scale Mental Control subtest. The patients with dementia and psychosis performed significantly below the contrast group on the Mental Control subtest, suggesting problems with executive functioning.

Westervelt, Ruffolo, and Tremont (2005) studied the relationship between odor identification and cognition in older adults. The study evaluated 100 participants, 74 of whom were presenting for assessment of their memory concerns. The remaining 26 participants were healthy, community-dwelling older adults. In addition to completing the Brief Smell Identification Test (BSIT), participants completed several neuropsychological tests, including the WMS-III Digit Span and Mental Control subtests, which were used as an index of attention, and the WMS-II Logical Memory I and II subtests, which were used as part of an index of memory. The results of the study indicated that the BSIT had moderately significant correlations with the WMS-III indexes.

Gomez and White (2006) examined the ability of verbal fluency tasks to assess mild AD. Participants in the study were 76 healthy adults and 77 individuals with very mild AD. Study participants completed a number of tests including the Associate Learning and Logical Memory subtests from the WMS and a measure of semantic fluency. The semantic fluency measure and the Logical Memory subtest were found useful in discriminating between healthy controls and those with mild AD.

Baudic et al. (2006) examined the relationship between executive function deficits and episodic memory in persons with early AD. Episodic memory was assessed by the WMS-R Logical Memory subtest, and attention/executive function by the Mental Control (months backward) subtest. Both measures were found to discriminate between normal controls and those with mild and very mild AD.

Westervelt, Carvalho, and Duff (2007) examined the differences in clinical presentation in patients presenting with AD with and without olfactory deficits. In comparing 46 AD patients who were olfactory impaired to 44 AD patients whose olfaction was intact, the authors found no significant differences between the two groups on the WMS-III Digit Span, Mental Control, Logical Memory I and II, and Visual Reproduction I and II subtests.

Seelye, Howieson, Wild, Moore, and Kaye (2009) investigated the performance of 24 patients with mild cognitive impairment and 46 patients with mild Alzheimer's disease on the WMS-III Faces subtest. They hypothesized that these two groups would be relatively impaired compared to controls on this measure. The authors found no significant difference between controls and patients with mild cognitive impairment on the Faces subtest. They also found that patients with Alzheimer's performed significantly worse on the Faces subtest than did the mild cognitive impairment group and controls, suggesting patients with mild Alzheimer's are impaired in their facial recognition abilities.

Adachi et al. (2013) compared the utility of the Rivermead Behavioral Memory Test (RBMT) and the Alzheimer's Disease Assessment Scale-Cognitive part (ADAS-C) for the evaluation of mild cognitive impairment or very mild Alzheimer's disease in a Japanese population. The author used the criterion of at least one WMS-R index score below 77.5, or 1.5 standard deviations below age-adjusted normal values, as an indicator of mild cognitive impairment. Using this criterion, the researchers found the RBMT was more useful than the ADAS-C in evaluating patients with mild cognitive impairment or very mild AD.

Alegret et al. (2013) investigated the ability of a neuropsychological battery for Spanish individuals to detect cognitive impairment in adulthood. The battery included the WMS-III Word List subtest. The authors found the Word List subtest along with a measure of semantic verbal fluency were most useful in distinguishing healthy from demented subjects.

Hori, Sanjo, Tomita, and Mizusawa (2013) investigated whether the Visual Reproduction subtest of the WMS-R could be used as a predictor of Alzheimer's disease in Japanese patients with mild impairment. They found this subtest was a useful and sensitive measure for predicting the conversion from MCI to Alzheimer's within a two-year period.

Frisch et al. (2013) attempted to dissociate the neural correlates of memory disorders in 19 patients with Alzheimer's disease and 11 patients with frontotemporal lobar degeneration using a German version of the WMS-R Logical Memory I and II and Visual Reproduction I and II subtests. Although both groups were found to be impaired on the WMS relative to controls, the tests did not differentiate between the two groups. However, the study found that patients with Alzheimer's presented with deterioration in the parieto-mesial cortex, and patients with frontotemporal lobar degeneration had deterioration in the frontal cortical and subcortical regions. The study indicates that poor performance on these subtests may occur for different neuroanatomical reasons.

Clark et al. (2016) investigated the utility and performance of internally developed norms and standard norms in identifying cognitive impairment in late middle age. The research was completed as part of the Wisconsin Registry for Alzheimer's Prevention Study. The WMS-R Logical Memory I and II subtests were among the neuropsychological measures investigated, and both were found useful in the identification of mild cognitive impairment.

Emsaki, NeshatDoost, Tavakoli, and Barekatain (2017) investigated the impact of memory specificity training on working and prospective memory in 20 patients who met the criteria for amnestic mild cognitive impairment. The patients were randomly assigned to either a control or a treatment group that consisted of five sessions of training on memory specificity. The participants were evaluated using a variety of measures, including Iranian versions of the WMS-III Spatial Span, Logical Memory and Verbal Paired Associates I and II subtests to assess working memory and auditory memory, and the WMS-IV Visual Reproduction and Designs I and II subtests to assess visual memory. The results of the study indicated that memory specificity training had a positive effect on WMS-III working memory measures.

Gonçalves et al. (2017) used selected subtests of a Portuguese version of the WMS-III to see if they would distinguish between the performance of 36 patients with Alzheimer's disease, 16 patients with subcortical vascular dementia (SVD), and 40 controls. The results of the investigation revealed that when controlling for education, the SVD group performed significantly better on the majority of the indexes and delayed recall subtests than did the AD group, except for Working Memory.

Earlier in this book, it was noted that the three WMS revisions use different periods to evaluate delayed recall. For the WMS-R, the time between the immediate and delayed recall subtests is 30 minutes; for the WMS-III 25–35 minutes; and for the WMS-IV 20–30 minutes. Montgomery, Harris, Stabler, and Lu (2017) have observed that consistency in the administration of neuropsychological tests is critical to obtaining reliable and valid results and that any deviation from standard administration procedures may negatively impact the test's reliability and validity. The authors also note that there is a paucity of research evaluating the effects of non-standard administration on patients' test performances. The authors completed an archival study using data from the National Alzheimer's Coordinating Center's Uniform Data Set. They compared the test administration of the WMS-R and WMS-III Logical Memory I and II subtests to 21,376 subjects and calculated the proportion of the subjects who were administered the tests according the standard test guidelines. Of the total sample, only 49.7% administered the tests consistent with standard test guidelines. Concerning the ability of the subtests to identify impaired performance, the authors found that patients with probable vascular dementia were more affected by the variability in time delay than were those with probable Alzheimer's disease. Based on an analysis of their data, the authors recommended that using a 20-minute delay (with a range of 18–25 minutes) between immediate and delayed recall yielded optimal data for diagnostic decisions.

Sahin et al. (2017) attempted to differentially diagnose depressive pseudodementia from Alzheimer's disease using selected subtests from the Turkish version of the WMS, other neuropsychological tests, and measures of hippocampal volume. They found that the Personal and Current Information, Orientation, Memory Span (Digit Span Backwards), and Visual Reproduction subtests successfully differentiated between these two groups.

Scheltens et al. (2018) presented the results of an exploratory clinical study of p 38 mitogen-activated kinase inhibitor on the memory functioning of 16 patients suffering from early Alzheimer's disease. Episodic memory was assessed by the WMS (version unknown) immediate and delayed recall composite scores. The authors found a significant increase over baseline in immediate and delayed recall at days 28 and 44.

Studies of Subcortical Conditions, Including the Vascular Dementias

Hypertension is a known risk factor for impaired cognitive and intellectual functioning. Vanderploeg, Goldman, and Kleinman (1987) examined the relationship between systolic and diastolic blood pressure and cognitive functioning in 15 hypertensive subjects who underwent biofeedback to treat their condition. Higher blood pressure levels were associated with poorer performance on a variety of measures, including the WMS-I MQ and the Visual Reproduction subtest.

Stambrook et al. (1988) presented a case history study of the neuropsychological changes associated with the neurosurgical treatment of normal pressure hydrocephalus (NPH). NPH is associated with gait and balance disturbance, urinary incontinence, and cognitive impairment. Fourteen patients were evaluated. All patients demonstrated significant pre- to post-surgery improvement on Russell's (1975) version of the WMS.

Sapin, Frishberg, and Sherman (1990) presented a case report of the neuropsychological and MRI correlates of dementia in Binswanger's disease (BD). The patient, who was a 60-year-old female, had displayed neurological symptoms for two years prior to a neurological consultation. The patient underwent an extensive neuropsychological evaluation, which included the WMS-I and Russell's (1975) revision. The results of testing revealed impairment on the Logical Memory II, Associate Learning, and Mental Control subtests.

Haut, Young, Cutlip, Callahan, and Haut (1995) presented a case history of an individual with bilateral thalamic lesions and anterograde amnesia and impaired implicit memory. The patient was neuropsychologically evaluated twice over a 13-month interval. During this period, the patient displayed improvements in her performance on WMS-R Logical Memory I and Visual Reproduction I and II subtests.

Lazar, Weiner, Wald, and Kula (1995) discussed a case history of a female with visuoconstructive deficits following an infarct in the right basal ganglia. Using a process approach with the Visual Reproduction subtest of the WMS-R to obtain additional quantitative information, the authors were able to demonstrate that her visuoconstructive deficit was not due to defects in visual perception. The patient's performance on the Visual Reproduction subtest fell at or below 1.5 standard deviations below average.

Deckel and Morrison (1996) examined the frequency of denial of illness in 19 patients diagnosed with Huntington's disease (HD), 17 of whom underwent neuropsychological evaluation, which included the WMS-R Logical Memory I and II and Visual Reproduction I and II subtests. The test performance of HD patients was compared to a control group ($N = 14$). On memory testing, there was no significant difference between HD patients and the control group on any WMS-R measure.

Libon et al. (1997) examined the neuropsychological functioning of 27 patients diagnosed with probable/possible ischemic vascular disease and 33 subjects with probable Alzheimer's disease using several tests, including the Boston Revision of the WMS Mental Control subtest, a measure of executive control. Persons with IVD obtained significantly lower scores than did AD patients on the WMS Mental Control subtest.

Karimian, Asgari, Neshat Doost, Oreizi, and Najafi (2018) used the WMS-III Logical Memory I and II and Visual Reproduction I and II subtests, along with other neuropsychological measures, to investigate the performance of 35 ischemic stroke patients compared to controls. The mean scores of the control group were significantly higher than that of the stroke group. Although all measures of memory were affected, the Visual Reproduction I and II subtests were affected to a greater degree than were the Logical Memory I and II subtests.

Studies of Parkinson's and Lewy Body Dementia

As might be expected, the WMS has been used to assess the memory dysfunction that often accompanies Parkinson's disease (PD). Lewy bodies (the name given to eosinophilic intracytoplasmic inclusions) in the brainstem are associated with the movement symptoms seen in PD. They are also present in other cortical and subcortical brain sites, often resulting in cognitive and psychiatric symptoms. Persons with PD are at risk for Lewy body dementia (LBD), a disease characterized by attention deficits, bradyphrenia, impaired spatial working memory, fluctuating consciousness, impaired verbal fluency, recognition memory better than free recall, and executive dysfunction (Larner, 2008).

Paolo, Tröster, Axelrod, and Koller (1995) investigated the construct validity of the Wisconsin Card Sort Test (WCST) in 187 normal elderly and 181 persons with Parkinson's disease. All subjects were volunteers in an ongoing study of neurodegenerative diseases. In addition to the WCST, subjects were administered a battery of tests including the WMS-R Logical Memory II subtest. The authors reported that WCST scores did not significantly load on any attention or memory measures for either group.

Wagner and Bachman (1996) presented a case history of a 60-year-old man with biopsy-proven Lewy body disease. He was seen over a 24-month period at a university-based memory clinic, during which time he underwent serial neuropsychological testing at 6 months, 10 months, 12 months, and 24 months after symptom onset. Neuropsychological testing included Russell's (1975) revision of the WMS and the Information and Orientation subtest from the WMS-R. Information and orientation questions were observed to be remarkably preserved through much of the patient's disease course. Performance on the Logical Memory I and II subtests was described as weak throughout of the course of the disease, and performance on the Visual Reproduction I and II extremely impaired.

Downes et al. (1998) compared groups of patients with PD and LBD to controls on a range of neuropsychological tests to evaluate their functioning. These tests included the WMS-R Logical Memory and Visual Reproduction subtests, with emphasis on immediate memory and an index of forgetting as assessed by the following formula: (immediate memory score − delayed memory score/ immediate memory score). The results of their study revealed that patients with early PD were impaired relative to controls on Logical Memory I, Logical Memory forgetting, and Visual Reproduction forgetting indices. Patients with advanced PD were impaired relative to controls on Logical Memory I and Visual Reproduction I measures. There was no significant difference between patients with advanced PD and those with LBD on any of the measures.

Tröster, Woods, and Morgan (2007) studied test-retest stability and practice effects for several commonly used neuropsychological tests used to evaluate persons with Parkinson's disease. Among the measures studied were the WMS-R Logical Memory I and II subtests. The authors did not find evidence of substantial practice effects in most neurocognitive measures, including the LM I and II.

Biars et al. (2019) investigated the performance of 24 patients with Parkinson's disease and 24 patients with Parkinson's disease with impulse control disorders on the Iowa Gambling Test (IGT). They found no significant difference in the two groups on their performance on the IGT or on the WMS-III Logical Memory I and II subtests.

Foster, Yung, Drago, Crucian, and Heilman (2013) investigated the effects of depression and side of onset of motor symptoms on working memory in patients with PD. Working memory was assessed by the WMS-III Digit Span

Backwards subtest. The authors compared 30 PD patients with left hemi-body onset to 35 PD patients with right hemibody onset. The authors found that poorer working memory was associated with left hemibody onset and depression, and noted that depression is often associated with left frontal dysfunction.

Sawada et al. (2018) investigated the use of donepezil against psychosis and decline in PD over a two-year period. Donepezil yielded no protective effect against psychosis but did positively affect auditory memory, as assessed by a Japanese version of the WMS. The subtests used to assess auditory memory were not disclosed in the research report.

Other Studies

Varney, Campbell, and Roberts (1994) examined the long-term neuropsycho-logical sequelae of fever associated with amnesia in 36 combat veterans who reported having experienced a febrile illness, which resulted in an elevated body temperature of 104 degrees or higher and a period of amnesia lasting 24 hours or more. Among the tests administered to the group of veterans was the WMS-I. Compared to 40 healthy controls, the veterans performed signifi-cantly worse on the Logical Memory and Associate Learning subtests and in addition had significantly lower MQs.

In regard to studies of amnesia, perhaps the most famous is the study of memory after bilateral hippocampal lesions by Scoville and Milner (1957). In this paper, the authors present test results of the now famous H. M., along with two other patients who had undergone a radical bilateral medial temporal lobe resection. When evaluated post-surgery, the three subjects' WMS-I Memory Quotients ranged from 60 to 70.

Bowden (1990) performed an interesting and enlightening review of the lit-erature regarding the relationship between neurologically asymptomatic alco-holism and Wernicke-Korsakoff syndrome. At the time he conducted his study, he noted that a 20–30 point scatter between IQ and MQ was often considered a psychometric hallmark of alcoholic Korsakoff patients. After reviewing the available evidence, he concluded that the psychometric hallmark might have created a neuropsychological stereotype not representative of the broader clini-cal group. He noted that Wernicke-Korsakoff patients are a more heteroge-neous group than generally recognized.

Channon and Daum (2000) investigated the effect of semantic categori-zation on recall memory in amnesia. They compared a group of 13 patients (seven with alcoholic Korsakoff's syndrome, three post-encephalitic patients with bilateral temporal lobe damage, two patients with medial temporal lobe damage from closed head injuries, and one patient with bilateral thalamic infarcts) to 15 controls. Among the recall measures used was a German version of the WMS Logical Memory I and II subtests. The amnestic group performed significantly worse than did controls on Logical Memory I and II.

Gass, Luis, Meyers, and Kuljis (2000) presented a neuropsychological case history of familial Creutzfeldt-Jacob disease, a rare hereditary form of prion disease. The patient was a 42-year-old male who had presented with signs of increasing impairment over a year. A neuropsychological evaluation revealed mild impairment on the WMS-R Logical Memory I subtest compared to severe impairment on Logical Memory II and moderate impairment on Logical Memory Recognition. No impairment was found in the Visual Reproduction I or II subtests.

The research presented in this section is representative of the many ways the WMS and various revisions have been used to assess persons with mild cognitive impairment, various forms of dementia, the cognitive sequelae of Parkinson's disease, and persons presenting with amnesia. The review that has been presented is by no means exhaustive, and interested readers are encouraged to conduct their own literature searches to identify other potentially pertinent references to the reader's area(s) of interest. The following key points are offered.

Key Points

- All WMS versions have been successfully used to diagnose dementia and mild cognitive impairment.
- Subjects with AD are frequently impaired on the Logical Memory and Visual Reproduction subtests, as are subjects with frontotemporal lobar degeneration. Although both groups perform poorly on these measures, it appears they do so for different neuroanatomical reasons.
- The Memory Quotient from the original WMS has shown some utility in identifying people with probable AD.
- Intrusion errors on the Visual Reproduction subtest have been useful in distinguishing patients with Huntington's disease from patients with Alzheimer's disease.
- The WMS-I Logical Memory, Associate Learning, and total score might be sensitive to impairment in individuals with E280A presinilin-1 mutations.
- The WMS-III Faces subtest may be a useful measure to distinguish between persons with AD and mild cognitive impairment.
- A cutoff score of 1.5 standard deviations below the mean on age-adjusted WMS-R index scores can be a useful criterion of mild cognitive impairment.
- Based on one large study, the optimum time between WMS immediate and delayed subtests appears to be 20 minutes (with a range of 18–25 minutes) to identify probable vascular and Alzheimer's dementia. The authors of the study remind clinicians of the importance of using consistent standard administration procedures to obtain reliable and valid results.
- The WMS-I appears useful in distinguishing depressive pseudodementia patients from patients with AD.
- The WMS has utility in identifying memory deficits in patients with Parkinson's disease and Lewy body dementia.

- WMS tests of working memory may be useful in distinguishing between patients with cortical versus subcortical dementia.
- The WMS has been used to assess the efficacy of medication on the memory of people suffering from AD.

Investigations of Aging

As might be expected, the WMS has been a popular instrument used by researchers to investigate various aspects of aging. What follows is a selection of papers illustrating the range of such investigations. These papers will generally be presented based on the year they were published.

In 1980, Bak and Greene published the results of an investigation into changes in neuropsychological functioning in an aging population. Two groups of 15 subjects between the ages of 50–62 and 67–86 were administered portions of the Halstead-Reitan Neuropsychological Test Battery, the WAIS, and the Logical Memory (LM), Visual Reproduction (VR), and Associate Learning (AL) subtests from the WMS-I, with a half hour readministration of the WMS-I subtests using Russell's (1975) scoring procedures and a scoring procedure devised by Bak for the AL subtest. In regard to the WMS, the authors found that the only significant difference between the two groups was that the younger group performed significantly better than the older group did on the VR I and II subtests. It should be noted that other researchers have suggested that the VR subtest may be a sensitive measure of early cognitive decline, possibly because it appears to tap more cognitive functions than other WMS measures of verbal memory.

Siegler, McCarty, and Logue (1982) reported on the results of a study of WMS scores, selective attrition, and distance from death of a subset of 160 of the initial participants who were part of the Duke First Longitudinal Study of aging. They found that the hard associates from the Associate Learning subtest and the Visual Reproduction subtests declined late in life. In a healthy group of nondemented older persons, the initial superiority of WMS scores was related to longer-term survival.

In a similar study, Haaland, Linn, Hunt, and Goodwin (1983) completed a normative study of Russell's (1975) variant of the WMS in a healthy elderly population in an effort to provide elderly normative data. Russell's (1975) WMS was administered to 175 participants ranging in age from 65 to 80 and above. The participants were divided into age groups of 65–69, 70–74, 75–79, and 80 and above. The authors found a clear age-related decline in Visual Reproduction I and II, with a significant aging effect present for Visual Reproduction I but not Visual Reproduction II. In addition, they found a significant memory decline from immediate to delayed recall for both the Logical Memory and Visual Reproduction subtests, noting that while age affects the amount immediately recalled, it does not affect the rate at which information is lost. The result was interpreted as reflecting a greater age-related decline in visual-nonlinguistic memory than auditory-linguistic memory with age, consistent with the findings of Bak and Greene (1980) and other researchers.

Crosson et al. (1984) provided a critique of Russell's (1975) norms for the Logical Memory and Visual Reproduction subtests of the WMS. The norms for the Logical Memory subtest were criticized as too stringent, as they tended to classify too many non-neurological subjects as impaired. The authors cautioned clinicians about making comparisons between differences in Logical Memory I versus Visual Reproduction I using Russell's (1975) norms, because they are not comparable.

Citing the need for ecological validity in memory testing, Crook, Youngjohn, and Larrabee (1990) attempted to replicate and extend the findings of Hill, Crook, Zadiek, Yesavage, and Sheikh (1989), who reported a significant correlation between TV News Test performance, two items from the Memory Assessment Clinic's Self-Rating form (MAC-S), and a self-report scale of everyday memory. Three hundred sixty-four normal volunteers were administered the TV News Test and the Logical Memory (LM) or Associate Learning (AL) subtests from the WMS-I, along with selected items from the MAC-S, and other neuropsychological tests. The results of the study revealed a strong relationship between the TV News Test and LM, and that the former was more sensitive to the effects of aging than the latter.

Cullum, Butters, Tröster, and Salmon (1990) investigated normal aging and forgetting rates on the WMS-R in groups of healthy older adults ages 50–70 and 75–95. The older group displayed significantly more rapid forgetting rates on the Visual Reproduction, Verbal Paired Associates, and Visual Paired Associates subtests.

Mitrushina and Satz (1991) studied the changes in cognitive functioning associated with normal aging using a test battery that included Mental Control, Logical Memory, and Visual Reproduction subtests, with a 45-minute delayed recall without warning on the first two WMS-I measures in a group of healthy aged volunteers ranging in age from 57 to 85. The number of subjects who participated in the first round of testing was 156. Of this group, only 122 subjects participated in three rounds of testing. People who dropped out of the study were characterized by poorer performance on Logical Memory I and II subtests and slower psychomotor speed compared to those who completed during the three test periods. The 122 participants were divided into four age groups: 57–65, 66–70, 71–75, and 76–85. The results of the study found that longitudinal performance on measures of verbal and visual memory were due to improvement in scores for the younger three groups and a decrease in performance for the older group. The "improvement" was attributed to practice effects for the youngest three groups and a failure to benefit from experience for the oldest group.

Crook et al. (1992) conducted a cross-cultural study of aging and everyday memory in Belgian and American samples matched on age and gender. Participants were administered the Memory Assessment Clinical (MAC) battery (a computerized test), along with traditional psychometric measures. In addition, the Logical Memory and Associate Learning subtests from the WMS-I were administered to American subjects. In this study, the only memory measure that did not show a significant age decline was the Logical Memory subtest, suggesting this subtest may not be the most sensitive measure with which to measure aging effects on secondary (i.e., long-term) memory.

Ivnik, Smith, Malec, Petersen, and Tangalos (1995) investigated the long-term stability and intercorrelations of cognitive abilities in older persons using the WAIS-R, WMS-R, and Rey Auditory-Verbal Learning Test. They investigated the assumptions that most psychologists make when interpreting adult cognitive tests, namely that for cognitively normal people, performances in one cognitive domain correlates well and predicts functioning in other cognitive domains, and that in the absence of pathology, cognition is stable. The authors note that age-related changes have been demonstrated for measures of intelligence, learning, and memory. Their study was conducted as part of the Mayo's Older Americans Normative Study (MOANS) research program. Three hundred ninety-seven participants from the 1988–1989 cohort were recontacted in 1992–1993 and invited to participate in repeat testing. Three hundred people or 75% of the original sample were retested, and of these 52 were excluded, leaving valid test data on 248 people. The mean test-retest interval was 3.7 years. Long-term stability coefficients for the WMS-R Verbal Memory, Visual Memory and General Memory Indexes were found to be 10 to 20 points lower than the 2- to 7-week stability coefficients presented in the WMS-R manual (Wechsler, 1987). The authors note that while many researchers have found that poor performance on formal memory testing is among the best predictors of degenerative neurological conditions for older persons, the final diagnosis of pathologic cognitive conditions cannot reliably be made from a single measurement, underscoring the need for repeat testing and convergent sources of information. While noting that the cognitive abilities of normal older adults are remarkably stable over several years, the authors also note that group differences mask individual differences. The authors found that while measures of attention/concentration and new learning were moderately stable over time, measures of delayed recall or retention were somewhat less stable.

Gage, Burns, Sellers, Roth, and Mittenberg (1995) examined the convergent/divergent properties and compatibility of the CVLT and WMS-R in a mixed sample of 30 normal and 30 psychiatric elderly individuals. The researchers found both tests were similar in discriminating between normal and psychiatric elderly subjects, and that the global indices (i.e., index scores) of the WMS-R were similar to the global and process indices of the CVLT.

Glisky, Polster, and Routhieaux (1995) report a study that provides evidence for a double dissociation between item and source memory. The subjects for the study consisted of 48 elderly (aged 65–87) participants without depression, dementia, or previous neurological problems who were divided preexperimentally into two groups on their basis of a composite measure of frontal lobe function. The subjects had completed a variety of neuropsychological tests, including measures executive and memory function (the WMS-R). The authors concluded that item and source memory rely on different underlying brain mechanisms.

Fastenau, Denburg, and Abeles (1996) investigated age differences in retrieval in 90 community-dwelling adults aged 30–90 using a variety of measures, including the WMS-R Logical Memory, Visual Reproduction, Digit Span, and Visual Memory Span subtests. The authors found that retrieval was less efficient in older adults, as predicted, and that age effects were reduced when controlling for differences in processing resources. The authors did not find that the age effect was larger for visual-spatial retrieval than for auditory-verbal retrieval. These findings suggest that while both verbal and visual-spatial information becomes less efficient with age, visual-spatial retrieval may require fewer processing resources.

Moore and Lichtenberg (1996) examined the relationship between neuropsychological measures and a measure of activities of daily living (ADLs) upon completion of an inpatient rehabilitation stay. One hundred fifty-four geriatric patients aged 60 and over were administered a variety of tests, including the WMS-R Logical Memory I and II subtests. Although the WMS-R measures were found to be positively correlated with other neuropsychological measures, an inability to perform ADLs, and functional independence, the value of measures like Logical Memory in predicting functional independence was judged to be modest.

When working with older adults, it is not unusual for clinicians to be asked to assess changes in cognitive functioning over time, including memory. Frerichs and Tuokko (2005) examined the change in scores on four memory tests, one of which included the WMS-I Information subtest, over a five-year period. The utility of six change scores were examined using five-year test-retest data. The authors found that reliable change indexes with a correction for practice and aging effects were useful when making diagnostic discriminations in older adults.

Helmes and Miller (2006) compared the performance of older adults on the computer-based MicroCog and the WMS-III. Although the WMS-III General Memory Index correlated moderately with the MicroCog Memory and General Cognitive Functioning indexes, the authors concluded that the correspondence between the two measures was not sufficient to substitute one for the other for clinical decision-making as to the memory functioning of adult adults.

Rogers, McPherson, Lu, and Cummings (2007) examined the ability of the WMS-III Logical Memory and Visual Reproduction norms for those 80 and over to accurately discriminate between individuals with amnestic mild cognitive impairment and Alzheimer's disease. In an investigation of 382 older adults ranging in age from 46 to 90, the authors found that these two subtests may overestimate long-delay memory in individuals with AD, undermining the discriminatory ability of the WMS-III in detecting dementia.

Teraishi et al. (2013) note that rare mutations in phenylalanine hydroxylase (PAH) contribute to phenylketonuria (PKU). PKU is a disease characterized by neuropsychiatric symptoms, including intellectual impairment. The authors studied whether there is an association between common single nucleotide polymorphisms (SNP) of PAH and memory performance as assessed by the WMS-R in a Japanese population. The results of the study indicated a significant association between an SNP and the age-corrected Verbal Memory Index. The results of the study suggest that common genetic variations in PAH are associated with verbal memory in healthy adults.

Kremen et al. (2014) investigated the genetic complexity of memory using the WMS-III Logical Memory and Visual Reproduction subtests and other cognitive measures to study episodic memory change in cognitive aging. Using a twin study approach from late middle-aged participants in the Vietnam Era Twin Study, the authors found phenotypic correlations between global cognitive ability and memory measures ranged from .28 to .33 for the Visual Reproduction and Logical Memory subtests, suggesting these measures are partially genetically determined.

Oberlin et al. (2015) examined whether the combined presence of the APOE e4 allele and elevated blood pressure was associated with lower cognitive performance in cognitively healthy middle-aged adults. The subjects were administered several tests, including the Visual Reproduction I and II and Logical Memory I and II subtests from the WMS-III. The authors found that elevated systolic blood pressure was predictive of poorer episodic memory performance (as assessed by the WMS-III) only in APOE e4 carriers.

Ezzati et al. (2016) studied the differential association of left and right hippocampal volumes with verbal episodic (as assessed by the WMS-R Logical Memory subtest) and spatial memory in older adults. The researchers found no significant correlation between the Logical Memory subtest and left hippocampal volume.

Bosnes et al. (2016) completed a confirmatory factor analytic study of the WMS-III in an elderly Norwegian sample. They found that a three-factor model consisting of working memory, visual memory, and auditory memory best fit their data.

Niwa et al. (2016) investigated whether regional cerebral blood flow (rCBF) using single-photon computed tomography was useful in the early diagnosis of dementia. They looked at the association between rCBF and various domains of memory as assessed by the Mini Mental Status Exam and the WMS-R. The correlation analysis indicated that WMS-R indices were most strongly correlated with rCBF in the left inferior frontal gyrus.

Kinno et al. (2017) examined the factor structure of the WMS-R for Japanese patients over 75 years of age in a memory clinic setting. They found that four factors appeared to best fit their model. These factors were recognition memory, paired associate memory, visual and working memory, and attention.

Hiscox et al. (2018) studied hippocampal viscoelasticity and episodic memory performance (as measured by the Verbal Paired Associates subtest of the WMS-R) in 11 healthy adults aged 66–73 examined with magnetic resonance elastography. A significant negative correlation was found between the left hippocampal damping ratio and Verbal Paired Associates recall score, and no correlation was found between right hippocampal measures and Verbal Paired Associates scores.

O'Shea et al. (2018) examined whether educational attainment, as a proxy of cognitive reserve, moderated the association between hippocampal volumes and episodic memory performance (as assessed by the WMS-III Logical Memory and total correct words recalled over four trials of the CVLT-2nd Ed.-Short Form) in healthy older adults. The researchers found that total hippocampal volume and larger left hippocampal volumes were associated with delayed recall of the Logical Memory. In addition, better recall was associated with greater educational attainment.

Summary

As can be seen from the previous section, various iterations of the WMS have been used in a remarkably wide range of studies investigating the correlates of normal and abnormal memory functioning in the aging. It is significant to note that nearly all of the studies cited used "core" WMS measures, especially the Logical Memory, Visual Reproduction, and Associate Learning (Verbal Paired Associates) subtests. The studies warn against making comparisons of differences in the Logical Memory and Visual Reproduction subtests using the Russell (1975) norms. In addition, they suggest that the poor performance on the Visual Reproduction may be a hallmark of emerging neurocognitive impairment. One of the studies (Helmes & Miller, 2006) should caution clinicians in using computerized testing using tests of unknown validity to assess elderly individuals. As might be expected, several studies in the past 20 years have investigated the neurology of normal and pathological memory functioning. This is not surprising, in light of the rapid advance in imaging technology.

Investigations of Seizure Disorders

The WMS has long been used to investigate seizure disorders. The WMS-R provides scant information on patients with seizure disorders. Table 5.7 is derived from information in the WMS-R manual (Wechsler, 1987). It should be noted that the maximum score for the Information and Orientation subtest is 14. As can be seen from Table 5.7, persons with seizure disorders scored one standard deviation or more below average on the General Memory, Attention/Concentration, Visual Memory, and Delayed Memory Indexes. The Verbal

Table 5.7 WMS-R Performance of Patients With Seizure Disorders (N = 58)

Index	Mean	Standard Deviation
General Memory	84.0	15.9
Attention/Concentration	85.0	18.9
Verbal Memory	88.8	13.9
Visual Memory	82.9	16.5
Delayed Recall	81.6	15.9
Information and Orientation	13.0	1.2

Table 5.8 WMS-III Performance of Patients With Temporal Lobe Epilepsy Undergoing Right (N = 12) or Left (N = 15) Temporal Lobectomies (Adapted from Wechsler, 1997)

Index	Left Lobectomy		Right Lobectomy	
	Mean	SD	Mean	SD
Auditory Immediate	77.9	16.3	95.0	11.3
Visual Immediate	88.5	15.4	83.5	9.1
Immediate Memory	78.1	16.2	87.2	10.7
Auditory Delayed	75.4	14.5	93.5	11.9
Visual Delayed	85.3	16.5	84.3	11.7
Auditory Recognition Delayed	83.0	18.5	92.1	15.7
General Memory	77.3	15.1	87.6	12.7
Working Memory	95.4	15.6	97.8	12.9

Memory Index fell grossly in the low average range. The index scores suggest that persons in this clinical sample presented with a mild global decline in their memory functioning, as assessed by the WMS-R.

Table 5.8 presents information on the WMS-III performance of patients with temporal lobe epilepsy undergoing right or left temporal lobectomies. The information contained in the table is derived from Wechsler (1997). As can be seen from the table, patients undergoing left temporal lobectomies displayed greater impairment on the Auditory Immediate, Immediate Memory, Auditory Delayed, Auditory Recognition Delayed, and General Memory Indexes than did patients undergoing right temporal lobectomies. Patients undergoing right temporal lobectomies were most impaired (as defined by scores which fell one or more standard deviations below average) on the Visual Immediate and Visual Delayed Memory Indexes. As a group, patients undergoing right temporal lobectomies were clearly less impaired than were patients undergoing left temporal lobectomies.

The data from Table 5.9 was adapted from Wechsler (2009b) and presents information on WMS-IV Index scores for patients with left or right temporal lobe epilepsy. The data suggests patients suffering from left temporal lobe

Table 5.9 WMS-IV Index Scores for Patients With Left (N = 8) and Right (N = 15) Temporal Lobe Epilepsy (TLE) (Adapted from Wechsler, 2009b)

Index	Left TLE Mean/SD	Matched Controls Mean/SD	Right TLE Mean/SD	Matched Controls Mean/SD
Auditory Memory	77.9 (20.1)	99.5 (16.4)	94.8 (17.7)	104.1 (13.6)
Visual Memory	98.3 (15.8)	103.5 (17.3)	86.0 (13.0)	107.2 (15.4)
Visual Working Memory	87.8 (10.9)	102.6 (9.3)	92.1 (13.2)	106.7 (14.1)
Immediate Memory	87.8 (13.6)	100.3 (14.9)	88.4 (14.6)	106.7 (14.2)
Delayed Memory	85.8 (20.4)	102.5 (17.1)	90.5 (16.0)	106.0 (16.2)

epilepsy (LTLE) scored approximately one standard deviation lower on all indexes except Visual Memory compared to matched controls. Using a criterion of one standard deviation below average of the mean scores of the matched control group, the hardest hit indexes were Auditory Memory and Delayed Memory. Patients suffering from right temporal lobe epilepsy (RTLE) also scored lower than matched controls on all indexes. Using a criterion of one standard deviation below the mean scores of matched controls, RTLE patients performed more poorly than matched controls on the Visual Memory, Immediate Memory, and Delayed Memory indexes. Comparing the two groups directly, and using a criterion of one standard deviation (15 points), patients with LTLE performed more poorly on the Auditory Memory Index.

One of the first uses of the WMS scales to study possible memory dysfunction associated with epilepsy was reported by Small, Milstein, and Stevens (1962), who investigated whether 25 patients with psychomotor epilepsy were more likely to suffer from psychopathic disturbances than 25 patients with equally severe nonpsychomotor seizure disorders. Each group was administered a variety of tests, including the WMS, none of which distinguished between the groups.

Glowinski (1973) compared the performance of 30 patients with unilateral temporal lobe epilepsy and 30 patients with centrencephalic epileptics to controls on the WMS (version unknown) and found that the former group performed more poorly on the Logical Memory subtest than did centrencephalic epileptics. Other WMS subtests did not discriminate between the two epileptic groups.

Saykin, Gur, Sussman, O'Connor, and Gur (1989) investigated the effects of laterality and age of onset of memory deficits before and after temporal lobectomy. On the WMS, left temporal lobectomy (LTL) patients earned worse scores on the Logical Memory than Visual Reproductive subtests preoperatively. Patients with early onset left temporal lobe epilepsy displayed a marked postoperative decline on the Visual Reproduction subtest, as compared to late onset left temporal lobe epilepsy patients who displayed a decline on Logical Memory. Right temporal lobectomy (RTL) patients improved postoperatively on both Logical Memory and Visual Reproduction regardless of age of onset.

Sass et al. (1992) used the Visual Reproduction I and II subtests of Russell's (1975) version of the WMS to evaluate the performance of 28 patients with left temporal lobe epilepsy to 31 persons with right temporal lobe epilepsy before surgery. Subjects in the latter group were found to be more impaired on immediate recall. After mesial temporal structures were excised, there were no correlations between Visual Reproduction scores and hippocampal neuronal density. The authors noted that while the Visual Reproduction I and II subtests should not be considered indices of hippocampal injury and disease, the Logical Memory Percent Retention might be an index of left hippocampal injury or disease.

Ivnik et al. (1993) compared the use of traditional versus computerized assessment procedures to assess memory after temporal lobectomy. A consecutive series of 40 lobectomy patients were studied: 20 with right and 20 with left resections. The WMS-R was among the traditional psychometric tests administered. Patients undergoing a left temporal lobectomy declined on the Verbal Memory, General Memory, and Attention Concentration Indexes and improved on Visual Memory Index from pre- to post-surgical measures. Patients undergoing right temporal lobectomies improved on all four indexes from pre- to post-surgical measures.

Chelune, Naugle, Lüders, Sedlak, and Awad (1993) investigated the impact of practice effects and base-rate information for assessing meaningful cognitive changes after epilepsy surgery for 47 LTL and 49 RTL patients. They found that LTL patients experienced declines in the WMS-R General Memory and Verbal Memory Indexes compared to RTL patients and epileptic patients who had not undergone surgery. After controlling for practice effects, RTL patients exceeded base-rate expectations for negative declines on the Verbal Memory Index.

In a similar study, Naugle, Chelune, Cheek, Lüders, and Awad (1993) investigated changes in material-specific memory as assessed by the WMS-R following temporal lobectomy. They compared Verbal-Visual Memory Index discrepancy scores and discrepancy scores using the LM I and II and VR I and II subtests in 30 patients with right temporal lobectomies to 30 patients with left temporal lobectomies and 50 epileptic, nonsurgical controls. On retesting, LTL patients displayed a marked change in short-term and delayed memory discrepancy scores, primarily due to a decline in performance on the Logical Memory subtests.

O'Shea, Saling, Bladin, and Berkovic (1996) investigated whether naming deficits underlied interictal memory complaints in persons with TLE. They administered the Memory Complaint Questionnaire, an Australian adaptation of the Logical Memory subtest, and subtests from an aphasia exam to 39 patients with left and right TLE and 38 controls with idiopathic generalized epilepsy. They found scores on Logical Memory were unrelated to memory self-report.

Moore and Baker (1996) performed a validation study of the WMS-R in a sample of 138 people with intractable TLE. Patients with a left temporal lobe focus performed significantly worse on the Verbal Memory Index, Logical Memory I and II, and Digit Span scores. Using the visual/verbal discrepancy approach, this procedure incorrectly identified most patients with a right temporal focus. The WMS-R was capable of identifying left hemisphere impairment, however.

Trenerry, Jack, Cascino, Sharbrough, and Ivnik (1996) investigated the relationship between sex and visual memory as assessed by the WMS-R Visual Reproduction I and II subtests after right and left temporal lobectomy. They found that pre- and postoperative scores were significantly related to the difference in hippocampal volumes in women, but not men. In other words, right temporal lobectomy resulted in a decline in visual memory, as assessed by the Visual Reproduction subtest, in women only.

Barr (1997) investigated the ability of the WMS-R to correctly classify patients with left temporal lobe ($N = 47$) and right temporal lobe ($N = 35$) seizure onset. Based on his investigation, he concluded that the WMS-R scores in isolation or in combination provided poor discrimination between these two populations.

Moore and Baker (1997) examined the psychometric properties and factor structure of the WMS-R in a sample of 181 patients with epilepsy. The results of their analysis confirmed that the WMS-R has acceptable levels of reliability as measured by internal consistency. Factor analysis revealed three factors: Visual Memory, Attention/Concentration, and Verbal Memory. Further analysis, however, raised the question as to whether the Visual Memory factor was a pure measure of nonverbal memory functioning (consistent with research reported earlier in this book).

Wachi et al. (2001) investigated the neuropsychological changes after surgical treatment for TLE in 26 patients before and after unilateral temporal lobectomy. The patients were assessed preoperatively and at one month and one year after surgery on a variety of measures, including the WMS-R. The authors found improved scores post-surgically at both intervals compared to pre-surgery scores on the WMS-R Verbal Memory Index, General Memory Index, and Verbal Paired Associates II subtest.

Dulay et al. (2002) used the WMS-III Family Pictures to assess visual memory and learning in 125 patients who were investigated for epilepsy surgery. The results of their study indicated that Family Pictures relies heavily on auditory-verbal based cognitive abilities as well as visual memory, suggesting it may be a good measure of memory performance.

In a related study, Chapin, Busch, Naugle, and Najm (2009) used the WMS-III Family Pictures subtest to investigate its relationship to verbal and visual memory following temporal lobectomy. The authors found that performance on Family Pictures was most strongly related to the WMS-III Logical Memory subtest, and that it measures both verbal and visual memory. In addition, it was found to be minimally sensitive to the lateralization of temporal lobectomy.

Doss, Chelune, and Naugle (2004) investigated the performances of 51 RTL patients and 56 LTL patients on the WMS-III. The results of the study revealed that post-surgery, the RTL group scored significantly lower on visual than auditory indexes, and the LTL group scored significantly lower on the auditory than visual memory indexes. The authors concluded the WMS-III was sensitive to modality-specific performance associated with unilateral temporal lobectomy.

In a rare study of forgetting after a period much longer than 30 minutes, Bell (2006) compared immediate memory and retention after 30 minutes to forgetting after a two-week delay in a control group (N = 25) and a group with TLE (N = 25) by using the raw free recall, thematic unit, and recognition memory scores from the Logical Memory subtest of the WMS-III. The TLE group performed significantly worse than controls on all trials.

Ladowsky-Brooks (2016) studied what has been called accelerated long-term forgetting (ALF). Noting that clinical neuropsychology is "blind" to certain abnormalities of consolidation that occur beyond standard 30-minute delays, the author investigated whether ALF could be identified in a small sample of subjects with head injuries or other neurological disorders (N = 42) by a four-hour delayed recall condition of the WMS-III Logical Memory subtest. The author found that 11% of their sample showed increased forgetting when compared to average retention scores after a four-hour delay.

Busch et al. (2011) investigated the effect of depression on memory following temporal lobectomy. They found that depressed patients undergoing left temporal lobectomies had greater declines in verbal delayed recall as assessed by the WMS-III than non-depressed patients undergoing left and right temporal lobectomies. Verbal delayed recall was assessed by the Auditory Delayed Memory Index.

Soble et al. (2014) investigated the clinical utility of the WMS-IV to predict the laterality of TLE among surgical candidates. The WMS-IV and other psychometric measures, including the Rey Auditory-Verbal Learning Test (RAVLT), were administered as part of a comprehensive pre-surgical investigation. The researchers found that that various WMS-IV measures offered little significant incremental validity in distinguishing seizure laterality in TLE beyond what could be obtained with the RAVLT.

Umfleet et al. (2015) studied the sensitivity and specificity of memory and naming tests for identifying left TLE in 143 patients with either left or right TLE using the Logical Memory I and II and Visual Reproduction I and II subtests from the WMS-R, WMS-III, and WMS-IV. There were no significant differences on these measures with patients suffering from right or left TLE. This study is noteworthy in that it is one of the very few to investigate the use of the Logical Memory and Visual Reproduction across the three revisions of the WMS.

Soble et al. (2015) investigated the utility of Green's Word Memory Test Free Recall (WMTFR) subtest as a conventional memory test. They compared the performance of 19 patients with left TLE and 16 patients with right TLE on the WMTFR, Rey Auditory-Verbal Learning Test (RAVLT), and the WMS-IV Logical Memory subtest during a pre-surgical evaluation. LTLE epilepsy patients performed significantly worse on the WMTFR and RAVLT Trial 7, but not on the LM subtest. In addition the receiver operating characteristic curves used to classify seizure laterality for the RAVLT and WMTFR were significant, but not for the LM.

As can be seen from the literature review, the WMS has been a popular tool used by researchers to investigate the memory functioning of patients with various types of epilepsy. Based on the studies, what conclusions can be drawn?

Key Points

- While patients with a seizure focus in the left temporal lobe are usually more impaired on WMS measures of verbal memory like Logical Memory I and II than patients with a seizure focus in the right temporal lobe, patients with a seizure focus in the right temporal lobe are not always impaired on measures of purported visual memory like the Visual Reproduction I and II subtests compared to patients with a seizure focus in the left temporal lobe.
- Verbal memory measures like the Logical Memory I and II subtests appear to be good measures of left hippocampal integrity. Visual measures like the Visual Reproduction I and II subtests are not good measures of right hippocampal integrity, since they contain a verbal memory component.
- The Visual Reproduction subtests measure auditory-verbal memory and visual memory, as do the WMS-III Family Pictures I and II subtests.
- The Visual Reproduction subtest should not be used as a pure measure of visual memory.
- Comparisons between measures of verbal memory (index and subtest scores) and measures of purported visual memory (index and subtest scores) do not reliably discriminate between laterality of seizure focus.
- Depression appears to be a unique risk factor for decline in verbal memory.

Investigations of Schizophrenia, Depression, and Related Disorders

As our state of knowledge about depression and schizophrenia has advanced, it has become increasing apparent that each of these conditions is associated with neurocognitive dysfunction. It will be recalled that schizophrenia was originally termed dementia praecox by Arnold Pick in 1891, a term that meant premature dementia. Pick, like other prominent clinicians of the day, was aware that people with schizophrenia often presented with significant cognitive difficulties.

The WMS-R presents limited information of the performance of persons suffering from depression and schizophrenia. This information is contained in Table 5.10. As can be seen from the table, persons suffering from depression performed grossly within normal limits on all WMS-R indexes. In contrast,

Table 5.10 WMS-R Performance by Persons Suffering From Depression and Schizophrenia

Index or Subtest	Depression (N = 18) Mean and SD	Schizophrenia (N = 14) Mean and SD
General Memory	90.6 (18.7)	71.4 (20.2)
Attention/Concentration	95.1 (14.6)	79.6 (17.1)
Verbal Memory	94.7 (16.0)	75.2 (15.8)
Visual Memory	87.9 (20.7)	77.6 (20.0)
Delayed Recall	91.4 (17.9)	76.9 (15.7)
Information/Orientation	13.3 (1.0)	13.3 (1.4)

Table 5.11 WMS-III Performance of Samples With Schizophrenia (N = 42)

WMS-III Primary Index	Mean	Standard Deviation
Auditory Immediate Memory	83.3	15.6
Visual Immediate Memory	82.3	14.3
Immediate Memory	79.1	15.7
Auditory Delayed Memory	84.4	15.9
Visual Delayed Memory	79.3	14.8
Auditory Recognition Delayed Memory	86.1	14.9
General Memory	79.7	15.8
Working Memory	85.6	13.9

persons suffering from schizophrenia scored over one standard deviation below average on all indexes. Especially hard hit was General Memory. The data in Table 5.10 was obtained from the WMS-R manual (Wechsler, 1987).

The WAIS-III and WMS-III technical manuals (Psychological Corporation, 1997; Tulsky et al., 2002) do not present any information regarding the performance of people with depression on the instrument. They do, however, have some limited information of the performance of 42 individuals with schizophrenia. That information is presented in Table 5.11 and it is derived from Tulsky et al. (2002). As can be seen from the table, patients with schizophrenia scored about a standard deviation below the mean on all the WMS-III memory indexes.

The WMS-IV Technical and Interpretive Manual (Wechsler, 2009b) presents information on the performance of 55 individuals with schizophrenia (see Table 5.12). As can be seen, people with schizophrenia performed worse than matched controls on all indexes. The index scores suggest global decline in memory functioning as assessed by the WMS-IV.

The WMS-IV Technical and Interpretive manual (Wechsler, 2009b) also presents limited information on the performance of a small group (N = 10) of older adults diagnosed with major depressive disorder compared to matched controls on the WMS-IV Older Adult Battery. The result of the study is presented in Table 5.13. As can be seen from the table, although this small group

Table 5.12 WMS-IV Performance of Persons With Schizophrenia (*N* = 55) and Matched Controls Adapted From WMS-IV Standardization Data (Wechsler, 2009b)

	Auditory Memory	Visual Memory	Visual Working Memory	Immediate Memory	Delayed Memory
Schizophrenia	78.8 (15.7)	81.8 (15.3)	79.5 (13.1)	77.1 (13.9)	78.4 (15.6)
Matched Controls	92.8 (14.8)	94.6 (14.7)	93.7 (16.1)	92.7 (15.1)	93.6 (16.8)

Table 5.13 WMS-IV Performance on the Older Adult Battery of Persons With Major Depressive Disorder (*N* = 10) and Matched Controls Adapted From WMS-IV Standardization Data (Wechsler, 2009b)

	Auditory Memory	Visual Memory	Immediate Memory	Delayed Memory
Major Depressive Disorder	101.1	97.0	97.1	100.1
Matched Controls	110.8	105.6	105.8	108.8

of patients with major depressive disorder scored below matched controls on all WMS-IV indexes, their performance still fell within the normal range.

People with depressive conditions represent a heterogeneous group, just as do those who suffer from schizophrenia. In addition, many people diagnosed with these conditions suffer from co-morbid psychiatric and medical problems. As a result, it is not logical to assume that there would be just one pattern of memory functioning unique to persons suffering from depression. What follows is a review of some of the literature that investigated the performance of individuals with schizophrenia and depression and related disorders on the WMS.

In the early 80s, Stuss et al. (1982) investigated the impact of the orbitofrontal cortex on memory by administering memory tests, including the WMS-I with modifications including multiple choice recognition, cued recall, and delayed recall, to a group of 16 patients with schizophrenia who had undergone a prefrontal lobotomy approximately 25 years earlier. The results of their study suggested that the presence or size of orbitofrontal lesions did not appear to negatively impact memory functions.

Tardive dyskinesia (TD) is a movement disorder frequently associated with the use of antipsychotic medication and a condition often afflicting individuals with schizophrenia. DeWolfe, Ryan, and Wolf (1988) investigated the cognitive sequelae of TD in 29 male VA patients, 15 of whom had schizophrenia and 14 of whom suffered from affective disorders. The patients were administered the WMS-I and the WAIS along with the Simpson Rating Scale, which is an instrument used to assess TD symptoms. Patients with schizophrenia obtained a mean MQ of 76.07 (SD = 18.25) compared to a mean MQ of 88.07 (SD = 21.21) for patients with affective disorders.

Gold, Randolph, Carpenter, Goldberg, and Weinberger (1992) examined the performance of 45 patients with schizophrenia on the WMS-R. The patients' intellectual functioning was also assessed. The authors report that the subjects demonstrated relatively flat performance across the five major WMS-R indexes, indicating similar levels of impairment in memory and attentional processes. It was also noted that a large portion of the sample had Full Scale IQs exceeding the General Memory Index by 15 points or more.

Gass, Burda, Starkey, and Dominguez (1992) investigated the relationship between MMPI indices of attention, concentration, and memory and the performance of three different groups of persons with schizophrenia on the WMS Digit Span, Visual Reproduction, and Logical Memory subtests. Analysis revealed weak correlations, suggesting that the MMPI was not a reliable basis for inferring attention and memory problems.

O'Carroll (1995) compared the performance of eight acutely deluded schizophrenic patients with eight matched recovered patients on the 10 word pairs "easy associates" of the Verbal Paired Associates subtest of the WMS-R, as well as additional paired associate tasks. The author found recovered patients performed better on both tasks, contraindicating the results of prior research that had found acute schizophrenia was characterized by a weakening of the effect of previous experience on new learning.

DeLisi et al. (1997) studied anomalous cerebral asymmetry and language processing in schizophrenia using neuroimaging and performance on a neuropsychological battery, which included the WMS-I as well as a 30-minute delayed recall on the Logical Memory and Visual Reproduction subtests. Patients with schizophrenia scored significantly below controls on the immediate recall of Logical Memory and Visual Reproduction, as well as Visual Reproduction delayed measures. Verbal memory as assessed by the Logical Memory subtest correlated with right > left anterior frontal asymmetry and with posterior left > right asymmetry.

Ilonen, Mattlar, and Salokangas (1997) compared well-defined groups of patients with first-episode psychotic unipolar depression to non-psychotic unipolar depression and first episode schizophrenia using a comprehensive neuropsychological battery, which included the WMS-R and the Rorschach. The authors found that schizophrenic patients performed at a significantly lower level than did the non-psychotic depressive group on the Verbal Memory Index, Delayed Recall Index, and the Logical Memory II subtest. The patients with psychotic depression did not differ from the other patient groups on any neuropsychological measure except the Wisconsin Cart Sort Test.

Willson (1997) studied the nature of accelerated forgetting in schizophrenia using the Logical Memory I and II and Visual Reproduction I and II subtests from the WMS-R, as well as the CVLT and Complex Figure Test. She found that people with schizophrenia forget both verbal and nonverbal information at a faster rate than do controls with no difference in magnitudes across modalities.

Finkelstein (1999) studied attention and working memory in schizophrenia using a discordant twin design and the Digit Span and Visual Memory Span subtests from the WMS-R, as well as the Continuous Performance Test, the Posner task, and the Stroop Color Word Test. The author found schizophrenic twins had shorter verbal and visual memory spans as assessed by the WMS-R subtests. The author also determined that the WMS-R Visual Memory Span was a sensitive measure of the level of genetic vulnerability to schizophrenia.

Hawkins has published several studies of memory deficits in people afflicted with schizophrenia. Hawkins, Sullivan, and Choi (1997) compared data from the WMS-R and the WAIS-R generated by 17 schizophrenia-spectrum patients and 33 psychiatric controls, and compared their findings in detail with all published WMS-R/WAIS-R studies of persons with schizophrenia. The authors noted that while the literature suggested that the acquisition of new information was disrupted in schizophrenia, there was little support for claims that memory deficits are especially pronounced relative to other weaknesses. The authors found that since patients with schizophrenia exhibit reasonable retention following an intervening activity, theories which suggested hippocampal dysfunction in schizophrenia were not well supported.

Hawkins (1999) also examined whether the WMS-III data of persons with schizophrenia presented in the WMS-III technical manual were consistent with data from studies using the WMS-R. Hawkins (1999) found that studies using the WMS-III indicated patients with schizophrenia did exhibit new learning difficulties. This was in contrast to studies using the WMS-R, which failed to find support that people with schizophrenia, as a group, displayed pronounced deficits in new learning and memory. She found that although patients with schizophrenia did not perform as well as the standardization group on material presented just once, their learning slope with repeated material exposure indicates they could absorb and consolidate increasing amounts of material, inconsistent with a pronounced memory impairment.

Touloupoulou, Rabe-Hesketh, King, Murray, and Morris (2003) studied episodic memory in 62 schizophrenic patients and their relatives ($N = 98$) using the WMS Logical Memory, Visual Reproduction, and Verbal Paired Associates (VPA: abstract associates) subtests, as well as parts of the WAIS-R and a visual analog to VPA. The researchers found that patients with schizophrenia performed significantly worse than controls on nearly all measures, and that their relatives showed significant deficits on Logical Memory I and II, Visual Reproduction I, and the Verbal Paired Associates (abstract associates). Logical Memory I was substantially more impaired than the other measures for both groups.

Conklin, Calkins, Anderson III, Dinzeo, and Iacono (2002) investigated facial recognition in 39 schizophrenic patients, 33 of their first-degree relatives, and 56 controls using the WMS-III Faces I and II subtests. Conklin et al. (2002) found that people with schizophrenia and their relatives were impaired relative to controls in recognition for faces after partialing out group differences in spatial attention and verbal memory.

In a related study, Moosavian and Hadianfard (2014) investigated whether facial affect recognition is a distinct function, since accurate facial recognition requires several cognitive abilities to support the ability to recognize faces correctly. The authors administered the WMS-R Verbal Paired Associates subtest, a continuous performance test, Picture Arrangement from the WAIS, and images of facial emotions from Ekman and Friesen (1976) to 55 patients with schizophrenia. It was found that patients who were and were not impaired on facial recognition did not show any significant differences in terms of their cognitive performance. The authors concluded that facial recognition was a distinct cognitive feature that contributes to the heterogeneity of schizophrenia.

Herman (2004) investigated the neurocognitive functioning and quality of life in patients with schizophrenia and substance abuse and patients just with schizophrenia using the WMS-III, selected measures from the WAIS-III, and other tests. He found the two groups did not differ in memory or intellectual functioning.

Tuğal, Yazici, Yağcioğlu, and Göğüş (2004) investigated if donepezil could improve cognitive functions in schizophrenia. Twelve schizophrenic patients were randomly assigned under double-blind conditions to receive 5 mg/d donepezil or placebo per day for 6 and 12 weeks, and then were crossed-over to the alternate condition for an additional 6 weeks. At baseline and follow-up, patients were evaluated by the Positive and Negative Syndrome Scale, the WMS-R, and other measures. The results of the study revealed no significant treatment, period, or carry-over effects on any neurocognitive measurement except for the Figural Memory subtest.

Tuulio-Henriksson, Partonen, Suvisaari, Haukka, and Lönnqvist (2004) studied the relationship between age of onset and cognitive functioning in schizophrenia. They administered the CVLT, selected subtests from the WMS-R, and the WAIS-R to 237 people with schizophrenia and selected family members. The authors found impairment in verbal learning and memory were risk factors for early onset schizophrenia.

Pirkola et al. (2005) examined spatial working memory function in twins with schizophrenia and bipolar disorder compared to controls using the WMS-R Visual Memory Span and Digit Span subtests. The authors found that schizophrenic patients and their unaffected co-twins performed significantly worse than controls on the Spatial Span subtest, but only schizophrenic patients performed significantly worse than controls on Digit Span. Neither persons with bipolar disorder nor their relatives were impaired on either of these measures.

Wilk et al. (2005) investigated whether it is possible to have schizophrenia without neuropsychological impairment. Sixty-four patients with schizophrenia were compared to 64 healthy controls on the WAIS-III and WMS-III. Patients with schizophrenia were found to perform significantly lower on the WMS-III Immediate and General Memory Indexes.

In a study investigating dual-modality impairment of implicit learning in patients with schizophrenia, Chiu, Liu, Hsieh, and Hwu (2005) compared the performance of 63 Chinese patients with schizophrenia to 27 comparison sub-jects. The patients' explicit memory performances were assessed by the Verbal Paired Associates and Visual Reproduction subtests on a Chinese version of the WMS-R. The authors found patients with schizophrenia were impaired on the WMS-R measures.

Foley et al. (2008) explored whether memory deficits in schizophrenia are attributable to poor organization and encoding during initial learning or to memory decay. They compared the performance of 37 geriatric patients with schizophrenia/schizoaffective disorders (SSD), 41 patients with frontotempo-ral dementia, and 107 geriatric controls on the WMS-III. Discrepancy scores between the immediate/delayed recall tests were used to explore possible dif-ferences in patterns of performance. Although the results failed to show dis-tinctions between the groups on patterns of memory impairment when using discrepancy comparisons, the findings suggested that deficits in immediate encoding rather than memory decay characterized the performance of some types of memory ability among geriatric SSD patients.

Manglam, Ram, Praharaj, and Sarkhel (2010) studied working memory in schizophrenia by administering the WMS-III Letter-Number Sequencing (LNS) and Spatial Span subtests to 78 drug-naïve or drug-free patients with schizophrenia and 35 age-, sex-, and education-matched normal controls. Compared to controls, patients with schizophrenia performed significantly worse on Spatial Span forward, backward, and total scores, as well as on LNS. The findings were consistent with prior findings of impaired working memory in persons with schizophrenia.

Xiang, Shum, Chiu, Tang, and Ungvari (2010) examined the relationship between three subtypes of prospective memory, intelligence, and retrospective memory in 110 persons with schizophrenia compared to 110 healthy controls. The subjects were administered a variety of measures, including the WMS-R Logical Memory I and II subtests. For patients with schizophrenia, perfor-mance on time- and event-based prospective memory tasks correlated with both WMS-R measures.

Substance abuse is not uncommon in patients with schizophrenia. Although nicotine is among the most frequently abused substances, cannabis abuse is also common. Scholes and Martin-Iverson (2010) investigated the effects of cannabis abuse on working memory, attentional control, and execu-tive functioning in patients with schizophrenia. They compared 36 canna-bis users who were otherwise healthy to 22 cannabis-using persons with schizophrenia and 49 non-abusing persons with schizophrenia on the Stroop Test, Letter-Number Sequencing and Spatial Span subtests of the WMS-III, and the Wisconsin Card Sort Test (WCST). Although persons with schizo-phrenia performed worse than did controls on all measures, there was no significant difference between the cannabis-using and non-cannabis-using schizophrenic groups in any of the cognitive domains, with the exception that cannabis-using schizophrenic patients had increased non-perseverative errors on the WCST.

Guo et al. (2013) investigated the relationship between obesity and neuro-cognitive functioning in 896 outpatients with schizophrenia using a Chinese version of the WMS-R Visual Reproduction subtest and a variety of other neuropsychological measures. For the 54% of the sample who were overweight or obese, they found a higher body mass index was associated with significantly lower scores on the Visual Reproduction subtest.

El-Missiry et al. (2015) studied the relationship between medication non-compliance and cognitive impairment in a sample of patients with schizophrenia. They found that medication compliance was associated with higher Verbal, Performance, and Total IQ scores and performance on the WMS-R Information and Orientation, Verbal Paired Associates, Digit Span, and Visual Memory Span subtests.

Cammisuli and Sportiello (2016) compared the performance of schizophrenic patients on the WMS-IV to that of matched obsessive-compulsive (OC) patients and healthy controls. As expected, schizophrenic patients scored significantly lower than healthy controls on all WMS-IV measures and significantly worse than OC patients on the Auditory Memory, Visual Memory, and Immediate and Delayed Memory Indexes.

Noting that memory performance is compromised in people with schizophrenia, Koshiyama et al. (2018) investigated the relationship between memory performance and subcortical regional volumes in a large sample of patients with schizophrenia. The researchers administered a Japanese version of the WMS-R to 174 persons with schizophrenia and 638 healthy controls. Patients with schizophrenia had significantly lower scores on all indexes than controls, with relatively greater impairments on the Verbal Immediate, Delayed Recall, Visual Immediate Recall, and Attention/Concentration Indexes.

Wannan et al. (2018) completed a longitudinal study of changes in visuo-spatial and verbal associative memory in 38 first episode psychotic patients and 22 healthy controls over a 5- to 11-year period using the Cambridge Neuropsychological Test Automated Visuospatial Paired-Associate Learning task and the WMS-R Verbal Paired Associates subtest. At follow-up, although they found deterioration in visuospatial associated memory for patients with psychosis compared to controls, Verbal Paired Associate scores improved to a similar degree as observed in hospital controls.

As noted previously, Park and Jon (2018) investigated whether working memory as assessed by the WMS-IV and WAIS-IV better fit a one- or two-factor model in a heterogeneous psychiatric sample of 115 Korean patients, 18 of whom suffered from schizophrenia, 39 from major depressive disorder, 6 from bipolar disorder, and 10 from a neurocognitive disorder. They note that routine administration of both forms of working memory is not recommended since they are strongly intercorrelated and functionally similar (Wechsler, 2009a). Confirmatory factor analysis revealed that a two-factor model of auditory working memory and visual working memory better fit the data than a one-factor model of working memory did, confirming the modality-specific working memory systems assessed by each measure.

Breslow, Kocsis, and Belkin (1980) studied memory deficits in 21 hospitalized depressed patients compared to matched controls on the WMS. Depressed subjects showed deficits on the Mental Control and Visual Reproduction subtests, as well as verbal learning.

Prigatano, Parsons, Levin, Wright, and Hawryluk (1983) investigated the neuropsychological test performance of mildly hypoxemic patients with COPD using a variety of tests including Russell's version of the WMS and WMS Verbal Paired Associate I and II subtests. Patients with COPD were significantly impaired compared to controls on all WMS measures. Depression, as assessed by the MMPI Depression scale, could not account for the poor performance.

Gass and Russell (1986) investigated the effects of depression and brain damage on the WAIS Digit Span and WMS-R Logical Memory subtests. It was found that performance on both tests was affected by brain damage but not depression.

In a related study, Gass et al. (1990) examined the validity of MMPI scores and MMPI-based cognitive complaints as indicators of memory and concentration difficulties in 70 closed-head-trauma patients. The researchers looked at scores from the MMPI Depression, Schizophrenia, and other scales compared to actual performance on the WAIS-R Digit Span and Russell's (1975) revision of the WMS. The authors found a lack of relationship between any MMPI scores and performance on these cognitive tests.

Bornstein, Baker, and Douglass (1991) investigated the relationship between depression and memory in 23 patients with major depressive disorder through administration of the WMS, MMPI, and Hamilton Rating Scale for Depression (HRSD). Although there was no relationship between the MMPI and any WMS scores, poor memory functioning was related to elevated scores on the HRSD.

Gass (1996) also studied the relationship between MMPI-2 variables, which included measures of depression and anxiety, and performance on the WMS-R in 48 individuals with closed head injury and 80 patients with psychiatric disorders. Concerning the psychiatric sample, 47 suffered from major depression, 10 from bipolar disorder, 5 from generalized anxiety disorder, and 2 had other conditions. All subjects were administered a variety of neurocognitive tests, including the Logical Memory (LM) I and II and Visual Reproduction (VR) I and II subtests. In the closed-head-injury group, there was no significant relationship between performance on VR and MMPI variables. Poor performance on LM was significantly related to performance on the Fears and Bizarre Mentation subscales of the MMPI. For the psychiatric group, poor performance on VR was significantly related to the MMPI Fears and Bizarre Mentation scale, and poor performance on LM was significantly related to the Depression, Psychasthenia, Schizophrenia, Depression, Anxiety, Obsessional, and Bizarre Mentation scales.

Schwartz (1997) investigated complaints about attention/concentration and memory in 20 female patients who reported chronic daily headaches. They were administered selected subtests from the WMS-R and other tests, as well as the Beck Depression Inventory (BDI). The author found that the subjects' overall subjective complaints did not significantly correlate with measurable impairment, although higher numbers of subjective complaints correlated with high scores on the BDI.

Kalska, Punamäki, Mäkinen-Pelli, and Saarinen (1999) examined memory and metamemory functioning among 30 adult patients suffering from depression and 30 controls in Finland. The patents met the criteria for unipolar major depression. They were administered a battery of tests including the WMS-R. Depressed patients were significantly impaired compared to controls on the WMS-R Visual Memory and Delayed Recall Indexes, and the Figural Memory, Visual Paired Associates I and II, Visual Reproduction I and II subtests.

Burriss, Ayers, Ginsberg, and Powell (2008) investigated the relationship of depression to learning and memory impairment in combat veterans with and without PTSD. They were administered measures of anxiety and depression as well as parts of the WAIS and the Logical Memory and Verbal Paired Associates subtests from the WMS-III. Veterans with PTSD were impaired on the WMS-III measures compared to those without. Performance on the Zung Self-Rating Depression Scale predicted WMS performance.

Zappert (2008) studied the effect of 12 weeks of treatment with an antidepressant on the cognition of middle-aged women with depression. The author found that effective treatment was associated with improvement on the WMS-III Logical Memory I and Visual Reproduction I subtests.

Azuma et al. (2009) studied the neural correlates of memory in depression measured by brain perfusion SPECT at rest in patients with depression. They found that the WMS-R Verbal Memory, Visual Memory, and General Memory Indexes were inversely correlated with brain perfusion in the right anterior cingulate cortex, left premotor cortices, and both regions, respectively.

As mentioned earlier, noting that between-group comparisons are permissible and meaningfully interpretable only if diagnostic instruments are proved to measure the same latent dimensions across different groups, Pauls et al. (2013) investigated the factor structure and measurement invariance of the WMS-IV across a clinical sample of people with depression and healthy controls. They found a three-factor structure of auditory memory, visual memory, and visual working memory best fit the data in both samples, but noted that possible differences in visual working memory between the depressed group and healthy controls could restrict comparisons on the WMS-IV Working Memory Index.

Medication overdoses are not uncommon in individuals suffering from affective disorders. Eizadi-Mood et al. (2015) investigated memory impairment following acute tricyclic antidepressants overdose. The authors compared the WMS-IV performance of two groups of patients, those that had suffered from mild to moderate overdoses versus severe tricyclic antidepressants overdoses, on a Turkish version of the instrument. All patients were tested immediately and 24 hours after returning to consciousness after admission to a hospital.

The authors found that 24 hours after initial consciousness, memory test scores were significantly correlated with intoxication severity.

In another study investing the effects of drugs on cognition, Sabater et al. (2016) investigated the neurocognitive effects of lithium and anticonvulsants in long-term stable bipolar I and II patients. The patient group was divided into three subgroups depending upon their medication regime: Group 1 had been taking lithium monotherapy; Group 2 had been taking lithium plus one or more anticonvulsants; and Group 3 had been taking one or more anticonvulsants. Neurocognitive testing included administration of the WMS-III (Spanish version). Sabater et al. (2016) found that patients in Group 1 performed similar to controls on the Immediate Auditory Memory, Delayed Memory, and Working Memory Indexes, and Group 3 patients performed worse than did controls on the Immediate Visual Memory and Working Memory Indexes as well as the Spatial Span subtest.

Cankorur et al. (2017) also investigated the effects on cognitive functioning of novel antipsychotics or mood stabilizers on euthymic bipolar patients using the WMS-R Logical Memory subtest. They found patients in both groups performed poorly, compared to controls, on this measure.

Gonzales et al. (2017) investigated whether cortical atrophy is associated with accelerated cognitive decline in mild cognitive impairment (MCI) with subsyndromal depression (SSD). They compared 32 individuals with MCI and SSD to 69 individuals with just MCI on repeated measures of cortical atrophy and memory over a four-year period. They found that SSD was associated with accelerated decline on the WMS-R Logical Memory II subtest.

Borderline personality disorder (BPD) is a severe chronic psychiatric disorder and is considered to fall in the affective (bipolar) spectrum by some writers. Korfine (1998) examined memory functioning in persons with BDP using the WMS-R. She found that relative to controls, persons with BPD performed more poorly on the Visual Paired Associates I, Visual Memory Span, and Visual Reproduction II subtests.

Crouse (2005) examined emotional regulation and verbal memory in BPD through the use of the Affective Control Scale to measure the former and the WMS-III Logical Memory subtest to measure the latter. She found no relationship between emotional dysregulation and performance on the WMS. Controls performed better than did those with BPD on Logical Memory immediate recall, delayed recall, and recognition measures.

Beblo et al. (2006) examined deficits in visual functions and neuropsychological inconsistency in BPD by comparing the performance of 22 patients with BPD to 22 matched controls on the WMS-R Visual Paired Associates and Visual Reproduction subtests, as well as other memory measures. Patients with BPD presented with deficits in visual function as assessed by the WMS-R subtests.

Bosinelli, Cantone, Sportiello, and Cammisuli (2017) compared the performance of 25 outpatients with BPD to 25 people with schizophrenia and 5 nonclinical controls on the WMS-IV. Patients with BPD scored lower than controls on all memory tasks except for the Auditory Memory Index. They also performed better than did persons with schizophrenia on the Auditory Memory, and Immediate and Delayed Memory Indexes.

Summary

There is a great deal of literature in which investigators have used various versions of the WMS to study the memory functioning of individuals with depression, schizophrenia, and related disorders. The aforementioned studies demonstrate some of the novel ways in which the WMS has been deployed to assess verbal and visual memory, attention/concentration, and learning in various clinical populations. It is remarkable that all versions of the WMS are still used for these purposes. It is rare, however, for researchers to use the whole test battery. Researchers typically use two or three subtests to investigate their area of interest, and the subtests that appear to be most frequently used are Logical Memory, Visual Reproduction, and Verbal Paired Associates.

The assessment of visual memory is a difficult task, since no WMS subtest is a pure measure of such. All WMS measures of purported visual memory can be verbalized and thus are contaminated measures, although WMS-IV measures of visual memory appear "purer" than those that are part of prior versions of the test. In some ways, purported measures of visual memory may be considered as indices of General Memory, as conceptualized by Carroll (1993), since they tap multiple domains of cognition.

It was noted earlier in this work that the new subtests introduced with each revision have not survived to the following revision. There is little reason to believe that this also won't be the case when the WMS-V appears in the market. A recent literature search (Kent, 2018) on the use of the WMS to study various clinical populations revealed that nearly all of the new subtests have been rarely used for research purposes compared to the seven core WMS subtests. For instance, there is relatively little research on the clinical use of the Spatial Addition subtest from the WMS-IV, a subtest that is difficult to administer. The subtests unique to each revision are not as well researched as are the core subtests, not only because they are newer, but also because they appear to lack validity and clinical utility compared to the core measures. In light of this, it appears that the lasting contributions of successive revisions will have been better standardization and scoring procedures, improved norms, the introduction of recognition procedures to tease out retrieval versus encoding difficulties, and the introduction of validity measures.

Key Points

- It has long been known that people with schizophrenia, and depression to a lesser extent, have cognitive challenges.

- Information presented in the WMS-R, WMS-III, and WMS-IV test manuals indicate that for the small sample of persons with schizophrenia tested, the subjects generally performed at least one standard deviation below average on all index scores. This is consistent with an early study by DeWolfe et al. (1988), who found that a group of 15 male VA patients with schizophrenia obtained a mean MQ score of 76.07 on the WMS-I.
- Several studies have investigated the relationship between MMPI indicators of attention/concentration and memory complaints compared to actual performance on various versions of the WMS. In general, it appears that the MMPI is not a highly reliable instrument for inferring attention and memory problems.
- It appears that the most used WMS subtests to investigate memory functioning in people with depression or schizophrenia are Logical Memory and Visual Reproduction.
- Delayed Recall Index scores significantly higher than Immediate Recall Index scores suggest attention problems.
- Some studies have suggested that people with schizophrenia suffer from accelerated forgetting of verbally and visually presented information.
- It appears that performance on Logical Memory II and Visual Reproduction II subtests has some utility in predicting individuals at risk for the early onset of schizophrenia and cognitive decline.
- Facial recognition, as assessed by the WMS-III Faces subtest, appears to be a distinct cognitive feature that contributes to the heterogeneity of schizophrenia.
- Cannabis does not appear to contribute to significant cognitive dysfunction in persons diagnosed with schizophrenia.
- Depressed patients often perform poorly on measures of attention and working memory.
- Depression has not been consistently related to poor performance on memory tests, however, although several investigators have reported that being depressed is a risk factor for poorer memory test performance. Depression appears to be a unique risk factor, however, associated with accelerated cognitive decline.
- Studies have demonstrated that some versions of the WMS are sensitive to drug effects, like the use of tricyclic antidepressants, anticonvulsants, and mood stabilizers.

Investigations of Miscellaneous Medical and Psychiatric Conditions

What follows is a look at how researchers have used the WMS to investigate various medical and psychiatric conditions.

Alcohol and Substance Abuse

It has long been known that alcohol and other psychoactive substances can have deleterious effects on one's cognitive functioning. As previously noted, Wechsler's first research study (Wechsler, 1917) investigated retention in persons suffering from Korsakoff psychosis.

Godding, Fitterling, Schmitz, Seville, and Parisi (1992) examined the discriminative ability of a quick assessment procedure for quantifying the cognitive status and the impact of existing cognitive status on acquiring information during treatment in 112 male patients who were admitted to an inpatient alcohol treatment program. The subjects were administered a variety of measures, including the WMS-R Digit Span, Logical Memory I, and Visual Reproduction I subtests. The researchers found that while the selected WMS-R measures were able to detect differences in cognitive performances related to age and recent drinking, the Digit Span and Visual Reproduction subtests were most sensitive to recent acute intoxication.

O'Mahony and Doherty (1993) investigated patterns of intellectual and memory performance in 43 patients referred for assessment because of suspected cognitive impairment associated with alcohol abuse. The study was conducted in Ireland and used seven subtests from the WAIS-R and the WMS-R Logical Memory I and II and Visual Reproduction I and II subtests. The second story of the WMS-I Logical Memory subtest was substituted for the second story of the WMS-R Logical Memory subtest. At the time of assessment, all patients were inpatients at a hospital alcohol treatment program. The results of the study found that all patients performed significantly below normative data on all WMS-R subtests. There was no evidence of a modality-specific deficit.

Franzen et al. (1995) investigated the factor structure of the WMS-R and several neuropsychological screening instruments in 352 recently detoxed substance abusers. The subjects were tested within one week of the termination of their detoxification period. The authors found that the WMS-R General Memory, Delayed Memory, Verbal Memory, and Visual Memory Indexes all loaded on a general memory factor. In addition, the authors found empirical support for the Attention/Concentration Index and support for the distinction between verbal and nonverbal memory.

Observing that neurological and neuropsychological deficits, including executive, visuospatial, and dysfunctions of gait and balance, are detectable in men even after a month of sobriety, Sullivan, Fama, Rosenbloom, and Pfefferbaum (2002) used an extensive test battery, which included the WMS-R, to investigate the cognitive and motor functions in 43 women who abused alcohol and were sober an average of 3.6 months. Declarative memory was assessed by the General Memory Index (GMI) of the WMS-R. The authors found no significant differences in GMI scores between women who abused alcohol and controls.

It has been observed that offspring from families with multiple cases of alcohol dependence have a greater likelihood of developing alcohol dependence and substance abuse disorders. Since posterior regions of the cerebellum are associated with cognitive abilities (Koziol & Budding, 2009), Hill, Lichenstein, Wang and O'Brien (2016) investigated if high-risk offspring would display regionally specific differences in cerebellar morphology and whether these differences would be related to working memory as assessed by the WMS-III Working Memory Index. The authors found that individuals with high risk for alcoholism showed poorer working functioning than low-risk offspring.

Heirene, John, and Roderique-Davies (2018) conducted a comprehensive search for tests deemed useful in identifying and evaluating alcohol-related cognitive impairment. The authors reported that the WMS-I, WMS-R, and WMS-III were all useful for assessing episodic memory.

AIDS and HIV

Van Gorp, Miller, Satz, and Visscher (1989) examined the neuropsychological performance in HIV-1 immunocompromised patients using selected subtests from the WMS, an abbreviated WAIS-R, and other measures. They compared the performance of 34 HIV-positive Stage 4 patients with 14 individuals with AIDS-related complex and 13 control subjects. Patients with AIDS-related complex were unimpaired relative to controls.

Hamby, Bardi, and Wilkins (1997) reported on the results of a neuropsychological investigation of a relatively intact sample of HIV+ individuals. One hundred seventeen HIV+ individuals were administered 26 different neuropsychological measures, including a version of Russell's (1975) WMS and the WMS-I Mental Control subtest. Measures of skewness and kurtosis were used to identify non-normal sampling distributions, and all the WMS measures were found to demonstrate adequate ability to assess this sample's performance. The performance of this sample, using Lezak (1983) norms, was generally normal.

Fazeli et al. (2014) studied the profile of memory deficits driving instrumental activities of daily living (IADL) declines across the lifespan in individuals with HIV. They studied 145 younger adults (less than 50 years of age) and 119 older (more than 50 years of age) adults with HIV on a variety of measures, including the WMS-III Logical Memory I and II subtests. The authors found that poorer immediate and delayed recall on LM subtests was significantly associated with increased IADL dependence.

Muniyandi, Venkatesan, and Jayaseelan (2012) studied the prevalence, nature, and extent of cognitive impairment in a sample of 33 people living with AIDS. The study was conducted in India. Study participants were interviewed and administered a variety of tests, including the WMS-I. The authors found that 55% of study participants had low scores on one or more WMS subtests. The subtests sensitive to impairment were Memory Span, Visual Reproduction, Mental Control, and Associate Learning.

Attention Deficit Disorder

Horton (1996) presented the results of a pilot project that investigated neuropsychological deficits in 11 adults diagnosed as having adult attention deficit disorder (ADD). The subjects were administered a variety of tests including Russell's (1995) version of the WMS. Horton found his subjects had impairment in the initial acquisition of verbal information, as assessed by Logical Memory I subtest, and borderline impairment in delayed recall as assessed by Logical Memory II and Visual Reproduction II subtests.

In a more comprehensive study, Johnson et al. (2001) investigated the neuropsychological performance of 56 adults between the ages of 20 and 53 with attention deficit hyperactivity disorder (ADHD). Their performance on a neuropsychological battery, which included the WMS-R Logical Memory-I and II and Visual Reproduction I and II subtests, was compared to a control group of 38 adults. Significant differences between adults with ADHD and the control group were found on the WMS-R Logical Memory I and II and Visual Reproduction-II subtests.

Riccio, Wolfe, Romine, Davis, and Sullivan (2004) examined the performance of adults with ADHD on the Tower of London (TOL) test, a purported measure of executive function. The study participants were also administered other psychological tests including the WMS-III. The 106 participants in the study were divided into three groups: 34 met the criteria for ADHD, 39 met the criteria for some other clinical disorder, and 33 did not meet the criteria for any disorder. For all participants, the WMS-III Working Memory Scale significantly correlated with the TOL Total Time score, and the TOL Rule Violations score significantly correlated with the WMS-III Immediate Memory Index. In this study, although females with ADHD had more difficulty with Rule Violations than males with ADHD, there was no significant difference in the performance on the TOL by the three groups.

Larochette, Harrison, Rosenblum, and Bowie (2011) examined the possible additive neurocognitive deficits in adults with ADHD and serious depression. The 54 university students participating in the study were divided into a group with ADHD and depression ($N = 18$), a group with only depression ($N = 18$), and a group with ADHD only ($N = 18$). All subjects were administered several tests, including the WMS-III. The group with ADHD and depression performed significantly worse on the WMS-III Logical Memory II subtest.

Schneider, Thoering, Cludius, and Moritz (2015) examined the rate of endorsement of ADHD symptoms and the association with neuropsychological performance in a psychiatric sample of 71 adults who had been referred for neuropsychological evaluation. The patients were divided into two groups:

the first group ($N = 36$) endorsed fewer than 10 symptoms on the ADHD-Self Report Scale; the second group ($N = 35$) endorsed 10 or more symptoms on the same scale. All participants were administered a variety of measures, including the WMS-I Logical Memory I and II subtests. The authors found no significant difference between the groups on WMS-III measures.

Anorexia Nervosa

Phillipou, Gurvich, Castle, Abel, and Rossell (2015) used a comprehensive cognitive battery that included the WMS-III Spatial Span and Letter-Number Sequencing subtests as measures of working memory to investigate the neuro-cognitive functioning of 26 individuals with anorexia nervosa (AN) compared to 27 health controls. The authors reported no significant differences in WMS-III test scores between the AN group and controls.

Autism

Williams, Goldstein, and Minshew (2005) used the WMS-III to study the auditory and visual memory of 29 high-functioning adults with autism compared to 34 group-matched controls. It was found that persons with autism were impaired on the Faces I and II, Family Pictures I and II subtests, as well as spatial working memory (Spatial Span). The authors noted that the deficits in memory for faces and common social scenes, and complex visual/spatial stimuli demonstrated the contribution of memory dysfunction in autism to deficits in real-life functioning.

Cancer and Leukemia

Lee, Hung, Woo, Tai, and Cho (1989) studied the effects that radiation therapy had on the neuropsychological functioning of patients with nasopharyngeal carcinoma (NC). Sixteen patients with NC who were treated with radiation therapy were followed up after a median duration of 5.5 years and given a battery of tests, which included an unknown version of the WMS Logical Memory (LM) I and II and Associate Learning subtests. Their test results were compared to a comparable group of newly diagnosed NC patients awaiting radiation therapy. The post-treatment group showed impairment relative to controls on LM I.

Kleinman and Waber (1994) studied the prose memory strategies of children treated for leukemia. Thirty-four children who had been treated for acute lymphoblastic leukemia (ALL) and 33 matched controls (MC) were administered the Anna Thompson passage from the WMS-R, and they were asked to repeat it. The ALL group were administered immediate and delayed recall versions of the test, compared to the MC group who were administered only the immediate recall subtest. The results of the study indicated that ALL subjects compared to controls produced fewer and sparser story structures and committed more errors in recall. The authors also noted that the error profile of children treated for ALL suggested that they were less effective at using story schemas in encoding the story.

Carbon Monoxide Poisoning

Carbon monoxide (CO) poisoning is associated with a number of neuropsychiatric disorders, including memory impairment. It is not unusual for the effects of CO poisoning to have a delayed onset of days to weeks or even months. Ryan (1990) presented the results of a case study of a 48-year-old right-handed married female who had a three-year history of constant headaches, lethargy, and memory problems following a six-year period where she ran a typing service out of her home, doing most of her work in the basement, which housed her furnace. During this time, she was exposed to CO poisoning over three times the OSHA-mandated permissible level. She was administered a variety of neurocognitive measures, including the Visual Reproduction I and II subtests, and was found to be impaired on each, and she obtained a score of 7 on the Visual Reproduction I subtest and a score of 5 on the Visual Reproduction II subtest.

Pinkston, Wu, Gouvier, and Varney (2000) presented another case history of a married couple who also sustained CO poisoning over a period of three years due to faulty furnace exhaust/ducting. The couple underwent PET imaging and serial neuropsychological testing over a three-year period. The testing included the WMS (version unknown). Remarkably, the couple did well on standardized memory testing. Patient MR obtained MQs of 118, 137, >143, and 132 and Patient MS obtained MQs of 120, 135, >143, and >143 on serial testing, despite the fact that memory problems were reported both by others and by each individual!

Delirium

Da Mota, Delgado, Schumacher-Schuh, and Chaves (2016) investigated the prevalence of delirium in patients over 18 years of age who were admitted to an emergency department in Brazil during a six-month period using the Confusion Assessment Method, Mini-Mental Status Exam (MMSE), and the WMS-III Logical Memory (LM) I and II subtests. They found that patients with delirium had significantly lower MMSE and LM I and II scores than non-delirium patients. Of the patients with delirium, 97.4% displayed impairment in episodic memory as assessed by the WMS-III.

Diabetes

Having diabetes increases one's risk for a variety of medical disorders, including various types of dementia (Whitmer, 2007). Christman, Vannorsdall, Pearlson,

Hill-Briggs, and Schretlen (2009) performed an analysis of the cranial volume, cognitive deficits, and functional limitations of diabetes by comparing 150 nondiabetic and 28 diabetic participants living in the community. All participants were administered a battery of neuropsychological tests, including the Logical Memory I and II and Visual Reproduction I and II subtests from the WMS-R. The diabetic participants ranged in age from 44 to 86 with a mean age of 66.39, and the nondiabetic group ranged in age from 40 to 92 with a mean age of 63.43. The authors found no significant difference on any of the WMS-R measures between the two groups, although individuals with diabetes were found to perform lower than controls on a variety of other neuropsychological variables.

Gorji, Ghahremanlu, Haghshenas, Sadeghi, and Gorji (2012) examined the memory impairments between two groups of patients with diabetes with different disease durations. They studied 120 Iranian patients over a 14-month period. The subjects were divided into two groups as to whether their disease duration was more than five years or less than one year. Subjects were administered the WMS-R. It was hypothesized the two groups would differ in their performance on the WMS-R. The authors found no significant difference on any WMS-R Index between the two groups.

Wang et al. (2015) note that Type 2 diabetes is often associated with cognitive dysfunction. They investigated the performance of 188 Type II diabetics compared to 266 controls on a Chinese version of the WMS-R, which apparently yields a Memory Quotient (MQ). The authors found no significant differences in MQ between the two groups. Nonetheless, it should be noted that the Type II diabetic group had a mean MQ of 78.2 (SD = 21.9) compared to 88.5 (SD = 18.7) for matched controls, suggesting the former group displayed some memory dysfunction.

Dissociation

Dissociation has been described as a discontinuity in the normally integrated functions of memory, identity, perception, and consciousness (American Psychiatric Association, 2000). Özdemir, Özdemir, Boysan, and Yilmaz (2015) investigated the relationship between dissociation, attention, and memory dysfunction in 45 low dissociators and 15 high dissociators using the WMS-R, Rey Auditory-Verbal Learning Test, and Stroop Color Word Interference Test. The authors found that high dissociators were significantly more impaired on the WMS-R Verbal Memory, Delayed Recall, and General Memory Indexes than low dissociators.

Hard Metal Disease

Occupational exposure to a wide variety of industrial toxins has been found to result in numerous medical conditions. Jordan, Whitman, Harbut, and Tanner (1993) studied the memory complaints of 12 adult former tungsten and cobalt workers with hard metal disease and 26 healthy matched controls on a test battery that included the WMS-R. Hard metal exposure has been found to result in skin disorders and cardiac and lung disease. Exposed workers performed significantly lower than controls on Verbal Memory and Attention/Concentration Indexes.

Hypothyroidism

Subclinical hypothyroidism (SH) is known to be associated with cognitive problems. Aghili et al. (2012) evaluated the impact of levothyroxine on the cognitive functioning as assessed by the WMS-I of patients with SH compared to controls. SH patients demonstrated significant improvements in the Logical Memory, Associate Learning, and Mental Control subtests as well as their Memory Quotient as a result of treatment.

Multiple Sclerosis

Multiple sclerosis (MS) is an autoimmune disease in which the immune system attacks the brain and spinal cord, often with devastating effects leading to chronic disability and death. It can result in changes in intellectual and memory functioning, including cognitive slowing and memory problems.

Lokken et al. (1999) investigated the effect of importance level, delay, and rate of forgetting on prose recall in multiple sclerosis using selected subtests on the WMS-R. Memory deficits are frequently seen in patients with MS, and this study examined semantic encoding and the rate of forgetting in MS patients using the Wechsler Memory Scale-R Logical Memory I and II subtests. The stories were divided into high, medium, and low idea units. MS patients were found to recall fewer idea units than controls, but both groups retained more main ideas relative to the nonessential details on Logical Memory I and II subtests. MS patients also forgot information at a much faster rate than did controls.

Drew, Tippett, Starkey, and Isler (2008) reported on the results of an investigation into executive dysfunction and cognitive impairment in a large community-based sample of persons with multiple sclerosis in New Zealand. Ninety-five participants completed a number of neuropsychological measures, including the WMS-III. Although the group as a whole displayed no significant impairment on any of the domains of memory assessed by scores lower than one standard deviation on this instrument, paired sample t-tests confirmed significant modality (visual versus auditory) differences for both the Visual and Auditory Immediate Indices, and the Visual and Auditory Delayed Indices. In other words, participants performed more poorly on visual measures.

Anhoque, Neto, Domingues, Teixeira, and Domingues (2012), noting that while the cognitive abnormalities had been studied extensively in MS, less is known about patients with clinically isolated syndrome (CIS), a condition defined as the first episode of a demyelinating inflammatory disease of the central nervous system. Eighteen CIS patients were compared to 18 controls on measures that included the WMS-R Logical Memory I and II and Digit Span subtests. Patients and controls did not significantly differ on any WMS-R measures.

Gerstenecker et al. (2017) examined financial capacity and its cognitive predictors in progressive MS. They evaluated the performance of 22 people with progressive MS and that of 18 healthy adults on a variety of measures, which included the WMS-III Logical Memory I subtest. The healthy control group significantly outperformed the MS group on this measure, and 72.7% of the MS sample were impaired on the Logical Memory I subtest. Individuals with progressive MS were also found to have significantly poorer financial capacity.

Masuda et al. (2017) investigated whether cognitive function and brain function differed in MS and neuromyelitis optica spectrum disorder (NMOSD) in Japanese patients using the WMS-R and other selected measures. They found MS patients performed significantly lower than did NMOSD patients on the General Memory, Verbal Memory, and Delayed Recall Indexes.

Fujimori et al. (2017) note that cognitive impairment has been found in Japanese patients with NMOSD. They evaluated the cognitive functioning of 12 patients with NMOSD and 14 MS patients using the WMS-R, WAIS-III, and Rao Brief Repeatable Neuropsychological Battery. Cognitive impairment was defined as performance two standard deviations or more below average on test measures. NMOSD patients with no or non-specific brain lesions were found to have intact performance on the WMS-R.

Obsessive-Compulsive Disorder

Abbruzzese, Bellodi, Ferri, and Scarone (1993) investigated memory functioning in 82 subjects with obsessive-compulsive disorder (OCD) and 39 matched controls using the WMS-R. The performance of OCD subjects and controls was evaluated by comparing their scores on three WMS factors as described by Kear-Colwell (1973): learning and recall, attention and concentration, and orientation and long-term information. Among the WMS factor scores, only orientation and long-term information were significantly lower in OCD patients.

Pulmonary Disease

COPD is a condition that involves the obstruction of airflow usually as a result of chronic bronchitis, emphysema, or both. Krop, Cohen, and Block (1972) investigated the neuropsychological functioning of 16 subjects with COPD who participated in a study of the effects of continuous oxygen therapy. 8 subjects were assigned to a treatment group and 8 to a comparison group. All subjects were administered a variety of IQ, memory and other tests, including the WMS-I as a pre-measure and the WMS-II as a post-measure. There were no pre-post differences for WMS MQs for either group.

Prigatano et al. (1983) examined the neuropsychological test performance of mildly hypoxemic patients with chronic COPD with controls on Russell's (1975) version of the WMS and the WMS-R Verbal Paired Associate I and II subtests. Patients with COPD were impaired relative to controls on all WMS measures.

Kelly and Doty (1995) completed a review of the literature of the neuropsychological dysfunction accompanying several disorders, including COPD. They report the results of several studies demonstrating that COPD is often associated with memory impairment as assessed by the WMS.

Crews, Jefferson, Broshek, Barth, and Robbins (1999) investigated the neuropsychological sequelae in a series of patients ($N = 18$) with end-stage cystic fibrosis who were evaluated for lung transplant using portions of the WMS-I and WMS-R, as well as a variety of other measures. The authors found 22.22% of the participants displayed impairment on Logical Memory I and 11.11% displayed impairments on Logical Memory II. On Visual Reproduction I, only 1 of 15 patients obtained an impaired score, and 2 of 15 were found to be impaired on Visual Reproduction II.

Crews et al. (2003) also presented the results of a similar study of 59 males and 75 females with end-stage pulmonary disease who had been referred for a neuropsychological evaluation as part of a lung transplant screening protocol. Once again, the participants were administered a variety of neuropsychological measures, including the Logical Memory I and II and Visual Reproduction I and II subtests from the WMS-R and WMS-III. Of those participants completing these measures, 13.76% were impaired on Logical Memory I; 16.51% on Logical Memory II; 12.75% on Visual Reproduction I; and 25.49% on Visual Reproduction II.

In a similar study, Crews et al. (2001) studied the neuropsychological functioning in 47 patients with end-stage COPD with a variety of tests, which included the WMS-R Logical Memory I and II and Visual Reproduction I and II subtests. The results of the study revealed a third of the patients who completed the Visual Reproduction II subtest exhibited impaired performance.

Trauma-Induced Weight Loss

Sutker, Galina, West, and Allain (1990) investigated trauma-induced weight loss and cognitive deficits among former prisoners of war (POWs) compared to controls on three cognitive measures, one of which was Russell's Version of the WMS. High-weight-loss POW veterans performed more poorly than did other veterans on immediate and delayed recall measures.

In a related study, Sutker, Allain, Johnson, and Butters (1992) examined the memory and learning performance of POW survivors with a history of malnutrition to combat veteran controls on the WMS-R. POWs who sustained the greatest degree of trauma-induced weight loss performed significantly worse on all WMS-R indexes except for the Attention/Concentration Index.

Summary

Various editions of the WMS have been used to investigate a remarkable range of psychiatric and medical conditions. As can be seen from this short survey, the subtests that appear over and over in research studies are basically the core subtests that make up the original WMS and composite indexes from various revisions. Although the review is not strictly a random sample of the literature, it is random in the sense that it reflects a convenience sample of articles that are open access, posted on such websites as ResearchGate, or easily obtained through APA PsychNet Gold. There is no reason to believe that articles which are freely available are inherently biased towards publication of research studies using the core subtests. The core subtests have persisted across time because they have been found to be useful in investigating diverse research topics. This does not mean to imply that there is universal agreement about what all the subtests assess, especially the Visual Reproduction subtest.

The next chapter will address issues in interpreting the WMS, including efforts to assess suboptimal effort and malingering.

Chapter 6

Clinical Interpretation
of the Wechsler Memory
Scales

In this chapter, we will review the results of several studies that have investigated issues relating to the clinical interpretation of the various versions of the Wechsler Memory Scale. For instance, assuming one were assessing a patient for suspected memory problems and the patient was administered a WAIS-IV that yielded a Full Scale IQ of 127 and a WMS-I that yielded a Memory Quotient of 78, what would be the significance of these findings? Or if one were conducting a study of patients who sustained brain damage to the left or right temporal lobes, and each group was administered the WMS-R, what differences might one expect to find based on the available research?

The studies that will be presented are not meant to be a comprehensive review of all those available for each version of the test. Like before, they represent a selective review of the literature. Some studies were chosen because they examine a particular facet of the WMS. Each study is presented because it is felt to have some research or clinical significance.

In order to organize the studies presented, it was decided to present the studies based on the version of the WMS used. This was done to make the reader sensitive to some of the controversies concerning interpretation that have been associated with each version of the test. The studies will generally be presented in chronological order, so the reader can glean some idea of the general issues that have interested investigators over time.

In addition to specific studies of clinical interpretation of the WMS, this chapter will also present the results of selected studies that used the WMS to assess malingering and incomplete performance. Validity testing is now considered an essential part of routine clinical testing. In the past two decades, a proliferation of books and papers have presented guidelines on what currently is called evidence-based practice and numerous guides on how to detect malingering. An example of an excellent guide to evidence-based practice is a paper by Bowden (2017b), which presents a cogent discussion of why we need to engage in evidence-based practice. In addition, one might wish to consult Larrabee (2007) and Boone (2007).

In this examiner's opinion, however, many books and papers presenting guidelines for evidence-based practice overemphasize the importance of quantitative indicators and fail to fully appreciate the importance of collecting detailed qualitative information about the person at hand. They also fail to appreciate Matarazzo's (1990) distinction between testing and assessment. When looking at the test results of any given individual, it is always important for the clinician to ask the question: do these test results make neuropsychological sense in light of the patient's presenting complaints and medical history? In other words, if the patient has experienced a brain insult, are these the test results one might reasonably expect based on what is known regarding the known neuropsychological correlates of such insults? It is also very important to have a good grasp of a person's developmental, cultural, and educational history when performing an assessment, as illustrated by the works of Klawans (2000), Luria (1987), and Sacks (1985). Sensitive consideration of qualitative factors not only humanizes the assessment procedure, it is also good clinical practice and likely to lead to more valid findings.

WMS Investigations

Stone (1947), one of the authors of the WMS-II (Stone, Girdner, & Albrecht, 1946), was among the first to publish a paper using the WMS in a research investigation. He investigated the effects of ECT on memory functioning. He also was one of the first writers to use both versions of the original instrument in a research study. 15 patients were administered the WMS-I within 18–24 hours prior to their first ECT treatment and 14 of these patients were administered the WMS-II within 24–30 hours after their last ECT treatment. The subjects were administered three ECT treatments per week with the maximum number of treatments being 20. Some patients did not receive the full 20 treatments. The majority of the patients had schizophrenia or severe depression. The author found that patients undergoing ECT showed a 15% loss of memory as assessed by the WMS, and he noted that the recovery of memory functioning was slow and, at times, incomplete. This study is important not only because it is one of the few studies to use parallel versions of the WMS, but also because it was one of the first to point to the importance of having objective quantitative information regarding a subject's premorbid functioning when assessing memory dysfunction. In the late 1940s, it was uncommon for examiners to make objective premorbid estimates of a subject's cognitive functioning. Wechsler (1939) attempted to address this issue with his first book on intellectual testing, in which he discussed "hold" and "don't hold" tests. Although the validity of Wechsler's hold-don't hold distinction has been strongly criticized by Challman (1952), Matarazzo (1972), and others, Wechsler was one of the first researchers to suggest objective criteria by which premorbid functioning could be assessed.

Toal (1957) was one of the first writers to criticize the WMS-I for not having information available concerning its reliability and validity. As the reader may recall, Wechsler (1945) provided no information regarding these properties when he published the test. Toal (1957) provided reliability information on the WMS-I based on a population of 150 healthy males aged 25–34 who were evaluated at a VA hospital in New York City between 1946 and 1949. In his paper, he presents internal consistency scores (alpha coefficients) for the Mental Control, Logical Memory, Digit Span, Visual Reproduction, and Associate Learning (AL) subtests, and the total score. The Mental Control and Associate Learning subtests were found to be the least reliable of the subtests, and the Logical Memory, Digit Span, and Visual Reproduction subtests were the most reliable. The author noted that the easy and hard associates of the AL subtests were not equivalent. Toal (1957) also found low intercorrelations among the WMS subtests indicating that score differences were so common and large that they had no practical predictive value. The author found that in 2.5% of the cases in his study, IQ exceeded MQ by 24 or more points, suggesting that the degree of compatibility between the two quotients is not great enough for use in individual diagnosis. Toal was thus one of the first writers to criticize the practice of making IQ-MQ comparisons when assessing for memory dysfunction, a practice that continues to the present day.

Zaidel and Sperry (1974) have observed that patients with cerebral commissurotomy appear to be remarkably free of behavioral impairment in ordinary activities. They studied eight patients with a complete commissurotomy and two patients with a partial commissurotomy who had completed a variety of neuropsychological tests including the WMS-I, and found that for the former group, the average MQ was 65 (score range 50–80), and for the latter the average MQ was 60 (scores were 63 and 58).

Russell (1975) presented a multiple scoring method for the assessment of complex memory functions, which continues to be used. Observing that a major aspect of verbal memory is located in the left temporal lobe and figural memory is primarily located in the right temporal lobe, he developed a version of the WMS that purportedly assessed the immediate and delayed recall of the Logical Memory and Visual Reproduction subtests. He reports data from the examination of 30 normal and 75 brain-damaged individuals that he claimed demonstrated his scale was both reliable and valid. In addition, he presented a memory impairment rating scale, ranging from 0 to 5, where 0 indicated normal functioning and 1–5 increasing degrees of impairment, directly comparable to the then-popular Halstead-Reitan Battery Impairment Index. It is noteworthy that Russell (1975) believed his delayed recall measures assessed long-term memory. As has been observed earlier in this book, Russell's concept of the lateralization of memory functioning, specifically that the Visual Reproduction subtest would be uniquely sensitive to right temporal lobe insult, has been found to be overly simplistic and was invalidated by several studies. In addition, his norms have been found to be lacking in clinical utility (see McCarty, Ziesat, Logue, Power, & Rosenstiel, 1980).

Brooks (1976) reported the results of a study that compared the performance of 82 patients with severe brain injury and 34 normal subjects who were tested with a slightly modified version of the WMS-I. The Logical Memory and Associate Learning subtests were readministered without warning one hour after their initial administration. The aims of the study were to determine the incidence and severity of memory problems in the brain-injured patients and examine the importance of the severity of diffuse injury, focal brain injury, presence of skull fracture, time after injury, and age of patient in memory recovery. The author reported that the head-injured patients had severe memory impairments on the Logical Memory and Associate Learning subtests, suggesting these subtests were very sensitive to severe brain injury.

Rawling and Lyle (1978), in a review of factor analytic studies of the WMS, note that the Logical Memory (LM), Associate Learning, and Visual Reproduction subtests of the WMS load on a factor involving the acquisition and immediate recall of complex stimuli, and that of the seven subtests of the WMS, these three appear to be most useful in the detection of cerebral dysfunction (Bachrach & Mintz, 1974; Kear-Colwell, 1973). They also noted that the LM subtest has several weaknesses in its administration and scoring that affect its reliability. They devised a cued recall version of the LM that discriminated significantly better than the original subtest between memory-impaired and control groups resulting in improved clinical utility.

Noting that the Russell (1975) revision of the WMS lacked an alternate form, McCarty et al. (1980) sought to develop such an instrument using subtests derived from the WMS-II (Stone, Girdner, & Albrecht, 1946). In addition, the authors investigated the potential utility of the alternate form with an elderly population, since the question of dementia in older patients is frequently encountered in clinical settings. The authors found that while the reliabilities for the immediate recall of both subtests were adequate, those for delayed recall were less adequate and the percentage-retained scores unacceptable. The authors also compared the immediate recall scores from the two subtests with those reported for various age groups in other investigations. The authors concluded that the Russell (1975) norms were not ideal to discriminate between normal and demented older adults. Citing previous research by Hulicka (1966) and Kear-Colwell and Heller (1978), who had demonstrated that older age groups scored lower than younger age groups on the Logical Memory and Visual Reproduction subtests, they also noted that Logue and Wyrick (1979) had demonstrated elder normal subjects produced significantly higher scores on these subtests than elder demented patients. Recommendations for the development of an alternate form of Russell's (1975) revised revision were made. The author cautioned against the use of Russell's (1975) revision of the WMS when assessing elderly persons with suspected impairment.

In an examination of then existing protocols for assessing memory dysfunction, Lawrence (1984) criticized the (implicit) assumption that memory and amnesia are an undifferentiated phenomenon that could be characterized by a single score such as the WMS MQ. Lawrence was strongly critical of the questionable procedure of diagnosing memory impairment based on IQ-MQ differences. Lawrence's article, although a bit dated, still bears reading by clinicians and researchers who assume IQ and memory score differences are characteristic only of patients with memory disorders.

Gass and Russell (1986) investigated the differential impact of brain damage and depression on memory test performance using the Logical Memory subtest from Russell's (1975) version of the WMS in four sample groups: those with depression and brain damage; those who were just depressed; those who were just brain damaged; and those who were not depressed or brain damaged. Depression was assessed by scale 2 of the MMPI-Form R. The authors found that performance on the LM II was substantially affected by brain damage but not by depression.

Pheley and Klesges (1986) examined the relationship between experimental and neuropsychological measures of memory. Although the authors report using the WMS-R in their study, they appear to have actually used a generic version of the WMS along with Russell's (1975) revision of the WMS, since the WMS-R was not published until 1987 and the results of their study are in line with known WMS and Russell (1975) measures. The authors report that the Luria Memory Scale significantly correlated with all WMS measures, including Russell's (1975) measures and the Associate Learning and MQ from the WMS.

Ryan and Geisser (1986) studied the diagnostic accuracy of an alternative form of the Rey Auditory-Verbal Learning Test. In their study, they used a memory impairment criterion that consisted of WMS-I MQ being less than or equal to 89 and/or the MQ was 12 or more points below the Full Scale IQ of the WAIS-R as suggested by Prigatano (1978). In discussing the use of these criteria, they note that the 12-point IQ-MQ discrepancy was established for the WAIS, not the WBIS, and because the WAIS-R yields lower IQs than the WAIS, it can be assumed that IQs from the WAIS-R will also be lower than the MQ. Their study points to the perils of using the WMS-I in comparison to WAIS-IV scores in an effort to determine memory impairment.

Mitchell (1987) studied scoring discrepancies on the Logical Memory (slightly modified for a British population) and the Visual Reproduction subtests of the WMS-I. They noted that there were clinically significant discrepancies between scores given by different raters on both subtests and offered suggestions for improved scoring. The results of their study suggest that if the original WMS-I subtests are used in research or clinical studies, special attention needs to be given to scorer reliability.

As noted in a prior chapter, Gass et al. (1990) evaluated the accuracy of MMPI-based inference regarding memory and concentration in closed-head-trauma patients when using Russell's (1975) version of the WMS. They note a lack of correspondence between any MMPI indices and memory test performance.

It was noted previously in this book that Crook et al. (1990) examined the relationship between a computerized measure of everyday verbal memory (the TV News Test) and the WMS-I Logical Memory subtest. Subjects were 364 normal, well-educated volunteers who were screened for significant psychological and medical impairment, and a drug sample study of 30 individuals over age 50 who met the screening criteria for age-associated memory impairment. Among the criteria used for age-associated memory impairment were cut off scores of 6 or less on the Logical Memory subtest or a score of 13 or less on the Associate Learning subtest. The authors found a strong relationship between the TV News Test and the Logical Memory subtest in both samples, and that the former (i.e., the TV News Test) appeared more sensitive to the effects of aging, but only in the 70+ age group. The authors also found that the Logical Memory and Associate Learning subtests had a moderately strong correlation in the drug study sample, but there was no such relationship between the TV News and Paired Associate Learning.

Trahan and Quintana (1990) looked at gender effects on the immediate recall and a 30-minute delayed recall version of the Visual Reproduction subtest of the WMS-I. The study used 70 male and 70 female adult volunteers. The study found that male volunteers outperformed female volunteers on the Logical Memory I, but not the Logical Memory II.

It was noted previously that Bowden (1990) completed a review of the literature investigating whether IQ-MQ differences can reliably distinguish between patients with cognitive impairment and neurologically asymptomatic alcoholism and patients with Wernicke-Korsakoff syndrome. Based on an extensive review of the literature, he made a compelling argument that such differences are not representative of the broader clinical group, thus questioning the practice of using IQ-MQ differences in identifying persons with the Wernicke-Korsakoff syndrome.

Williams (1997) published the results of a study that was the first empirical investigation of the estimation of premorbid memory ability from demographic variables, a topic that had been curiously ignored in the literature. In this very interesting paper, Williams (1997) discusses the flaws in the nature of reasoning regarding intellectual and memory functioning that have plagued the profession. As an example, she cites a study by Kareken and Williams (1994) that found although many clinicians believe that the correlation between education and Verbal IQ is approximately 0.8, empirical studies have found it to be approximately 0.6. Williams (1997) also reports that everyday observations of clinical practice indicate that clinicians estimate premorbid memory ability using either premorbid IQ estimates or by comparing current memory test summary scores to current IQ test scores. Using the latter rationale, clinicians assume that among normal, unimpaired subjects, IQ and memory scores should be essentially the same, when research has demonstrated that the performance on IQ and memory tests is very complex.

Summary

As can be seen from the studies on WMS, some early researchers were aware of the importance of having valid measures of premorbid functioning when assessing whether a person was suffering for memory impairment, as was Wechsler (1939). As the science of assessment has advanced, so has our ability to estimate premorbid functioning (see, for instance, Scott et al., 1997). Previously, such measures as the "hold" tests from the Wechsler intelligence scales, the reading recognition test from the Wide Range Achievement Test, or the Vocabulary subtest from the Shipley Institute of Living Scale have served this function.

From relatively early on, several writers have questioned the validity of using IQ-memory score differences to identify memory impairment. The use of such score comparisons, which was advocated by Wechsler (1945), has continued to be advocated by the publisher for all official revisions. Clinicians and researchers using all versions of the WMS, including the WMS-I and II, need to be aware of the pitfalls associated with such comparisons. Several studies criticizing the use of such procedures have been cited in this book, and they should be consulted by examiners wishing to use this method. The paper by Williams (1997) is especially informative.

As research using the WMS-I accumulated, it became clear to investigators that the Logical Memory (LM), Visual Reproduction (VR), and Associate Learning (AL) subtests were the most useful of the "core subtests" to assess memory dysfunction. Although many researchers have used the LM subtest to assess the integrity of left temporal and hippocampal regions, and performance on the VR subtest to assess the integrity of the right temporal and hippocampal regions, poor performance on the VR subtest has not been found to be reliably indicative of right temporal and hippocampal dysfunction, because in addition to assessing visual memory, it also assesses verbal memory. The interested reader is encouraged to reread the earlier section of the book that examined studies of the lateralization of memory. Despite the limitations of the VR, all three subtests have been found to be sensitive and valid indicators of memory dysfunction in a variety of populations. Clinicians have to be careful to not assume that impairment on Visual Reproduction reflects impaired visual memory, since this subtest assesses verbal and visual memory.

Russell's (1975) revision of the WMS has been very popular with clinicians and researchers alike. Despite this, several writers have observed that the revision suffers from several shortcomings and does not meet its original goals: to be a valid measure of delayed recall and the lateralization of memory functions. In addition, the norms supplied by the author in the 1975 study have been found wanting, especially with older populations. Those wishing to use Russell (1975) are encouraged to become knowledgeable of the limitations of this revision and the importance of using more updated, valid norms. Although Russell provided updated norms in 1988, factor analytic studies have failed to provide support for the delayed recall measures. Clinicians and researchers wishing to use Russell's (1975) revision of the WMS are also strongly encouraged to become familiar with the most recent findings regarding the strengths and limitations of this version.

WMS-R Investigations

Just as various aspects of the WMS continue to be debated, the same is true of the WMS-R. The WMS-R remains in use primarily in research settings. As before, we will look at selected articles discussing various aspects of this instrument. The articles will be discussed in the order that they generally appeared in the professional literature.

Bornstein et al. (1989) examined IQ-memory score discrepancies in normal ($N = 110$) and clinical ($N = 192$) samples. The WMS was explicitly designed for that purpose, as it was assumed that MQ scores significantly lower than Full Scale IQ scores were indicative of memory deficits. Noting that Milner (1975), Prigatano (1974), and Quadfasel and Pruyser (1955) suggested that IQ-MQ discrepancies of 10 to 12 points may be indicative of memory problems, the authors investigated the clinical utility of IQ-memory discrepancies computed from the WAIS-R and WMS-R. As will be recalled, the WMS-R was revised to assess material-specific memory indexes for verbal and nonverbal types of memory tasks, and factor analytic studies had indicated verbal and nonverbal subtests loaded on separate factors. In their study, the authors found that only 10% of their normal sample and about a third of their clinical sample (patients who had a diagnosis likely associated with a memory problem) had a Full Scale IQ (FSIQ)-Delayed Memory Index (DMI) discrepancy of 15 points. As a result, they felt this computation was useful in making clinical judgments about the presence of a significant memory deficit. While discrepancies in FSIQ-DMI were found helpful in discriminating between the two groups, discrepancies between IQ and immediate recall memory scores and material-specific discrepancies did not. The authors also noted that FSIQ-DMI discrepancies could not be used to identify material-specific deficits. The paper by Bornstein et al. (1989) remains a useful guide for researchers wishing to use the WMS-R, and it discusses some of the pitfalls of using simple IQ-Memory Index discrepancies in isolation to identify memory deficits.

Loring, Lee, Martin, and Meador (1989) investigated the ability of verbal and visual memory index discrepancies from the WMS-R to predict laterality of previous temporal lobectomy in 33 patients due to seizure disorders. Of the 33 patients, 13 had undergone a left temporal lobectomy and 20 had undergone a right temporal lobectomy. They note that because the WMS-R General Memory Index is subdivided into Verbal and Visual Memory Indexes, there is an implicit assumption that these indexes were designed to assess lateralized memory dysfunction. Three verbal-visual index discrepancy criteria (16, 21, and 29 points) were used to predict laterality. The 16- and 21-point discrepancies represent .15 and .05 levels of significance determined from the measurement error of the Verbal and Visual Indexes. The 29-point difference was used to obtain the 95% degree of confidence. The authors reported that relying solely on WMS-R Verbal and Visual Memory Indexes to infer lateralized temporal lobe dysfunction results in incorrect conclusions at an unsatisfactorily high rate. They also reported that using even the most conservative criteria (29 points), one in four patients were incorrectly classified. The authors found, on average, that the verbal-visual index differences correctly detected left temporal lobectomy patients but not right temporal lobe lobectomy patients. The authors felt that the use of verbal and visual labels for the memory indexes created confusion between "modality-specific" memory functions and "material-specific" memory functions, since verbal memory may be assessed through either verbal or visual modalities. In addition, they observed that such measures as the Visual Paired Associate subtests contain a significant verbal component. In summary, the authors cautioned against using the Verbal and Visual Memory Indexes to infer laterality of lesion.

In a similar study, Barr (1997) performed a receiver operating characteristic curve (ROC) analysis of WMS-R scores in epilepsy surgery candidates. Eighty-two epilepsy surgery candidates were administered the WMS-R, and their scores were used in combination with ROC curves to classify patients with either left or right temporal lobe seizure onset. Barr found that WMS-R scores used in isolation or combination provided poor discrimination of right and left temporal lobectomy patients.

In order to aid in WMS-R interpretation, Atkinson (1991) published an article containing a table of revised WMS-R standard errors of measurement (SEMs) for defining confidence intervals as they bracket predicted true scores. His paper also contains a revised table of significant index-score differences. The original tables published by Wechsler (1987) were felt to be of limited value for various technical reasons. The values in the tables were obtained from WMS-R manual data for the standardization sample. Atkinson's (1991) tables are useful if a clinician has administered the WMS-R on two occasions and wants to assess if variation in index scores are due to measurement error alone or attributable to some event, like a head injury.

Atkinson (1992) also published a table for General Memory-Attention/Concentration, Verbal Memory-Visual Memory, and General Memory-Delayed Recall Index comparisons so the clinician can make a determination of the abnormality of the selected index differences. His tables can be used to answer the question: how unusual is a given discrepancy in the normative sample?

Mittenberg, Thompson, and Schwartz (1991) presented tables based on the standardization data of confidence intervals for the statistical abnormality between scales. The tables allow the clinician to evaluate the material-specific rates of forgetting on the Logical Memory and Visual Reproduction subtests, as well as the adequacy of overall retention as reflected by contrasts between the General and Delayed Memory Indexes. It should be noted that the tables include information for the following age groups: 16–17, 20–24, 35–44, 55–64, 65–69, and 70–74. Notably absent is data for 18–19, 25–34, and 45–54 age groups. Despite the fact that factor analytic studies have generally failed to find support for the delayed recall indexes, studies using earlier versions of these subtests (Butters et al., 1988; Russell, 1988) have found that contrasts between immediate and delayed recall conditions have been found to characterize patients with Alzheimer's, Korsakoff's syndrome, and Huntington's disease.

In an effort to fill a void in the WMS-R standardization data, Mittenberg, Burton, Darrow, and Thompson (1992) published normative data for 25- to 34-year-olds based on a stratified sample consisting of 50 volunteers. The volunteers were selected based on their match of 1980 U.S. census data. It will be recalled that the data for 25- to 34-year-olds presented in the manual was interpolated. The authors warn that the large differences between the estimated and empirical index scores that occur in some cases are of sufficient magnitude to result in possible diagnostic errors. The Mittenberg et al. (1992) study points to the danger of using interpolated norms in research and clinical studies and to a serious flaw in the development of the WMS-R.

McCaffrey, Ortega, and Haase (1993) examined the effects of repeated neuropsychological testing on 13 neuropsychological variables, including the Logical Memory and Visual Reproduction subtests from Russell's (1975) WMS. The subjects were part of a larger study designed to evaluate the neuropsychological sequelae of prophylactic cranial irradiation therapy in patients with small cell lung cancer. The study subjects' performance was evaluated across four assessment periods to examine issues of test-retest reliability, practice effects, and the intercorrelation matrices among the same neuropsychological variables. Assessments I and II occurred within a seven- to ten-day period, and Assessments III and IV took place approximately three and six months following Assessment II. Based on their study, the authors report that researchers and clinicians should expect Logical Memory I and II scores to steadily improve across multiple assessments regardless of interval, suggesting these measures show practice effects. They note that an absence of improved performance might have important diagnostic implications. For the Visual Reproduction I and II subtests, the authors found an alternating up and down performance across time. The absence of variability, in this instance, may be of diagnostic importance.

Randolph et al. (1994) completed a study that compared estimates of global memory functioning from the WMS-R and CVLT, two tests that are frequently used in clinical memory testing. Noting that past studies had indicated that the WMS-R and CVLT are highly correlated (Delis, Cullum, Butters, Cairns, & Prifitera, 1988), suggesting a high degree of convergence between the two tests in providing estimates of memory functioning, they hypothesized that this degree of convergence should provide comparable estimates of memory function. The authors completed a retrospective comparison of standardized scores obtained by two patient groups on the CVLT and WMS-R. They tried to determine if standard scores from these tests provided commensurate global estimations of memory functioning. Data on 161 subjects who had taken both tests were reviewed. Of these patients, 33 suffered from schizophrenia, 31 from temporal lobe epilepsy, and 97 were normal volunteers. The researchers found that the standardization samples for these two tests were not representative of the same population and that the CVLT normative sample appears to have been higher functioning than the WMS-R sample and characterized by a narrower range of memory function. The researchers also found that the parity between WMS-R indexes and estimated WAIS-R FSIQ suggests that the WMS-R standardization group was more representative of the general population than was the CVLT normative reference group. As a result, it was suggested that estimates of memory function based on the CVLT are more likely to suggest a deficit when the performance is actually in the normal range, particularly in subjects with below-average educational attainment.

Gass (1995) described a procedure for assessing storage and retrieval on the WMS-R. Noting that distinguishing deficient memory storage from compromised retrieval operations is an important clinical task, Gass (1995) presents a 21-item five-option multiple choice recognition test for Logical Memory and a cuing technique for the Visual Reproduction subtest. Gass's procedure can be used to address one of the shortcomings of the WMS-R, namely its relative lack of recognition procedures useful for identifying whether a person's poor performance on a given subtest is due to encoding or retrieval issues.

Noting that one of the shortcomings of the WMS-R was increased administration time as compared to the WMS, Woodard and Axelrod (1995, 1996) present two regression equations to predict weighted raw score sums for the General Memory and Delayed Recall Indexes using the WMS-R analogs of five subtests from the WMS. The authors presented data that suggest that use of these regression equations may prove useful in reducing WMS-R administration time without an appreciable decline in accuracy. The authors caution against using the scale in populations significantly different from their sample group.

Van den Broek, Golden, Loonstra, Ghinglia, and Goldstein (1998) attempted to cross-validate the formulas presented by Woodard and Axelrod (1995) and Axelrod, Putnam, Woodard, and Adams (1996) for estimating the WMS-R General Memory and Delayed Recall Indexes and deriving a formula using two rather than three subtests. The results of their study indicated excellent cross-validation for the original formulas with a correlation of .99. Using estimates based on only two subtests, the authors devised a formula to estimate the same indexes. The authors noted that while the new formula resulted in higher estimation errors, they felt the two-subtest short form of the WMS-R could be used when less accurate estimates were acceptable.

Hoffman, Tremont, Scott, Adams, and Mittenberg (1997) investigated the efficacy of the Woodard and Axelrod (1995) regression equation in the Mittenberg et al. (1992) normative WMS-R sample of 50 subjects between the ages of 25 and 34. The results of their study confirmed the Woodard and Axelrod (1995) equations in a separate clinical sample of 30 patients with closed head injury who were matched across age, education, and gender with the 30 subjects from that normative sample.

Palmer, Boone, Lesser, and Wohl (1998) examined the base rate of impaired neuropsychological test performance among healthy older adults in several measures, including the WMS-R. Impairment was defined as test performance falling greater than or equal to 1.3 standard deviations or 2 standard deviations below the mean. For some WMS-R Logical Memory measures, using the first criteria, between 10% and 20% of the study participants fell into the impaired range; using the latter criteria, 5% were found to be impaired on the Logical Memory percent retention score.

In a review of the literature, Hilsabeck, Schrager, and Gouvier (1999) note that five studies have shown that the three-subtest WMS-R short form equations allow for decreased testing time without sacrificing reliability or clinical accuracy. In their study, they attempted to cross-validate these results in a mixed clinical sample to expand the generalizability of these findings. The authors also studied the validity of two-subtest equations. While the results of Hilsabeck et al. (1999) provided support for use of three-subtest short forms to estimate memory in normal and cognitively impaired patients, it was felt that using two-subtest short forms resulted in a decline in predictive validity.

Noting that during testing of clinical patients many seemed to "freeze" following the standard instructions and administration of WMS-R Story A, Cannon (1999) investigated the possible relative interference on the Logical Memory I Story A versus Story B in a clinical sample. The author found that patients who showed poorer performance on Story A than Story B had significantly higher T-scores on the MMPI Social Anxiety scale.

Shores and Carstairs (2000) described the methodology used to complete the Macquarie Neuropsychological Normative Study (MUNNS), which involved the co-norming of the WAIS-R and WMS-R on a stratified random sample of 399 healthy young adults. In this study, the authors found that education was significantly correlated with WAIS-R measures, while lower correlations were evident with WMS-R measures. It is significant to note that this study was completed in Australia.

In a related study, Carstairs and Shores (2000) report problems with using interpolated norms citing Mittenberg et al. (1992). The latter study provided normative data for a representative sample of healthy young adults for the age ranges of 18–19, 20–24, 25–29, and 30–34. The purpose of the Carstairs and Shores (2000) study was to provide normative data for Australian young adults against which brain-injured patients could be compared.

Adams, Stanczak, Leutzinger, Waters, and Brown (2001) report the results of an archival study of 168 persons that investigated the impact of psychological disturbance on immediate memory. Selected measures from the WMS-I and WMS-R were used to study various domains of memory. The authors report that their study corroborates the hypothesis that psychological disturbance may impact immediate memory performance due to attention factors.

Steinberg, Bieliauskas, Smith, and Ivnik (2005) provided age- and IQ-adjusted norms for the WMS-R as part of Mayo's Older Americans Normative series. The age range of the sample was from 56 to 99.

Summary

As can be seen in this discussion, there have been numerous and diverse investigations of issues related to WMS-R interpretation. Several of the studies investigated the development of short forms of the WMS-R. Of the studies cited, it appears that a three-subtest version is most promising for clinical decision-making when time is an issue. Several studies investigated the validity of using Visual Memory versus Verbal Memory Indexes to assess the lateralization of memory dysfunction, especially in patients with epilepsy. As noted previously in this book, the evidence for the use of these indexes for determining the lateralization of memory dysfunction has been mixed. Several studies helped provide missing WMS-R normative data, and they indicated the interpolated norms that were presented when the instrument was published were flawed. In addition, some studies have provided normative data for older adults, thus extending the utility of the instrument for research and clinical purposes. Gass (1995) provided a recognition protocol that can be used to evaluate whether subjects have retrieval versus encoding and storage problems, thus compensating for one of the structural flaws of the instrument.

Some of the WMS-R indexes were found to have clinical utility in distinguishing between various clinical groups. Many studies investigated the problems associated with using IQ-memory score comparisons in attempting to identify memory dysfunction. Although a long-standing practice, the use of this procedure is fraught with many potential problems. Several studies provided improved norms for various versions of the WMS, such as Russell's (1975) adaptation, which has been widely used in clinical practice and research. And in a novel study, Cannon (1999) found that poor performance on Story A versus Story B of the Logical Memory subtest may be an embedded indicator of anxiety.

It is hoped that in reading the survey presented, interested clinicians and researchers will be motivated to dig deeper into the literature on the WMS-R. In addition, the articles cited should caution test users in assuming that test results from the WMS-R are comparable to test results from other instruments, like the CVLT, which is commonly used in clinical practice. The WMS-R is still being used in research settings in the U.S. and elsewhere. Despite having been published over 30 years ago, it lives on.

WMS-III Investigations

Like before, several studies will be presented that examine various clinical issues when interpreting WMS-III test results. As before, the studies reviewed come from a sample of convenience and will be presented roughly in the order in which they were published. The WMS-III introduced several new subtests into the clinical landscape. If the reader has not already done so, it is strongly recommended that they read and become familiar with the contents of the revised WMS-III technical manual (Tulsky et al., 2002) if they wish to use the

WMS-III for clinical or research purposes. The manual is an excellent source of information regarding the development of the WMS-III and many of its strengths and limitations.

Tulsky and Ledbetter (2000), who are associated with the development of the WMS-III, note that it sometimes is difficult for clinicians who test individuals on repeated occasions to switch over to a new version of a test because of difficulty in interpreting score discrepancy between two test versions. In addition, the authors note that switching to a new test version can create problems for investigators involved in longitudinal research. Tulsky and Ledbetter (2000) provide a good summary of how the WAIS-III and WMS-III were updated, and several things clinicians and researchers need to be aware of in moving from a prior version of the instrument to the new revision.

Professional guidelines urge psychologists to adopt the most recent version of a test, in part, to ensure the tests being administered have appropriate normative data (Aera, 1999). Norms become outdated due to what has been called the Flynn effect (Flynn, 2007). As argued repeatedly earlier in this book, although new revisions of tests are marketed as being improved and better measures of the domains of interest, oftentimes this isn't the case. It is important to be skeptical about the claims of new tests and revisions of existing measures and important to scrutinize the literature in an ongoing manner to stay up to date regarding the strengths and shortcomings of the measures we use. There are good reasons why tests like the Illinois Test of Psycholinguistic Ability, Luria Nebraska Neuropsychological Battery, and Bender Gestalt Test have faded from the clinical and research landscape. In addition, one can make the case that there are times when using previous versions of a test is justified. For instance, let's assume your patient was given a WMS-IV in 2020, one year before the WMS-V was released. You are asked to evaluate that patient in 2021 for suspected memory impairment. You have access to the WMS-IV test results. Should you administer the WMS-V, with its updated norms and content, or use the WMS-IV? In such a case, administering the WMS-IV can be justified to ensure one can make direct comparisons between the test results.

Ryan et al. (2000) note that the WMS-III yields 51 separate scores from 11 primary subtests and 8 primary indexes. As a result, compared to its two predecessors, the instrument takes more time to administer and is much more difficult to interpret. To aid in clinical interpretation, the authors provide a table that may be used to evaluate differences between subtest scores and the means of the 11 primary subtests. They also include the frequencies of differences obtained by 1%, 2%, 5%, 10%, and 25% of the WMS-III standardization sample. The authors suggest the table may be useful to identify strengths and weaknesses of the examinee and the relative infrequency of test scores.

Axelrod and Woodard (2000) present the results of a study of the WMS-III, which attempted to use the same principles that were applied in generating the prediction equations for the General Memory and Delayed Memory indices of the WMS-R (Woodard & Axelrod, 1995). Specifically, they tried to determine which of the WMS-III subtests included in the Immediate Memory Index were most predictive of immediate memory and which of the subtests included in the General Memory Index (a measure a delayed recall) were most predictive of delayed recall. In an effort to develop a shortened version of the WMS-III, the authors report that the Immediate Memory and General Memory Indexes can be accurately predicted by leaving out one of the two visual memory subtests (either Faces or Family Pictures).

Iverson (2001) notes that clinicians need to be aware that there is considerable variability in the reliabilities of the index and subtest scores derived from the WMS-III. In reviewing these reliabilities, he reports that the Auditory Immediate Index, Immediate Memory Index, Auditory Delayed Index, and General Memory Index are the most reliable in terms of internal consistency and test-retest reliability. Of the subtests, the Logical Memory I and Verbal Paired Associates I were the most reliable. The criteria for most reliable were internal consistency scores of 0.85–0.99 and test-retest reliability scores of 0.75–0.99. The author also presents a table of confidence intervals for test-retest measurement error to help the clinician determine whether patients have reliably improved or deteriorated on follow-up testing.

The Family Pictures subtest is unique to the WMS-III. It was one of the more controversial subtests of the new revision, with several writers expressing concerns about its clinical utility. Dulay et al. (2002) assessed the extent to which different cognitive abilities contribute to the performance on Family Pictures in 125 patients evaluated for epilepsy surgery. The results of their study indicated that performance on Family Pictures relies heavily on auditory-verbal based cognitive abilities as well as visual memory, raising questions about the appropriateness of including it in calculations of the WMS-III Visual Index score.

Noting that a major criticism of the WMS-III Faces subtest is the number of items, which can be daunting and time-consuming for an impaired patient, Migoya, Zimmerman, and Golden (2002) developed an abbreviated version of the subtest for clinical use. The abbreviated subtest has 32 items and can be used to predict Faces I and II raw scores.

Ryan, Kreiner, and Burton (2002) investigated whether high amounts of intersubtest scatter on the WAIS-III subtest profiles compromised the predictive validity of IQs for predicting WMS-III indexes. Using data from a sample of 80 male VA patients who were assigned to groups of high or low intersubtest scatter, the authors found that when differences in IQ are controlled, the validity of WAIS-III scores to predict memory performance does not depend upon the amount of intersubtest scatter.

Uttl, Graf, and Richter (2002) note that the normative data for the WMS-III Verbal Paired Associates subtest show clear evidence of performance ceiling effects that limit its clinical usefulness. In an examination of test manual normative scores, for instance, they report that the top-performing 25% of all individuals who are under 55 years of age have expected learning scores that cannot be achieved. As a result, the authors note that caution is needed in interpreting test scores.

Kreiner, Ryan, and Miller (2003) evaluated the ability of the WAIS-III Digit Symbol-Coding Free Recall score to determine if an individual should be referred for further memory evaluation on a test like the WMS-III. In their research, using persons with substance abuse as subjects, they evaluated the power of the Incidental Learning scores to identify WMS-III memory impairment, with the General Memory Index (GMI) used as a criterion of impairment. The GMI is considered by the publisher to be the best overall measure of abilities that are critical to effective memory in everyday life (Psychological Corporation, 1997). Kreiner et al. (2003) found that the WAIS-III Digit Symbol-Coding Free Recall score was useful as a screening instrument for this purpose using the equation they developed to predict WMS-III General Memory Index scores.

Dori and Chelune (2004) provide information on education-stratified, directional prevalence rates (base rates) of discrepancy scores between the major index scores for the WAIS-III, the WMS-III, and between the WAIS-III and WMS-III. Their article discusses the diagnostic use of these measures in clinical decision-making, and it is recommended reading for those wishing more information in this area.

Skeel et al. (2004) examined discrepancies between WAS-III and WMS-III scores for a group of 39 males and 48 females with a history of TBI using three methodologies: predicted-difference, simple-difference, and premorbid-estimation methods. The authors found that using a combination of estimates of premorbid functioning and regression-based predicted scores were best for interpreting IQ/memory score discrepancies, although the results of their study did not indicate dramatic differences in the overall impairment classification rates between the three classification methods.

Noting that acute mental stressors have been implicated as variables that may deleteriously affect test performance, Hoffman and al'Absi (2004) examined the performance of 25 subjects with no known neurological or psychiatric impairment on a short neuropsychological battery on alternate days following rest or induced mental stress in a counterbalanced design. Among the neuropsychological measures used were the WMS-III Logical Memory, Digit Span, and Visual Memory Span subtests. The results of their study indicated that there were no statistically significant differences in any of the neuropsychological measures when stress versus rest days were compared.

McDowell, Bayless, Moser, Meyers, and Paulsen (2004) examined the concordance between the CVLT and the WMS-III Words List Test (WLT). Both were administered to a diagnostically diverse group of 25 patients, and the authors report that the two tests were highly correlated. They found that correlations between corresponding measures of the CVLT and WLT ranged from .50 to .76. Despite the correlations, they also reported that decisions of recognition memory impairment were not consistent between the two test outcomes.

Levy (2006) notes that a recent examination of the test norms for the WMS-III Faces-I subtest reveal significant age-related floor effects implying excessive difficulty in the acquisition phase among unimpaired older adults. As a result, the author presented the results of a study of an alternative measure that demonstrated clinical utility in differentiating between the performance of 16 patients with Alzheimer's disease and 16 controls.

In another study of the Faces subtest, Barlow and Axelrod (2007) investigated the effect of racial response bias on the WMS-III Faces subtest. Using a sample of 159 male patients (98 Caucasian and 60 African American), the authors found that Caucasian and African American subjects had statistically greater recognition of their own race and poorer recognition of other races on Faces I. On Faces II, the only significant finding was that Caucasians have significantly poorer recognition of African American faces.

Brooks, Iverson, Holdnack, and Feldman (2008) examined the base rates of low memory scores in older adults ($N = 550$, age range 55–87) from the WMS-III standardization sample. Examining eight age-adjusted WMS-III scores simultaneously (the Auditory Recognition and Working Memory tests were not included), the authors found that 26% of the older adults had one or more scores at or below the fifth percentile. In looking at eight demographically adjusted scores, 39% had at least one score at or below the fifth percentile. Noting that there was an inverse relationship between intellectual abilities and the prevalence of low memory scores, the authors underscored the importance of understanding base rates of low scores in order to reduce the overinterpretation of low scores and minimize false-positive misclassification.

Frisby and Kim (2008) note that Profile Analysis via Multidimensional Scaling (PAMS) is a procedure for extracting latent core profiles in a multitest data set. One of the advantages it offers is that it estimates individual profile weights that reflect the degree to which an individual's observed profile approximates the shape and scatter of latent core profiles. The authors applied the PAMS procedure to WMS-III index scores of $N = 1,033$ nonreplicated participants from the standardization sample. The PAMS procedure extracted discrepant visual memory and auditory memory versus working memory core profiles for the complete 19- to 89-year-old sample, and discrepant working memory and auditory memory versus working memory core profiles for the 75- to 89-year-old cohort. The authors note that the use of this procedure allows for unique interpretive opportunities for researchers and clinicians.

Walker, Batchelor, and Shores (2009) conducted a literature review to study the effects of education and cultural background on the performance of WAIS-III, WMS-III, WAIS-R, and WMS-R measures in an Australian sample. They report that although the limited research available did not demonstrate improved diagnostic efficiency with the application of demographic corrections for the WMS-III, this was an area requiring further study.

Brooks, Strauss, Sherman, Iverson, and Slick (2009) published an excellent article on recent developments in neuropsychological assessment and clinical interpretive methods with a variety of tests, including the WMS-III. The authors emphasize how important it is for clinicians to understand the adequacy of the normative sample, the role of measurement error, issues of normal test score variability, and various methods for interpreting changes in test performance over time. Concerning the WMS-III, they note that normative scaled score distribution varies by subtest and age. For example, for a 20-year-old, the ceiling effect results in a maximum scaled score of 12 on Verbal Paired Associates II, compared with a maximum scaled score of 19 on Logical Memory II. For readers wishing to learn more about these issues, the paper by Brooks et al. (2009) is strongly recommended.

Brophy, Jackson, and Crowe (2009) present the results of two studies investigating the effect of interference on delayed recall scores of the WMS-III and other commonly used memory measures. Their study highlights the importance of considering interference effects in clinical practice and cautions against the use of memory-related materials during the delay interval in memory testing.

Binder, Iverson, and Brooks (2009) reviewed normative studies of variability in performance by healthy adults on neuropsychological batteries, including the WMS-R and III. Their paper is recommended reading for those wishing to learn more about this issue.

Brooks and Iverson (2010) compared actual to estimated base rates of "abnormal" scores on the Neuropsychological Assessment Battery and a battery consisting of the WAIS-III and WMS-III using Monte Carlo simulation software. The authors found that although Monte Carlo estimations of base rates of low scores had good accuracy compared with actual base rates of low scores for the two batteries, the estimated base rates lost considerable accuracy for individuals with low or high intelligence. The authors reported that the Monte Carlo program might underestimate the base rates for those with low intelligence and overestimate the base rates for those with high intelligence.

Lamb, Thompson, McKay, Waldie, and Kirk (2015) observe that recall and recognition are forms of memory proposed to have different neural substrates, with recall having greater dependence on the prefrontal cortex and hippocampus. Their research assessed recall and familiarity-based recognition in a sample of 100 healthy adults using the WMS-III Faces and Family Pictures subtests. The researchers found that subjects who carried the catechol-O-methyltransferase gene (COMT) did not perform poorly on either task, and that carriers of the brain-derived neurotrophic factor (BDNF) displayed poorer recall ability.

In a related study, Lamb, McKay, Singh, Waldie, and Kirk (2016) investigated the joint effect of sex and the COMT genotype on face recognition as assessed by the WMS-III Face I subtest. The authors found a significant two-way interaction between sex and COMT genotype on facial recognition. Male met homozygotes demonstrated a greater ability to determine whether faces had been previously encountered than male val carriers.

In a rare study of accelerated long-term forgetting (ALF), Ladowsky-Brooks (2016) investigated whether ALF could be identified in a small sample of subjects with head injuries or other neurological disorders (N-42) using a four-hour delayed recall condition of the WMS-III Logical Memory subtest. As noted previously, the author found that 11% of their sample showed increased forgetting when compared to average retention scores after a four-hour delay.

Summary

The studies on WMS-III reviewed cover a remarkably wide range of investigations into various factors which could influence the interpretation of WMS-III results. Because the WMS-III yields 51 separate scores, it is not surprising that many researchers have investigated ways to make test interpretation easier and less error-prone. Due to the amount of time it takes to administer the full WMS-III, as with the WMS-R, some investigators have derived formulas to estimate various index scores based on shorter batteries.

Numerous investigators have looked at the meaning of "abnormal scores," finding they are surprisingly common even among healthy adults. Investigators have also looked at gender and racial effects on test results, and the composition of such subtests as Family Pictures, which has been found to have loadings on verbal and visual memory factors. As with the WMS-R, the studies cited are but a fraction that appear in the literature examining various properties of the WMS-III, including its reliability, validity, and utility for clinical and research use. It is significant to note that there have been relatively few studies of the subtests unique to the WMS-III, especially after the WMS-IV was published, likely because the subtests new to the WMS-III were not retained in the WMS-IV.

With the advent of computer assisted scoring and interpretation, many clinicians rely on such to guide their test interpretation and report writing. The highlighted studies suggest that it is important for clinicians and researchers to be aware of the limitations of computerized test interpretations that rely on possibly questionable assumptions, like the frequency of abnormal test scores, and use them cautiously, especially in forensic assessments.

WMS-IV Investigations

As before, what follows is a presentation of selected papers that have examined various facets of the WMS-IV. And as before, the papers will be presented roughly in the order they were published.

Miller et al. (2012a) examined the validity of substituting scores from the CVLT-II for the Verbal Paired Associates (VPA) subtest. At the index level, Miller et al. (2012a) found that substitution resulted in significantly lower scores for the Auditory Memory Index but not for the Immediate Memory Index. For the subtest scores, substituted scaled scores for VPA were not significantly different for immediate recall.

Martin and Schroeder (2014) examined the chance performance and floor effects of the WMS-IV Designs subtest. They note that the test allows for the accumulation of points by chance alone, creating the potential for artificially inflated scores. The study indicates that clinicians should use caution in interpreting Designs II performance in the 45–69 age range.

In a similar study, Thiruselvam, Vogt, and Hoelzle (2015) investigated the interchangeability of CVLT-II and WMS-IV Verbal Paired Associates (VPA) scores. The authors found that VPA I and II scores were significantly greater than VPA substitute scores derived from CVLT-III performance. In addition, they found that Auditory Memory Index scores were significantly lower when CVLT-II scores were used in place of VPA scores.

Miller et al. (2012b) used archival data to attempt to predict the Immediate Memory Index (IMI) and Delayed Memory Index (DMI) from three of the four primary subtests used in calculation of the IMI and DMI. The results of their study demonstrated that the IMI and DMI can be reliably estimated using two or three subtests, with the three-test combination yielding better results. The authors found that there was little evidence to suggest there was any improvement in predictive accuracy with the inclusion of CVLT-II measures.

Miller, Axelrod, and Schutte (2012) conducted a related study of the parsimonious estimation of WMS-IV demographically adjusted Immediate Memory and Delayed Memory Index scores. The results of their research showed strong support for estimating demographically corrected index scores from the Advanced Clinical Solutions for the WMS-IV using parsimonious subsets of the most frequently administered subtests.

Stark, Fox, Roberts, Stewart, and Golden (2014) examined gender differences in individual performance on the WMS-IV. Using a mixed clinical sample of adults aged 17–70, the authors found that men scored statistically higher on the Visual Working Memory Index.

Bouman, Hendriks, Van Der Veld, Aldenkamp, and Kessels (2016) evaluated the reliability and validity of three short forms of the Dutch WMS-IV in a mixed clinical sample of 235 patients. The short forms were based on the WMS-IV Flexible Approach, specifically three-subtest and two-subtest combinations for the Older Adult Battery. The authors report that while all short forms showed adequate reliability, three-subtest short forms were consistently more accurate.

Carrasco, Grups, Evans, Simco, and Mittenberg (2015) examined apparently abnormal Wechsler Memory Scale-IV index score patterns in the normal population. The authors note that standardization data indicate that 15-point differences between any pair of index scores are relatively uncommon in normal individuals, but these base rates refer to a comparison between a single pair of indexes rather than multiple simultaneous comparisons among indexes. The authors conducted a study that provides normative data for the occurrence of multiple index score comparisons calculated by using Monte Carlo simulations and validated against standardization data. The authors note that when multiple comparisons are made, the probability of apparently abnormal differences increases due to chance, which may inflate false positive findings.

Etherton and Tapscott (2015) investigated the impact of laboratory-induced pain on selected visual and auditory subtests of the WMS-IV. They found that laboratory-induced pain in nonclinical volunteers did not significantly impair their performance on Visual Working Memory or on the immediate portions of the auditory memory subtests.

Ingram, Diakoumakos, Sinclair, and Crowe (2016) investigated proactive and retroactive interference effects between the WMS-IV using the flexible approach and the WAIS-IV. The author found that the WAIS-IV produced significant retroactive interference effects on the WMS-IV, but no proactive interference effect was observed. The retroactive effect was dependent on material specificity. The authors found that material presented during the delay period between immediate and delayed recall measures can have a significant effect on subsequent delayed recall.

Hinton-Bayre (2016) examined the responsiveness, or ability to detect change, of three reliable change index models using existing test-retest norms. In his paper, which reviews the pros and cons of the three models, the author presents a convincing case for using a regression-based model.

Brooks, Holdnack, and Iverson (2016), in an investigation of test-retest WMS-IV normative data, found that "abnormal" reliable change memory scores are common in healthy adults and older adults. Their study demonstrates that it is common for people to have at least one large change in performance on memory testing when several tests are administered, and that the changes in test performance were not unidirectional and reflective of practice effects, rather they were bidirectional. They also caution that determining whether there has been improvement or worsening in cognitive functioning is a complicated process that involves several steps and a good understanding of psychometric concepts.

Summary

As was the case for prior versions of the WMS, the papers reviewed here cover a range of topics from the use of reliable change models in clinical decision-making and the search for brief WMS-IV batteries, to investigations of pain and stress on test performance. A takeaway from the studies cited is that clinicians should use caution in substituting CVLT-II scores for Verbal Paired Associate scores. Doing so appears to introduce additional sources of error in to the interpretive process.

In this era of managed care, clinicians frequently feel pressured to administer as many tests as possible in the time available. The results of the Ingram et al. (2016) study should caution examiners that trying to cram too many tests into a given period may have unintended negative consequences. Doing so may not only result in test results with diminished validity, but also create undue stress on elderly or fragile patients.

Hopefully the studies discussed in this section will encourage clinicians and researchers to regularly review the literature regarding the tests they use.

In addition to reviewing studies contained in a variety of excellent clinical journals, like *Applied Neuropsychology, Neuropsychology*, and the *Archives of Clinical Neuropsychology*, the APA PsychNET Gold is an excellent and inexpensive source of up-to-date information and provides cost-effective access to all current and past copies of journals published by the American Psychological Association.

Investigations of Malingering and Incomplete Effort

The detection of malingering and incomplete effort is presently a very hotly debated topic in clinical neuropsychology. All clinicians examining subjects for suspected memory impairment have to make a determination that the test results produced by their clients are valid reflections of their actual functioning. This determination is of great importance in subjects who are pursing litigation or benefits. Most examiners these days try to include at least two measures of incomplete effort in their assessments, and a whole market has grown up around the assessment of malingering and incomplete effort. Numerous books and papers have been written and tests published to address these concerns (see, for instance, Bowden, 2017a; Chafetz et al., 2015). The following studies of incomplete effort and malingering will be presented by WMS version in the order they appeared in the literature. As before, this presentation does not purport to be comprehensive, although it is representative of various studies that have appeared in the literature over the years. In addition, as has been the case with prior presentations, a general overview of the studies will be presented. For more specific details, interested readers are encouraged to consult the original articles.

Studies Using the WMS and WMS-R

Rawling and Brooks (1990) attempted to detect simulated failures on the WAIS-R and WMS through a qualitative analysis of error types. In the first phase of their study, test protocols of a group of subjects who had sustained a severe head injury were compared to a group of patients claiming severe and persistent mental impairment following mild head injury. The authors identified error types unique to each group, which were assigned differential numerical weighting, and scores for the error types were summed to produce a Simulation Index that reportedly produced a perfect separation of the two groups. In the validation phase, the Simulation Index was applied to two new groups: one sustaining severe head injury and one presenting with independent clinical evidence of simulation. According to the authors, the same cutoff score produced only one misclassification error for the 20 patients sampled. It is significant to note that the Simulation Index developed by the author was partially based on subject's performance on the WMS and WAIS-R. Two limitations of the Rawling and Brooks (1990) study are small sample size and nature of the samples.

Bernard, McGrath, and Houston (1993) tested the hypothesis that malingering is distinguished by poorer performance on recognition relative to recall tasks by evaluating the ability of discriminant functions to distinguish between eight subjects simulating malingering and 44 subjects with a history of closed head injury (CHI) on the WMS-R. The authors found that a complex performance pattern on seven WMS-R subtests distinguished malingering subjects from those with CHI. The results of the study did not support the recognition versus recall hypothesis. It is noteworthy that malingering performance was associated with poorer performance on two relatively easy tasks (Visual Reproduction I and Visual Memory Span); better performance on two relatively easy tasks dependent on immediate recall (Visual Paired Associates I and Digit Span); poorer performance on two relatively difficult tasks of delayed recall (Logical Memory II and Visual Paired Associates II); and better performance on another task of delayed recall (Visual Reproduction II).

Mittenberg, Azrin, Millsaps, and Heilbronner (1993) compared the performance of 39 head-injured outpatients with 39 age-matched subjects who were instructed to malinger head trauma on the WMS-R and WAIS-R. The head-injured group was not involved in litigation or pursuing a workers compensation claim. A discriminant function analysis based on WMS-R subtests and indexes was able to accurately classify 91% of the head-injured group and 83% of the malingering group. The authors noted that the discrimination rested primarily on a tendency for the former group to do better and malingerers to do worse on measures of attention relative to their own measures of memory.

Fox (1994) evaluated a sample of 100 neuropsychologically normal worker's compensation claimants using the Logical Memory (LM) I and II WMS-R subtests to estimate the degree to which WMS-R norms may overestimate the degree of memory impairment when applied to litigating clients. He also investigated the role of clinical depression in memory performance. He found that the use of standard norms for the Logical Memory tests would result in a large number of neurologically normal worker compensation subjects (approximately 20%) appearing to suffer from memory impairment. He also found evidence that depression may artificially lower LM scores. His study points to the danger of using such norms uncritically in litigation cases.

Blackwood (1996) provided a critique of Fox's (1994) findings, however, and asserted that the data did not support such a conclusion. Instead, he suggested, based on the results of other research, that the data presented by Fox appeared to simply demonstrate that patients in litigation with potentially painful orthopedic and/or emotional injuries could, as a group, perform slightly below-average levels on memory tests.

Milanovich, Axelrod, and Millis (1996) expanded the findings of Rawling and Brooks (1990) by examining the specificity of the Simulation Index-Revised (SI-R) in a mixed clinical sample of 338 patients in which simulation was not expected. The SI-R evaluates qualitative errors on the WAIS-R and WMS. Examples of errors coded are omission or order errors on Mental

Control, and confabulations or generalizations on Logical Memory I. Mila-novich et al. (1996) found that the overall level of specificity was 62% in this sample, and noted that patients with schizophrenia, vascular dementia, and alcohol dependence had lower specificity scores than did the mean of the entire sample.

Franzen and Martin (1996) investigated whether people with knowledge fake better. They looked at the ability of graduate students and professors of psychology to malinger believable memory deficits in order to investigate the ability of sophisticated subjects to malinger memory deficits. The subjects were administered several tests including the WMS-R Logical Memory sub-test followed by a forced choice recognition procedure for elements of the paragraph narratives. While 33 out of the 37 subjects were classified as malin-gerers based solely on their Logical Memory recognition scores, only two of the subjects were classified as malingerers based solely on their performance on the 21-Item Word List.

Trueblood and Binder (1997) investigated neuropsychology practitioners' accuracy in detecting malingering based on neuropsychological test data alone. One hundred forty psychologists, selected from the National Academy of Neuropsychology, the American Board of Professional Psychology/American Board of Clinical Neuropsychology, and the American Board of Professional Neuropsychology received study materials via general mail. Of the 140 prac-titioners, 75 were included in the study based on their timeliness in return-ing study materials and other factors. The test materials included results from malingered and head-injured testing on the WMS-I and the WMS-R. Clinical malingerers were identified by subjects who performed at below-chance levels on forced choice test results. The error rates of detecting malingering ranged from 0% to 25% with an average of 10% across all four malingered cases.

Johnson and Lesniak-Karpiak (1997) investigated the effects of warning regarding detection of simulated cognitive and motor deficits on the WMS-R and Grooved Pegboard. Eighty-seven undergraduates were randomly assigned to one of three conditions: simulators without warning, simulators with warn-ing, and controls. The results of their study provided support for the effective-ness of warning in reducing malingering behavior.

Arnett and Franzen (1997) examined the performance of 149 inpatient subjects with substance abuse with impaired and unimpaired delayed mem-ory performance (as assessed by the WMS-R) on three measures (the 21-Item Wordlist, the Memorization of 16 Items Test, and the Rey Dot Counting Pro-cedure) typically used to detect malingering. Only subjects who could be assumed to be performing at their optimal effort were chosen for the study. Consistent with the study's hypotheses, the patient group with unimpaired delayed memory performance performed better than the patient group with impaired memory performance on several of the malingering indices. The study suggested that each of the three malingering measures appeared equally useful in the detection of malingering.

Denny (1999) developed a forced-choice, two-alternative recognition test for the Logical Memory subtests of the WMS-R that incorporated the statistical properties of symptom validity testing paradigm to demonstrate recognition ability for individuals claiming no such ability. He reports that his procedure is useful in detecting below-chance levels of performance in association with the WMS-R.

Rosenfeld, Sands, and Van Gorp (2000) observed that the search for reliable and valid methods of detecting malingering and distortion had become an increasingly important task for forensic psychologists and neuropsychologists and discussed the importance of examining the base rates of malingering on the accuracy of prediction models. They noted that the efficacy of the prediction model proposed by Mittenberg et al. (1993) is related to the base rate of malingering in a given setting. Noting that Mittenberg et al. (1993) suggest that a significant discrepancy between the WMS-R Attention/Concentration Index (ACI) and the General Memory Index (GMI) "does not make neuropsychological sense," Rosenfeld et al. (2000) cite research by Johnstone, Erdal, and Stadler (1995) who studied the validity of the ACI-GMI discrepancy to classify those with probable ADHD, in which the ACI was at least 15 points higher than the GMI. The authors found the mean difference between ACI and GMI scores for the ADHD group was actually 25.

Suchy and Sweet (2000) examined the utility of the Information/Orientation (IO) subtest of the WMS-R to identify insufficient effort. The performance of 50 benefit-seeking patients was compared to previously generated norms based on a clinical sample. The authors found that 12% of the benefit-seeking patients had IO scores that were outside the performance ranges of the entire clinical sample, and an additional 24% had performances that were comparable to less than 2% of the normative sample. The authors concluded that the IO subtest had some utility as an indicator of insufficient effort.

Slick, Hinkin, van Gorp, and Satz (2001) examined the base rate of a WMS-R malingering index in a sample of non-compensation-seeking men infected with HIV-1. The purpose of their study was to cross-validate the malingering index proposed by Mittenberg et al. (1993). The results of their study suggested the application of the GMI-ACI Malingering Index be cautiously used, particularly among patients who obtained above-average GMI scores, due to significant false-positive errors.

Ishikawa, Raine, Lencz, Bihrle, and Lacasse (2001) studied autonomic stress reactivity and executive functions in successful and unsuccessful criminal psychopaths from the community. They examined the hypothesis that successful psychopaths would show increased autonomic stress reactivity and better neuropsychological function compared to unsuccessful psychopaths on psychophysical measures recorded during an emotional manipulation and psychological testing on selected subtests from the WMS-R. The results of the study revealed that there were no significant differences between successful and unsuccessful psychopaths on the Visual Reproduction I and II and Logical Memory I and II subtests.

Hilsabeck et al. (2003) conducted a partial cross-validation of the index proposed by Mittenberg et al. (1993) in a sample of 200 nonlitigants. Nine diagnostic categories were examined, including participants with traumatic brain injury, brain tumor, stroke and vascular problems, dementia of the Alzheimer's type, depression/anxiety, medical problems, and no diagnosis. The researchers found that the General Memory Index-Attention/Concentration Index difference score misclassified 8.5% of the sample as malingering when a difference of greater than 25 points was used as a cutoff criterion.

Studies Using the WMS-III and IV

Langeluddecke and Lucas (2003) compared the WMS-III performance of 25 mild-head-trauma litigants who met the criteria for probable malingered neurocognitive dysfunction with 50 nonmalingering subjects. The results of their study revealed that malingerers produced significantly poorer scores on all WMS-III indexes and subtests.

Greve, Bianchini, Mathias, Houston, and Crouch (2003) examined the validity of Mittenberg et al.'s (2001) approach to detecting malingered performance on the WAIS in individuals who had sustained traumatic brain injury. The study participants were 151 TBI referrals for comprehensive neuropsychological evaluation for workers compensation/personal injury cases. As part of their evaluation, all patients completed either the WMS-R or III. Patients were classified based on the Slick, Sherman, and Iverson (1999) criteria for malingered neuropsychological dysfunction. Of the sample, 37 failed to meet all the Slick et al. (1999) criteria and were referred to as the control group. An analysis of variance revealed that the control group obtained significantly higher WAIS-R or -III and WMS-R or -III index scores than did the probable malingering group. Yet the probable malingering group sustained significantly less severe injuries than did the control group.

D'Amato and Denney (2008) examined the diagnostic utility of the Rarely Missed Index (RMI) of the WMS-III in detecting response bias in an adult male incarcerated setting. Archival data from a sample of 60 incarcerated males who presented for neuropsychological testing were reviewed. Subjects were assigned to one of two groups: possible malingerers ($N = 30$) and valid test responders ($N = 30$). The researchers found that when using the recommended cutoff score of 136 or less, the sensitivity of the RMI was only 33% and the specificity 83%. Their findings suggested that the RMI might not be a reliable index for detecting response bias in this or possibly other similar settings.

Ylioja, Baird, and Podell (2009) developed an embedded performance validity measure based on the WMS-III Spatial Span task in a sample of litigating persistent postconcussion complainants. Their measure, titled the Reliable Spatial Span (RSS), reportedly had specificity, sensitivity, and predictive validity power within the range of other embedded measures and was able to distinguish between persistent postconcussion complainants demonstrating valid and invalid performance. The authors suggested that the RSS had some potential for use as an embedded validity indicator.

Miller et al. (2011) investigated the ability of the WMS-IV Advanced Clinical Solutions (ACS) package, including the Word Choice test, to distinguish poor performance due to intentional response bias among simulators of traumatic brain injury (TBI) from poor performance due to actual TBI. Participates were 45 survivors of moderate to severe TBI and 39 healthy adults coached to simulate TBI. The authors found that the diagnostic efficiency of the full ACS model was excellent.

Armistead-Jehle and Buican (2012) evaluated the impact of evaluation context symptom validity testing performances in a U.S. military sample. The study included a convenience sample of 335 U.S. military service members who underwent a neuropsychological evaluation for TBI at an outpatient military clinic. Subjects were divided into those who passed the Word Memory Test ($N = 195$) and those who failed the measure ($N = 140$). As part of their neuropsychological evaluation, participants completed the WMS-IV. The Spatial Addition and Symbol Span subtests were used as measures of an attention composite; the Logical Memory I and II, Verbal Paired Associates I and II, Designs I and II, and Visual Reproduction I and II subtests were used as a composite of memory. Subjects who failed the Word Memory Test scored significantly lower on these composites compared to those who passed the Word Memory Test.

Young, Caron, Baughman, and Sawyer (2012) explored whether the Symbol Span subtest of the WMS-IV could be used to discriminate adequate effort from suboptimal effort. Using archival data collected from 136 veterans classified into Poor Effort ($N = 42$) and Good Effort ($N = 94$) groups, the Poor Effort group had significantly lower raw scores and age-corrected scores than the Good Effort group on the Symbol Span subtest. A raw score cutoff of less than 14 produced an 83% specificity and 50% sensitivity for the detection of Poor Effort. Sensitivity was 52% and specificity was 84% when employing a cutoff of less than 7 for Age-Corrected Scale Scores. The authors concluded that the Symbol Span subtest thus had utility as a measure of suboptimal performance in the population they studied.

Schroeder et al. (2013) investigated the efficacy of the Test of Malingering Trial 1, Trial 2, and Retention Trial, and the Albany Consistency Index to assess malingered neurocognitive dysfunction in 69 consecutive forensic cases. They used archival records. The authors found the WMS-III Auditory Immediate Index standard score of less than or equal to 80, WMS-IV Verbal Paired Associates II Recognition raw score of less than or equal to 27, and WMS-IV Visual Reproduction II Recognition raw score of less than or equal to 3 were useful to identify malingered performance.

Armistead-Jehle and Buican (2013) evaluated the classification statistics of the WMS-IV Advanced Clinical Solutions (ACS) embedded measures of symptom validity in relation to the Word Memory Test (WMT) in a sample of active duty military personnel with mild TBI. Relative to the WMT, the ACS embedded measures were felt to have adequate specificity, but lacked sensitivity.

Martin, Schroeder, Heinrichs, and Baade (2015) investigated whether true neurocognitive dysfunction, as indicated by impaired performance on either the WMS-III or IV, contributed to the MMPI-2-RS Cognitive Validity Scale scores before and after controlling for performance validity test (PVT) status in 120 individuals referred for neuropsychological evaluations. After controlling for PVT status, the authors found the Cognitive Validity Scale scores were useful in the evaluation of individuals reporting cognitive impairment.

Bouman, Hendriks, Schmand, Kessels, and Aldenkamp (2016) examined the utility of a Dutch version of the WMS-IV (WMS-IV-NL) for the identification of suboptimal performance using an analogue study design. The patient group consisted of 59 mixed-etiology patients; the experimental malingerers were 50 healthy individuals who were asked to simulate cognitive impairment as a result of traumatic brain injury. These two groups were compared to 50 healthy controls who were instructed to put forth full effort. The researchers found that experimental malingerers performed significantly lower on all WMSI-IV-NL tasks than did patients or healthy controls. The researchers found that using recognition and visual working memory tasks from the WMS-IV-NL and the Spatial Addition subtest provided clinically useful information for the detection of suboptimal effort.

Soble et al. (2018) evaluated the accuracy of the WMS-IV Logical Memory embedded validity index to detect invalid test performance. Examining a clinical sample of 97 individuals, 71 were classified as displaying valid test performance and 26 were classified as displaying invalid test performance. The researchers concluded that the Logical Memory embedded validity measure was not appropriate from an evidence-based perspective due to its poor concordance with criterion performance validity tests and unacceptable psychometric properties.

Summary

As can be seen from the previous sections, there have been numerous studies of possible indicators of suboptimal performance or malingering using all versions of the WMS. The detection of suboptimal performance and malingering remain hotly debated topics in the professional literature, and clinicians are urged to consult recent publications for the most up-to-date advice regarding the use of such measures. The purpose of the review was to give an example of the range of efforts made to assess underperformance with the WMS and to show that many purported measures of such, upon further investigation, have been found to be invalid or have minimal clinical utility.

Chapter 7

Afterword

Glancing Back and Looking Ahead to the WMS-V

The Wechsler Memory Scale and its three official revisions have been part of the clinical landscape during the past 80 years. In addition, numerous other variations of the WMS have been proposed and used in a wide range of clinical investigations. The Wechsler Memory Scale remains the most used and taught formal test of memory in the United States, and it is widely used internationally in English-speaking and non-English-speaking countries.

In this book, it was argued that for most of the past eight decades, the WMS has had an invariant conceptual core consisting of the original WMS-I subtests. Of the seven subtests making up the original WMS, only the Digit Span subtest, a measure of verbal working memory, did not appear in the last official revision, partly because the publisher assumed the clinician would have access to this information by administering the Digit Span subtest from the WAIS-IV or another Digit Span subtest variant. Thus, even though Digit Span did not appear in the WMS-IV, the publisher tacitly acknowledged the importance of assessing verbal working memory when assessing memory functioning, just as Wechsler (1945) had done when he published his original scale.

It was noted earlier that of all the new subtests introduced in the WMS-R, none were retained when the WMS-III was published. And of all the new subtests introduced in the WMS-III, none survived when the WMS-IV was published. It is anticipated that most of the new subtests introduced in the WMS-IV will suffer the same fate when the WMS-V appears.

It was also argued that the factor structure of the WMS-I bears an uncanny resemblance to the factor structure of the WMS-R, WMS-III, and WMS-IV, with the exception that the WMS-IV finally appears to reliably and validly assess visual memory. The available evidence also suggests the WMS-IV appears to validly assess visual working memory. Based on the results of most factor analytic studies, none of the revisions of the WMS appear to validly assess delayed recall, a fact acknowledged by the publisher (Wechsler, 1997, 2009b). Despite this, many clinicians and research studies continue to discuss the differences between indexes of immediate and delayed recall, a practice inconsistent with those who advocate evidence-based clinical practice (see, for instance, Bowden, 2017a, 2017b).

Although all revisions of the WMS have failed to validly assess delayed recall, each revision has been an improvement over the prior version of the test in several ways. The size of the standardization groups has increased over time and generally been more representative of the U.S. population. For example, the WMS-I was normed on what appears to have been a sample of convenience of "about" 200 individuals; the WMS-IV was normed on a 1,400 representative sample of the 2005 Census. While the WMS-I could only be used to assess the memory function of individuals in the 20–64 age range, the WMS-IV can assess individuals aged 16–90. Each revision of the WMS has also provided more objective scoring guidelines for the various subtests.

All revisions of the WMS have also been linked to theoretical notions of memory and our understanding of the neurological bases of memory. In addition, the administrative and technical manuals for the WMS have evolved in a manner to provide clinicians and researchers with better information regarding the psychometric properties of each scale and guides to clinical interpretation.

The last two revisions have also made a decided effort to assess memory performance through free recall *and* recognition paradigms, a distinction critical for identifying the reason for poor test performance. The last revision also made an effort to assess assessment validity (Larrabee, 2015).

Each revision of the WMS provides some information of the use of the scale with various clinical populations. This information has usually been presented in the context of supporting the scale's validity. Unfortunately, the information presented has often been based on ill-defined clinical groups and small samples, consisting of 20 patients or less. It is hoped when the next revision appears, the selection of various clinical groups will be based on bigger and more representative samples.

At the time this book is being written, it is anticipated that the WMS-V will appear in 2021 or 2022, assuming data from the 2020 Census is used for standardization purposes. Pearson is currently engaged in field trials of the new revision and presumably research highlighting the psychometric properties and the strengths and weaknesses of the next revision.

Based on what we know about the strengths and weaknesses of each WMS version, in an ideal world, what might the WMS-V look like? The following suggestions and rationale for each are offered.

Suggestion 1: The WMS-V Should Contain *All* the Subtests of the Original Scale as Part of the Standard Battery

Rationale: As noted previously in this book, the original WMS subtests map remarkably well on Carroll's (1993) seminal investigation of the factor structure of memory and learning. To recap his findings, Carroll found that individuals differ in a *general memory ability* that affects their performance across a variety of tasks (similar to Spearman's concept of "g"). He also found evidence for more specific factors of memory, which include *memory span, associate memory, free recall memory, meaningful memory,* and *visual memory.* His research demonstrated that there is a *general learning factor* that correlates with fluid and crystallized intelligence (Cattell, 1971) and evidence of unique factors of learning ability specific to particular kinds of learning situations. It was noted earlier that the finding of unique factors of learning is consistent with what we know about brain networks and cognition. Different cognitive tasks recruit different brain networks (Anderson, 2014). Retaining subtests that map well onto the theoretical findings of Carroll (1993) is consistent with sound evidence-based practice.

Making the next iteration of the Brief Cognitive Status Exam (BCSE) part of the standard battery ensures that the functions assessed by this subtest are done so in a uniform and consistent manner and allows the examiner to assess any change in functioning across time in a way that is not contaminated by comparing the results of measures that may be dissimilar in composition. One of the most significant and clinically useful changes introduced with the WMS-IV BCSE was the inclusion of normative information to help interpret this subtest.

A vast amount of research has accumulated in the past 80 years regarding the reliability and validity of each of the core subtests. These subtests, in their various iterations, have been used in thousands of studies investigating the nature of memory dysfunction in numerous clinical conditions. They have also been used to map the trajectory of memory functioning across the lifespan and identify the boundaries between normal and pathological aging.

Suggestion 2: The WMS-V Should Retain the WMS-IV Subtests (i.e., Spatial Span and Spatial Addition) Which Comprise the Visual Working Memory Index, in Addition to the Digit Span and Mental Control Subtests From Prior Versions

Rationale: Reestablishing the Digit Span subtest as part of the core battery will ensure that clinicians will obtain information regarding verbal working memory that has been normed with the other core subtests. The same applies to the Mental Control subtest. Patients who present with complaints about their memory and attention commonly complain of problems with verbal, not visual, working memory. This does not mean to imply that the assessment of visual working memory is unimportant. Rather, from a clinical standpoint, if one had to choose between assessing either one, verbal working memory appears to be the most clinically pertinent domain. Although patients do not commonly complain about problems with visual working memory, this also is an important capacity to assess since visual information is most commonly integrated with auditory information (Coolidge, 2020). In the past 15 years, the importance of working memory to everyday functioning has been examined by a variety of researchers, such as Baddely (2007) and Baddely et al. (2015). Working memory is a critical component of executive functioning (Banich & Compton, 2018; Lezak et al., 2012). Factor analytic studies have generally upheld the validity of the WMS-IV Visual Working Memory Index, just as they have supported the validity of the Attention/Concentration Index of prior revisions. Research has suggested that these subtests assess the integrity of frontal-parietal brain networks. An ideal memory test battery should assess both.

Suggestion 3: The WMS-V Should Contain Subtests That Validly Assess Delayed Recall of the Logical Memory, Visual Reproduction, and Verbal Paired Associates Subtests

Rationale: Factor analytic studies of each revision of the WMS have failed to establish the validity of purported measures of delayed recall, something the publisher has acknowledged in the technical manuals accompanying the last two revisions. Despite this acknowledgment, the lack of the validity of purported measures of delayed recall appears to have gone largely unappreciated in the clinical literature and when such measures are used in most research studies. The publisher chose to include (invalid) measures of delayed recall partially for "clinical" reasons and partly, this writer would argue, because of clinical tradition. Russell's (1975) revision of the WMS-I was the first serious attempt to assess delayed recall (in this case, of the Logical Memory and Visual Reproduction subtests), in an effort to address persistent criticisms of the original scale. At the time, it was assumed that the Logical Memory subtest was uniquely sensitive to left hemisphere lesions and the Visual Reproduction subtest was uniquely sensitive to right hemisphere lesions. We now know that there serious limitations to Russell's (1975) norms; that the Visual Reproduction subtest assesses both verbal as well as visual memory; and the Visual Reproduction subtest is not uniquely sensitive to right hemisphere lesions.

As previously noted, the Logical Memory, Visual Reproduction, and Verbal Paired Associates subtests have been the most used and best investigated of the core subtests. More is known about these subtests than any of the other core subtests, with the possible exception of Digit Span. In some ways, they represent the heart of the WMS.

It was suggested earlier in this book that the failure of most factor analytic studies of the three revisions of the Wechsler Memory Scale to provide validity for the delayed recall subtests and indexes might be a function of the use of a faulty methodology. The current measures of delayed recall appear to be assessing intermediate memory (Kent, 2017), a form of short-term memory rarely assessed clinically (Lezak et al., 2012). Depending on the revision used, delayed recall is assessed after a period ranging from 20 to 35 minutes. There are theoretical reasons to believe this interval is too short to assess delayed recall, if by delayed recall we mean long-term retention.

Valid measures of delayed recall (as determined by factor analytic studies) likely will have to involve significantly longer intervals between the administration of the immediate and delayed recall measures than is currently the practice. Although from a clinical standpoint this will add to the length of time it takes to administer the WMS, the payoff will be test findings that are valid and more clinically useful. In addition, the use of subtests that validly assess delayed recall may have an added benefit of redefining what we know about the nature of various neurological disorders impairing memory functioning, such as head injuries, strokes, and the dementias, and potentially aiding in the development of more effective treatment interventions.

Suggestion 4: The WMS-V Should Include Formal Measures of Semantic and Procedural Memory

Rationale: The deterioration in semantic memory is associated with many neurological disorders, including several dementing conditions like Alzheimer's disease. Presently the WMS-IV does not manifestly assess this type of memory. In addition, no version of the WMS has attempted to assess procedural memory in a systematic fashion. Deficits in procedural memory are often characteristic of subcortical dysfunction (Koziol & Budding, 2009). Including formal measures of each can help address some of the historic shortcomings of the instrument and aid in the differential diagnosis process.

Suggestion 5: The WMS-V Should Have Significantly Expanded Information on the Characteristic Memory Profiles of Individuals Who Present With Various Neuropsychological and Medical Disorders

Rationale: Beginning with the first revision, the publisher included limited information on WMS profiles of individuals with various frequently encountered clinical conditions, like mild cognitive impairment, head injury, and seizure disorders. When this information has been presented, the information appears to have been collected from samples of convenience yielding small sample sizes, limiting the usefulness of such information.

In the more than 75 years that that the WMS has been in clinical and research use, a vast amount of information has been collected about the performance of various clinical groups on each test battery. The WMS is the most researched clinical memory battery in the world. It is time to harness that information in a systematic fashion, as doing so will impact clinical practice and future research. Unfortunately, there have been relatively few studies attempting to synthesize what is known regarding the performance of various clinical conditions on each test version. One of the aims of this book was an effort to do just that. Unfortunately, the current academic atmosphere appears to privilege original, often narrowly based, trivial research efforts over efforts to synthesize what has already learned. As a result, the clinical literature contains a great deal of data but little information.

The publisher of the WMS-V could address the relative lack of synthesis of information regarding the use of the scale with various populations by partnering with graduate psychology departments across the world and providing financial support for students willing to complete meta-analytic and literature synthesis research projects for their thesis or dissertation. The results of such studies could be published in an online journal sponsored by the publisher devoted entirely to the Wechsler Memory Scales. This would result in a win for the publisher, since such information could be included in technical guides to the use of the various scales and disseminated by the publisher on a regular basis to users of the scales, an added benefit to clinicians wishing to use the scale. Graduate psychology students would benefit by completing a project that fulfills an essential requirement for graduation and being able to publish a report of significance to clinicians and researchers alike. It is well known that a major barrier to completing a doctoral degree is often the dissertation, especially in clinical training programs with modest financial resources and a limited research tradition.

Suggestion 6: The WMS-IV Should Be Explicitly Linked to Advances in Our Understanding of the Neurological Basis of Memory. In Addition, It Should Be Anchored in an Explicit Theory of Memory

Rationale: Starting with the first revision, the publisher made an attempt to link the development of the revision to advances in our understanding of the neurological basis of memory. It is strongly suggested that efforts be made to significantly improve this linkage with the new revision, with special emphasis on what we know about brain networks. In addition, it is time that the WMS is firmly anchored in an explicit, as opposed to an implicit, theory of memory.

Suggestion 7: The Standard WMS-V Battery Should Include Formal Measures of Malingering and Suboptimal Performance

Rationale: Professional assessment guidelines currently call for the assessment of malingering or suboptimal performance as part of every neuropsychological evaluation. It is time that measures of suboptimal effort and malingering are a *standard* part of the WMS.

Assuming the aforementioned recommendations are incorporated into the WMS-V, the next revision might look something like the following (see Table 7.1). As can be seen, by adopting the proposed new structure, several advantages are gained over the previous revision.

Table 7.1 Proposed WMS-V Structure and Content

Proposed Indexes	Suggest Content
Screening Index	*Brief Cognitive Status Exam*
Auditory Memory Immediate Recall Index	Logical Memory I; Verbal Paired Associates I
Auditory Memory Delayed Recall Index	Logical Memory II; Verbal Paired Associates III
Visual Memory Immediate Recall Index	Visual Reproduction I; Visual Paired Associates I
Visual Memory Delayed Recall Index	Visual Reproduction I; Visual Paired Associates II
Visual Working Memory Index	Spatial Addition; Spatial Span
Verbal Working Memory Index	Digit Span; Mental Control
Semantic Memory Index	Derived from Verbal Paired Associates?
Prospective Memory Index	Embedded in the Brief Cognitive Status Exam?
Procedural Memory Index	Possibly based on the WMS-III Spatial Span subtest
Malingering-Suboptimal Performance Index	Embedded measures from Advanced Clinical Solutions

First, clinicians will finally be able to make valid comparisons between the immediate and delayed recall subtests. This has not been the case with prior revisions.

Second, all subtests for the Auditory Memory Immediate Recall Index will have directly comparable measures in the Auditory Memory Delayed Recall Index. The same will be true of Visual Memory Immediate Recall Index and the Visual Memory Delayed Recall Index. This will result in valid clinical inferences that are evidence based.

Third, clinicians will be able to make meaningful comparisons between the immediate recall of auditorily presented versus the immediate recall of visually presented material. Likewise, clinicians will be able to make meaningful comparisons between the delayed recall of auditorily presented material versus the delayed recall of visually presented material.

Fourth, clinicians will be able to make meaningful comparisons between the subject's verbal and visual working memory capacities. A significant difference in these capacities would suggest that the subject might benefit from a treatment plan or intervention strategy that draws on the subject's strengths.

Fifth, formally assessing semantic and procedural memory within a common memory battery will allow the clinician to gain a better picture of the subject's strengths and weaknesses and aid in the differential diagnosis of cortical versus subcortical neuropsychological and neurological disorders.

Sixth, including measures of possible malingering or suboptimal test performance as part of the standard battery is clinically useful and consistent with current evidence-based assessment guidelines.

The new revision, as a result of incorporating old "tried and true" subtests, new measures of semantic, prospective, and procedural memory, and measures of malingering and suboptimal performance as part of the standard battery will likely increase the test administration time compared to the current WMS-IV Standard Adult Battery. A downside to expanding the time it takes to administer the WMS-V is that many clinicians will likely complain that the WMS-V is not as clinician or patient friendly as the prior revision. While this is a valid concern, it needs to be recognized that with prior revisions, clinicians were left with a test that purported to measure delayed recall (which was often confused with a deficit in long-term memory) when numerous factor analytic studies have indicated it did not. It is very likely that many clinicians using the prior revisions of WMS were not aware of this limitation of the instruments. Requiring clinicians to use invalid WMS measures of delayed recall, such as when conducting evaluations for Social Security disability determinations for persons complaining of memory problems, is grossly unfair to claimants where a failure to find impairment in delayed recall is used as evidence to deny disability or pension benefits.

Among older individuals not seeking disability determinations and who have concern about their memory, there is a trend these days to substitute memory screening for in-depth memory assessment. While memory screening clinics might be useful for perhaps 80% of the patient population, unfortunately such procedures may yield an unacceptable rate of false negatives, resulting in the underidentification of individuals with clinically significant memory problems. As a result, patients and families are left with a false sense of security, or a situation where there is a mismatch between the observations of patients and/or their caregivers as to the memory functioning of the afflicted person and quantitative "test results."

In these situations, one can make a compelling case for the importance of in-depth memory assessment for individuals who "pass" screening tests yet who continue to complain about memory problems, or family members who express significant concerns about the memory functioning of their loved ones despite apparently normal test findings. In addition, one can also make the case for in-depth memory assessment for most individuals in order to develop appropriate specialized intervention protocols. Memory screening clinics and medical personnel, when conducting short evaluations of patients complaining of memory dysfunction, often do a poor job of differentiating memory failure due to attention deficits, storage issues, retrieval deficits, or possible psychiatric problems like depression. Proper in-depth memory assessment can correct this problem. As a result, intervention plans can be tailored to the strengths and weaknesses of the person being evaluated, and behavioral interventions designed to help the person better cope and adapt to their unique environmental demands. This is especially important since it is highly unlikely that the pharmaceutical industry will ever develop a "silver bullet" to effectively treat all facets of memory problems. Memory problems, by nature, affect multiple neural networks and involve multiple neuropsychological domains. In addition to being neurological in nature, they also impact one's social networks and relationships with others. While it is conceivable that one day a pill may be developed to "rewire" all the brain's neural networks to some hypothetical ideal state, such rewiring will not rewire one's behavior resulting from that elusive construct we call "free will, which is a function of the interaction of nature and nurture, and each person's unique life experiences.

References

Abbruzzese, M., Bellodi, L., Ferri, S., & Scarone, S. (1993). Memory functioning in obsessive-compulsive disorder. *Behavioural Neurology, 6*(3), 119–122. https://doi.org/10.1155/1993/574872

Acker, M. B., & Davis, J. R. (1989). Psychology test scores associated with late outcome in head injury. *Neuropsychology, 3*(3), 123–133. https://doi.org/10.1037/h0091756

Adachi, H., Shinagawa, S., Komori, K., Toyota, Y., Mori, T., Matsumoto, T. . . . Ikeda, M. (2013). Comparison of the utility of everyday memory test and the Alzheimer's Disease Assessment Scale-Cognitive part for evaluation of mild cognitive impairment and very mild Alzheimer's disease. *Psychiatry and Clinical Neurosciences, 67*(3), 148–153. https://doi.org/10.1111/pcn.12034

Adams, R. A., Stanczak, D. E., Leutzinger, M. R., Waters, M. D., & Brown, T. (2001). The impact of psychological disturbances on immediate memory. *Archives of Clinical Neuropsychology, 16*(6), 605–618.

Aera, A. P. A. (1999). *Standards for educational and psychological testing.* New York: American Educational Research Association.

Aghili, R., Khamseh, M. E., Malek, M., Hadian, A., Baradaran, H. R., Najafi, L., & Emani, Z. (2012). Changes of subtests of Wechsler Memory Scale and cognitive function in subjects with subclinical hypothyroidism following treatment with levothyroxine. *Archives of Medical Science, 8*(6), 1096–1101.

Alegret, M., Espinosa, A., Valero, S., Vinyes-Junqué, G., Ruiz, A., Hernàndez, I. . . . Boada, M. (2013). Cut-off scores of a brief neuropsychological battery (NBACE) for Spanish individual adults older than 44 years old. *PLoS ONE, 8*(10): e76436. https://doi.org/10.1371/journal.pone.0076436

Altepeter, T. S., Adams, R. L., Buchanan, W. L., & Buck, P. (1990). Luria Memory Words Test and Wechsler Memory Scale: Comparison of utility in discriminating neurologically impaired from controls. *Journal of Clinical Psychology, 46*(2), 190–193. https://doi.org/10.1002/1097-4679(199003)46:2<190::AID-JCLP2270460211>3.0.CO;2-M

American Psychiatric Association. (2000). *Diagnostic and statistical manual-text revision (DSM-IV-TR).* Washington, DC: American Psychiatric Association.

Anderson, M. L. (2014). *After phrenology: Neural reuse and the interactive brain.* Cambridge, MA: MIT Press.

Anhoque, C. F., Neto, L. B., Aires Domingues, S. C., Teixeira, A. L., & Domingues, R. B. (2012). Cognitive impairment in patients with clinically isolated syndrome. *Dementia & Neuropsychologia, 6*(4). https://doi.org/10.1590/S1980-57642012DN06040011

Arbit, J., & Zagar, R. (1979). The effects of age and sex on the factor structure of the Wechsler Memory Scale. *The Journal of Psychology: Interdisciplinary and Applied, 102,* 185–190. https://doi.org/10.1080/00223980.1979.9923486

Ardila, A. (1992). Luria's approach to neuropsychological assessment. *International Journal of Neuroscience, 66,* 35–43.

Ardila, A., Lopera, F., Roselli, M., Moreno, S., Madrigal, L., Arango-Lasprilla, J. C. . . . Kosik, K. S. (2000). Neuropsychological profile of a large kindred with familial Alzheimer's disease caused by the E280A single presenilin-1 mutation. *Archives of Clinical Neuropsychology, 15*(6), 515–528. https://doi.org/10.1016/S0887-6177(99)00041-4

Armistead-Jehle, P., & Buican, B. (2012). Evaluation context and Symptom Validity Test performances in a US Military sample. *Archives of Clinical Neuropsychology, 27*(8), 828–839.

Armistead-Jehle, P., & Buican, B. (2013). Comparison of select Advanced Clinical Solutions embedded effort measures to the Word Memory Test in the detection of suboptimal effort. *Archives of Clinical Neuropsychology, 28*(3), 297–301.

Arnett, P. A., & Franzen, M. D. (1997). Performance of substance abusers with memory deficits on measures of malingering. *Archives of Clinical Neuropsychology, 2*(5), 513–518. https://doi.org/10.1016/S0887-6177(97)00010-3

Atkinson, L. (1991). Three standard errors of measurement and the Wechsler Memory Scale-Revised. *Psychological Assessment: A Journal of Consulting and Clinical Psychology, 3*(1), 136–138. https://doi.org/10.1037/1040-3590.3.1.136

Atkinson, L. (1992). The Wechsler Memory Scale-Revised: Abnormality of selected index differences. *Canadian Journal of Behavioural Science/Revue Canadienne Des Sciences Du Comportement, 24*(4), 537–539. https://doi.org/10.1037/h0078753

Axelrod, B. N. (1999). Administration duration for the Wechsler Adult Intelligence Scale-III and Wechsler Memory Scale-III. *Archives of Clinical Neuropsychology, 16,* 293–301.

Axelrod, B. N., Putnam, S. H., Woodard, J. L., & Adams, K. M. (1996). Cross-validation of predicted Wechsler Memory Scale-Revised scores. *Psychological Assessment, 8*(1), 73–75. https://doi.org/10.1037/1040-3590.8.1.73

Axelrod, B. N., & Woodard, J. L. (2000). Parsimonious prediction of Wechsler Memory Scale-III Memory Indices. *Psychological Assessment, 12*(4), 431–435.

Azuma, H., Segawa, K., Nakaaki, S., Murata, Y., Kawakami, K., Tohyama, J. . . . Uru-kawa, T. A. (2009). Neural correlates of memory in depression measured by brain perfusion SPECT at rest. *Psychiatry and Clinical Neurosciences, 63*(5), 685–692. https://doi.org/10.1111/j.1440-1819.2009.02013.x

Babcock, H., & Levy, L. (1940). *Test and manual of directions; The revised examination for the measurement of efficiency of mental functioning.* Chicago, IL: CH Stoelting.

Babcock, H., Shipley, W. C., Weider, A., Hunt, H. F., & Eisenson, J. (1953). Tests of Intellectual Impairment. In *Contributions toward medical psychology: Theory and psychodiagnostic methods* (Vol. II, pp. 741–771). New York: Ronald Press Company. https://doi.org/10.1037/11296-009

Bachrach, H., & Mintz, J. (1974). The Wechsler Memory Scale as a tool for the detection of mild cerebral dysfunction. *Journal of Clinical Psychology, 30*(1), 58–60. https://doi.org/10.1002/1097-4679(197401)30:1<58::AID-JCLP2270300115>3.0.CO;2-4

Baddely, A. (2007). *Working memory, thought, and action.* New York: Oxford University Press.

Baddely, A., Eysenck, M., & Anderson, M. (2009). *Memory.* New York: Psychology Press.

Baddely, A., Eysenck, M., & Anderson, M. (2015). *Memory* (2nd ed.). New York: Psychology Press.

Bak, J. S., & Greene, R. L. (1980). Changes in neuropsychological functioning in an aging population. *Journal of Consulting and Clinical Psychology, 48*(3), 395–399. https://doi.org/10.1037/0022-006X.48.3.395

Banich, M. T., & Compton, R. J. (2018). *Cognitive neuroscience* (4th ed.). New York, NY: Cambridge University Press.

Barlow, A. S., & Axelrod, B. N. (2007). Exploring racial response on the Wechsler Memory Scale-III faces subtest. *The Clinical Neuropsychologist, 21*(4), 690–690.

Barr, W. B. (1997). Receiver operating characteristic curve analysis of Wechsler Memory Scale-Revised scores in epilepsy surgery candidates. *Psychological Assessment, 9*(3), 171–176.

Baudic, S., Barba, G. D., Thibaudet, M. C., Smagghe, A., Remy, P., & Traykov, L. (2006). Executive function deficits in early Alzheimer's disease and their relations with episodic memory. *Archives of Clinical Neuropsychology, 21*(1), 15–21.

Beblo, T., Saavedra, A. S., Mensebach, C., Lange, W., Markowitsch, H. J., Rau, H. . . . Driessen, M. (2006). Deficits in visual functions and neuropsychological inconsistency in Borderline Personality Disorder. *Psychiatry Research, 145*(2–3), 127–135. https://doi.org/10.1016/j.psychres.2006.01.017

Bell, B. D. (2006). WMS-III Logical Memory performance after a two-week delay in temporal lobe epilepsy and control groups. *Journal of Clinical and Experimental Neuropsychology, 28*(8), 1435–1443. https://doi.org/10.1080/13803390500434367

Bell, B. D., Primeau, M., Sweet, J. J., & Lofland, K. R. (1999). Neuropsychological functioning in migraine headache, nonheadache chronic pain, and mild traumatic brain injury patients. *Archives of Clinical Neuropsychology, 14*(4), 389–399.

Bender, L. (1938). A visual motor gestalt test and its clinical use. *Research Monographs, American Orthopsychiatric Association, 3*, xi + 176.

Benton, A. (2000). *Exploring the history of neuropsychology: Selected papers.* New York: Oford University Press.

Berger, S. (1998). The WAIS-R factors: Usefulness and construct validity in neuropsychological assessments. *Applied Neuropsychology, 5*(1), 37–42.

Bernard, L. C., McGrath, M. J., & Houston, W. (1993). Discriminating between simulated malingering and closed head injury on the Wechsler Memory Scale-Revised. *Archives of Clinical Neuropsychology, 8*(6), 539–551. https://doi.org/10.1016/0887-6177(93)90054-5

Biars, J., Johnson, N., Nespeca, M., Busch, R., Kubu, C., & Floden, D. (2019). Iowa Gambling Task performance in Parkinson's disease patients with impulse control disorders. *Archives of Clinical Neuropsychology, 34,* 310–318.

Bigler, E. D., & Alfano, M. (1988). Anoxic encephalopathy: Neuroradiological and neuropsychological findings. *Archives of Clinical Neuropsychology, 3*(4), 383–396.

Bigler, E. D., Blatter, D. D., Anderson, C. V., Johnson, S. C., Gale, S. D., Hopkins, R. O., & Burnett, B. (1997). Hippocampal volume in normal aging and traumatic brain injury. *American Journal of Neuroradiology, 18*(1), 11–23.

Bigler, E. D., Johnson, S. C., Anderson, C. V, Blatter, D. D., Gale, S. D., Russo, A. A. . . . Abildskov, T. J. (1996). Traumatic brain injury and memory: The role of hippocampal atrophy. *Neuropsychology, 10*, 333–342. https://doi.org/10.1037/0894-4105.10.3.333

Bigler, E. D., & Snyder, J. L. (1995). Neuropsychological outcome and quantitative neuroimaging in mild head injury. *Archives of Clinical Neuropsychology, 10*(2), 159–174.

Binder, L. M., Iverson, G. L., & Brooks, B. L. (2009). To err is human: "Abnormal" neuropsychological scores and variability are common in healthy adults. *Archives of Clinical Neuropsychology, 24*(1), 31–46.

Blackwood, H. D. (1996). Recommendation for test administration in litigation: Never administer the category test to a blindfolded subject. *Archives of Clinical Neuropsychology, 11*(2), 93–95.

Blair, C. D., & Lanyon, R. I. (1987). Retraining social and adaptive living skills in severely head injured adults. *Archives of Clinical Neuropsychology, 2*(1), 33–43.

Bloom, B. L. (1959). Comparison of the alternate Wechsler Memory Scale forms. *Journal of Clinical Psychology, 15*(1), 72–74.

Boake, C. (2002). From the Binet-Simon to the Wechsler-Bellevue: Tracing the history of intelligence testing. *Journal of Clinical and Experimental Neuropsychology, 24*, 383–405.

Bolognani, S. A. P., Miranda, M. C., Martins, M., Rzezak, P., Bueno, O. F. A., de Camargo, C. H. P., & Pompeia, S. (2015). Development of alternative versions of the Logical Memory subtest of the WMS-R for use in Brazil. *Dementia & Neuropsychologia, 9*(2), 136–148. https://doi.org/10.1590/1980-57642015DN92000008

Boone, K. B. (Ed.). (2007). *Assessment of feigned cognitive impairment: A neuropsychological perspective*. New York: Guilford Press.

Boone, K. B., Pontón, M. O., Gorsuch, R. L., González, J. J., & Miller, B. L. (1998). Factor analysis of four measures of prefrontal lobe functioning. *Archives of Clinical Neuropsychology, 13*(7), 585–595.

Bornstein, R. A., Baker, G. B., & Douglass, A. B. (1991). Depression and memory in major depressive disorder. *The Journal of Neuropsychiatry and Clinical Neurosciences, 3*(1), 78–80. https://doi.org/10.1176/jnp.3.1.78

Bornstein, R. A., & Chelune, G. J. (1989). Factor structure of the Wechsler Memory Scale-Revised in relation to age and educational level. *Archives of Clinical Neuropsychology, 4*(1), 15–24. https://doi.org/10.1016/0887-6177(89)90003-6

Bornstein, R. A., Chelune, G. J., & Prifitera, A. (1989). IQ-memory discrepancies in normal and clinical samples. *Psychological Assessment: A Journal of Consulting and Clinical Psychology, 1*, 203–206. https://doi.org/10.1037/1040-3590.1.3.203

Bosinelli, F., Cantone, D., Sportiello, M. T., & Cammisuli, D. M. (2017). Logical inference and visual memory frailty in patients suffering from borderline personality disorder: A contribution from cognitive psychopathology. *Journal of Psychopathology/Giornale Di Psicopatologia, 23*(3), 119–127.

Bosnes, O., Troland, K., & Torsheim, T. (2016). A confirmatory factor analytic study of the Wechsler Memory Scale-III in an elderly Norwegian sample. *Archives of Clinical Neuropsychology, 31*(1), 12–17. https://doi.org/10.1093/arclin/acv060

Bouman, Z., Hendriks, M. P. H., Kerkmeer, M. C., Kessels, R. P. C., & Aldenkamp, A. P. (2015). Confirmatory factor analysis of the Dutch version of the Wechsler Memory Scale-Fourth Edition (WMS-IV-NL). *Archives of Clinical Neuropsychology, 30*(3), 228–235. https://doi.org/10.1093/arclin/acv013

Bouman, Z., Hendriks, M. P. H., Schmand, B. A., Kessels, R. P. C., & Aldenkamp, A. P. (2016). Indicators of suboptimal performance embedded in the Wechsler Memory Scale-Fourth Edition (WMS-IV). *Journal of Clinical and Experimental Neuropsychology*, *38*(4), 455–466. https://doi.org/10.1080/13803395.2015.1123226

Bouman, Z., Hendriks, M. P. H., Van Der Veld, W. M., Aldenkamp, A. P., & Kessels, R. P. C. (2016). Clinical validation of three short forms of the Dutch Wechsler Memory Scale-Fourth Edition (WMS-IV-NL) in a mixed clinical sample. *Assessment*, *23*(3), 386–394. https://doi.org/10.1177/1073191115593629

Bowden, S. C. (1990). Separating cognitive impairment in neurologically asymptomatic alcoholism from Wernicke-Korsakoff syndrome: Is the neuropsychological distinction justified? *Psychological Bulletin*, *107*(3), 355–366. https://doi.org/10.1037/0033-2909.107.3.355

Bowden, S. C. (Ed.). (2017a). *Neuropsychological assessment in the age of evidence-based practice: Diagnostic and treatment evaluations*. New York: Oxford University Press.

Bowden, S. C. (2017b). Why do we need evidence-based neuropsychological practice? In S. C. Bowden (Ed.), *Neuropsychological assessment in the age of evidence-based practice: Diagnostic and treatment evaluations* (pp. 1–14). New York: Oxford University Press.

Bowden, S. C., Carstairs, J. R., & Shores, E. A. (1999). Confirmatory factor analysis of combined Wechsler Adult Intelligence Scale-Revised and Wechsler Memory Scale-Revised scores in a healthy community sample. *Psychological Assessment*, *11*(3), 339–344. https://doi.org/10.1037/1040-3590.11.3.339

Breslow, R., Kocsis, J. H., & Belkin, B. (1980). Memory deficits in depression: Evidence utilizing the Wechsler Memory Scale. *Perceptual and Motor Skills*, *51*(2), 541–542. https://doi.org/10.2466/pms.1980.51.2.541

Brooks, B. L., Holdnack, J. A., & Iverson, G. L. (2016). To change is human: "Abnormal" reliable change memory scores are common in healthy adults and older adults. *Archives of Clinical Neuropsychology*, *31*(8), 1026–1036.

Brooks, B. L., & Iverson, G. L. (2010). Comparing actual to estimated base rates of "abnormal" scores on neuropsychological test batteries: Implications for interpretation. *Archives of Clinical Neuropsychology*, *25*(1), 14–21. https://doi.org/10.1093/arclin/acp100

Brooks, B. L., Iverson, G. L., Holdnack, J. A., & Feldman, H. H. (2008). Potential for misclassification of mild cognitive impairment: A study of memory scores on the Wechsler Memory Scale-III in healthy older adults. *Journal of the International Neuropsychological Society*, *14*(3), 463–478. https://doi.org/10.1017/S1355617708080521

Brooks, B. L., Strauss, E., Sherman, E. M. S., Iverson, G. L., & Slick, D. J. (2009). Developments in neuropsychological assessment: Refining psychometric and clinical interpretive methods. *Canadian Psychology/Psychologie Canadienne*, *50*(3), 196–209. https://doi.org/10.1037/a0016066

Brooks, D. N. (1976). Wechsler Memory Scale performance and its relationship to brain damage after severe closed head injury. *Journal of Neurology, Neurosurgery & Psychiatry*, *39*(6), 593–601.

Brophy, L. M., Jackson, M., & Crowe, S. F. (2009). Interference effects on commonly used memory tasks. *Archives of Clinical Neuropsychology*, *24*(1), 105–112.

Brown, L. B., & Storandt, M. (2000). Sensitivity of category cued recall to very mild dementia of the Alzheimer type. *Archives of Clinical Neuropsychology*, *15*(6), 529–534.

Burriss, L., Ayers, E., Ginsberg, J., & Powell, D. A. (2008). Learning and memory impairment in PTSD: Relationship to depression. *Depression and Anxiety, 25*(2), 149–157. https://doi.org/10.1002/da.20291

Burton, D. B., Mittenberg, W., & Burton, C. A. (1993). Confirmatory factor analysis of the Wechsler Memory Scale-Revised standardization sample. *Archives of Clinical Neuropsychology, 8*(6), 467–475. https://doi.org/10.1016/0887-6177(93)90047-5

Burton, D. B., Ryan, J. J., Axelrod, B. N., Schellenberger, T., & Richards, H. M. (2003). A confirmatory factor analysis of the WMS-III in a clinical sample with crossvalidation in the standardization sample. *Archives of Clinical Neuropsychology, 18*(6), 629–641. https://doi.org/10.1093/arclin/18.6.629

Busch, R. M., Dulay, M. F., Kim, K. H., Chapin, J. S., Jehi, L., Kalman, C. C. . . . Najm, I. M. (2011). Pre-surgical mood predicts memory decline after anterior temporal lobe resection for epilepsy. *Archives of Clinical Neuropsychology, 26*(8), 739–745. https://doi.org/10.1093/arclin/acr067

Butters, N. (1984). The clinical aspects of memory disorders: Contributions from experimental studies of amnesia and dementia. *Journal of Clinical and Experimental Neuropsychology, 6*(1), 17–36.

Butters, N. (1992). Memory remembered: 1970–1991. *Archives of Clinical Neuropsychology, 7*(4), 285–295.

Butters, N., Salmon, D. P., Cullum, C. M., Cairns, P., Tröster, A. I., Jacobs, D. . . . Cermak, L. S. (1988). Differentiation of amnesic and demented patients with the Wechsler Memory Scale-Revised. *Clinical Neuropsychologist, 2*(2), 133–148. https://doi.org/10.1080/13854048808520096

Cammisuli, D. M., & Sportiello, M. T. (2016). Cognitive psychopathology in schizophrenia: Comparing memory performances with obsessive-compulsive disorder patients and normal subjects on the Wechsler Memory Scale-IV. *Psychiatria Danubina, 28*(2), 118–126.

Cankorur, V. S., Demirel, H., & Atbasoglu, C. (2017). Cognitive functioning in euthymic bipolar patients on monotherapy with novel antipsychotics or mood stabilizers. *Archives of Neuropsychiatry/Noropsikiatri Arsivi, 54*(3).

Cannon, B. J. (1999). Relative interference on Logical Memory I Story A versus Story B of the Wechsler Memory Scale-Revised in a clinical sample. *Applied Neuropsychology, 6*(3), 178–180. https://doi.org/10.1207/s15324826an0603_6

Carrasco, R. M., Grups, J., Evans, B., Simco, E., & Mittenberg, W. (2015). Apparently abnormal Wechsler Memory Scale index score patterns in the normal population. *Applied Neuropsychology: Adult, 22*(1), 1–6. https://doi.org/10.1080/23279095.2013.816702

Carroll, J. B. (1993). *Human cognitive abilities: A survey of factor-analytic studies.* New York: Cambridge University Press.

Carroll, W. (1963, February). The differentiation of organic and non-organic hospital patients by use of the Wechsler Memory Scale. *Newsletter for Research in Psychology, 5*(1), 11. Retrieved from https:/10.1037/e535052008-011

Carstairs, J. R., & Shores, E. A. (2000). The Macquarie University Neuropsychological Normative Study (MUNNS): Rationale and methodology. *Australian Psychologist, 30*(1), 36–40.

Cattell, R. B. (1941). Some theoretical issues in adult intelligence testing. *Psychological Bulletin, 38*, 592.

Cattell, R. B. (1971). *Abilities: Their structure, growth, and action.* Boston, MA: Houghton Mifflin.

Chafetz, M. D., Williams, M. A., Ben-Porath, Y. S., Bianchini, K. J., Boone, K. B., Kirkwood, M. W. . . . Ord, J. S. (2015). Official position of the American Academy of Clinical Neuropsychology Social Security Administration policy on validity testing: Guidance and recommendations for change. *The Clinical Neuropsychologist, 29*, 723–740.

Challman, R. C. (1952). Review of The Clinical Method in Psychology. *The Journal of Abnormal and Social Psychology, 47*(4), 863–864. https://doi.org/10.1037/h0052073

Channon, S., & Daum, I. (2000). The effect of semantic categorisation on recall memory in amnesia. *Behavioural Neurology, 12*(3), 107–117. https://doi.org/10.1155/2000/354905

Chapin, J. S., Busch, R. M., Naugle, R. I., & Najm, I. M. (2009). The Family Pictures subtest of the WMS-III: Relationship to verbal and visual memory following temporal lobectomy for intractable epilepsy. *Journal of Clinical and Experimental Neuropsychology, 31*(4), 498–504. https://doi.org/10.1080/13803390802317575

Chelune, G. J., Naugle, R. I., Lüders, H., Sedlak, J., & Awad, I. A. (1993). Individual change after epilepsy surgery: Practice effects and base-rate information. *Neuropsychology, 7*, 41–52. https://doi.org/10.1037/0894-4105.7.1.41

Chiu, M.-J., Liu, K., Hsieh, M. H., & Hwu, H.-G. (2005). Dual-modality impairment of implicit learning of letter-strings versus color-patterns in patients with schizophrenia. *Behavioral and Brain Functions, 1*(1), 23. https://doi.org/10.1186/1744-9081-1-23

Chlopan, B. E., Hagen, R. L., & Russell, E. W. (1990). Lateralized anterior and posterior lesions and performance on Digit Span and Russell's revision of the Wechsler Memory Scale. *Journal of Consulting and Clinical Psychology, 58*(6), 855–861. https://doi.org/10.1037/0022-006X.58.6.855

Christensen, H., Hadzi-Pavlovic, D., & Jacomb, P. (1991). The psychometric differentiation of dementia from normal aging: A meta-analysis. *Psychological Assessment: A Journal of Consulting and Clinical Psychology, 3*, 147–155. https://doi.org/10.1037/1040-3590.3.2.147

Christman, A. L., Vannorsdall, T. D., Pearlson, G. D., Hill-Briggs, F., & Schretlen, D. J. (2009). Cranial volume, mild cognitive deficits, and functional limitations associated with diabetes in a community sample. *Archives of clinical neuropsychology, 25*(1), 49–59.

Clark, L. R., Koscik, R. L., Nicholas, C. R., Okonkwo, O. C., Engelman, C. D., Bratzke, L. C. . . . Asthana, S. (2016). Mild cognitive impairment in late middle age in the Wisconsin registry for Alzheimer's prevention study: Prevalence and characteristics using robust and standard neuropsychological normative data. *Archives of Clinical Neuropsychology, 31*(7), 675–688.

Cohen, J. (1950). Wechsler Memory Scale performance of psychoneurotic, organic, and schizophrenic groups. *Journal of Consulting Psychology, 14*(5), 371–375. https://doi.org/10.1037/h0062273

Compton, J. M., Sherer, M., & Adams, R. L. (1992). Factor analysis of the Wechsler Memory Scale and the Warrington Recognition Memory Test. *Archives of Clinical Neuropsychology, 7*(2), 165–173. https://doi.org/10.1016/0887-6177(92)90010-K

Conklin, H. M., Calkins, M. E., Anderson III, C. W., Dinzeo, T. J., & Iacono, W. G. (2002). Recognition memory for faces in schizophrenia patients and their first-degree relatives. *Neuropsychologia, 40*(13), 2314–2324. https://doi.org/10.1016/S0028-3932(02)00091-X

Cooley, E. L., & Stringer, A. Y. (1991). Self and observer predictions of memory performance in a brain-damaged sample. *Archives of Clinical Neuropsychology, 8*(6), 485–496. https://doi.org/10.1016/0887-6177(91)90011-W

Coolidge, F. L. (2020). *Evolutionary neuropsychology: An introduction to the evolution of the structures and functions of the human brain.* New York: Oxford University Press.

Cooper, P. V., Numan, B. K., Crosson, B., & Velozo, C. A. (1989). Story and List Recall Tests as measures of verbal memory in a head-injured Sample. *Neuropsychology, 3,* 1–8.

Cornell, E. L., & Coxe, W. C. (1934). *A performance ability scale.* New York: World Books.

Crews Jr., W. D., Jefferson, A. L., Bolduc, T., Elliott, J. B., Ferro, N. M., Broshek, D. K. . . . Robbins, M. K. (2001). Neuropsychological dysfunction in patients suffering from end-stage chronic obstructive pulmonary disease. *Archives of Clinical Neuropsychology, 16*(7), 643–652. https://doi.org/10.1016/S0887-6177(00)00075-5

Crews Jr, W. D., Jefferson, A. L., Broshek, D. K., Barth, J. T., & Robbins, M. K. (1999). Neuropsychological sequelae in a series of patients with end-stage cystic fibrosis: Lung transplant evaluation. *Archives of Clinical Neuropsychology, 15*(1), 59–70.

Crews Jr, W. D., Jefferson, A. L., Broshek, D. K., Rhodes, R. D., Williamson, J., Brazil, A. . . . Robbins, M. K. (2003). Neuropsychological dysfunction in patients with end-stage pulmonary disease: Lung transplant evaluation. *Archives of Clinical Neuropsychology, 14*(8), 646–647.

Crook III, T. H., Youngjohn, J. R., & Larrabee, G. J. (1992). Multiple equivalent test forms in a computerized, everyday memory battery. *Archives of Clinical Neuropsychology, 7*(3), 221–232.

Crook, T. H., Youngjohn, J. R., & Larrabee, G. J. (1990). TV News Test: A new measure of everyday memory for prose. *Neuropsychology, 4*(3), 135–145. https://doi.org/10.1037/0894-4105.4.3.135

Crook, T. H., Youngjohn, J. R., Larrabee, G. J., & Salama, M. (1992). Aging and everyday memory: A cross-cultural study. *Neuropsychology, 6,* 123–136.

Crosson, B., Hughes, C. W., Roth, D. L., & Monkowski, P. G. (1984). Review of Russell's (1975) norms for the Logical Memory and Visual Reproduction subtests of the Wechsler Memory Scale. *Journal of Consulting and Clinical Psychology, 52*(4), 635–641. https://doi.org/10.1037/0022-006X.52.4.635

Crouse, E. M. (2005). *Anna Thompson's starving children: Emotion regulation and verbal memory in borderline personality disorder.* ProQuest Information & Learning, US.

Cullum, C. M., Butters, N., Tröster, A. I., & Salmon, D. P. (1990). Normal aging and forgetting rates on the Wechsler Memory Scale-Revised. *Archives of Clinical Neuropsychology, 5*(1), 23–30. https://doi.org/10.1093/arclin/5.1.23

Cunningham, W. A. (1986). Psychometric perspectives: Validity and reliability. In L. W. Poon (Ed.), *Handbook of clinical memory assessment in older adults* (pp. 27–31). Washington, DC: American Psychological Association.

D'Amato, C. P., & Denney, R. L. (2008). The diagnostic utility of the Rarely Missed Index of the Wechsler Memory Scale-Third Edition in detecting response bias in an adult male incarcerated setting. *Archives of Clinical Neuropsychology, 23*(5), 553–561. https://doi.org/10.1016/j.acn.2008.05.007

D'Elia, L., Satz, P., & Schretlen, D. (1989). Wechsler Memory Scale: A critical appraisal of the normative studies. *Journal of Clinical and Experimental Neuropsychology, 11*(4), 551–568. https://doi.org/10.1080/01688638908400913

Da Mota, S. S., Delgado, V. B., Schumacher-Schuh, A. F., & Chaves, M. L. F. (2016). Association of education with occurrence of delirium in patients from an emergency

department. *Dementia & Neuropsychologia, 10*(3), 198–203. https://doi.org/10.1590/
S1980-5764-2016DN1003005

Davis, L. J., & Swenson, W. M. (1970). Factor analysis of the Wechsler Memory Scale.
Journal of Consulting and Clinical Psychology, 35(3), 430. https://doi.org/10.1037/
h0030273

Deckel, A. W., & Morrison, D. (1996). Evidence of a neurologically based "denial of
illness" in patients with Huntington's disease. *Archives of Clinical Neuropsychology,
11*(4), 295–302.

Delis, D. C., Cullum, C. M., Butters, N., Cairns, P., & Prifitera, A. (1988). Wechsler
Memory Scale-Revised and California Verbal Learning Test: Convergence and
divergence. *Clinical Neuropsychologist, 2*(2), 188–196. https://doi.org/10.1080/1385
4048808520100

Delis, D. C., Kramer, J. H., Kaplan, E., & Ober, B. A. (1987). *California Verbal Learning Test: Adult version: Manual*. San Antionio, TX: Psychological Corporation.

DeLisi, L. E., Sakuma, M., Kushner, M., Finer, D. L., Hoff, A. L., & Crow, T. J. (1997).
Anomalous cerebral asymmetry and language processing in schizophrenia. *Schizophrenia Bulletin, 23*(2), 255–271. https://doi.org/10.1093/schbul/23.2.255

Denny, R. L. (1999). A brief symptom validity testing procedure for Logical Memory
of the Wechsler Memory Scale-Revised which can demonstrate verbal memory in the
face of claimed disability. *Journal of Forensic Neuropsychology, 1*(1), 5–26. https://
doi.org/10.1300/J151v01n01_02

DesRosiers, G., & Ivison, D. (1988). Paired associate learning: Form 1 and Form 2 of
the Wechsler Memory Scale. *Archives of Clinical Neuropsychology, 3*(1), 47–67.
https://doi.org/10.1016/0887-6177(88)90026-1

DeWolfe, A. S., Ryan, J. J., & Wolf, M. E. (1988). Cognitive sequelae of tardive
dyskinesia. *Journal of Nervous and Mental Disease, 176*(5), 270–274. https://doi.
org/10.1097/00005053-198805000-00003

Dori, G. A., & Chelune, G. J. (2004). Education-stratified base-rate information on
discrepancy scores within and between the Wechsler Adult Intelligence Scale-Third
Edition and the Wechsler Memory Scale-Third Edition. *Psychological Assessment,
16*(2), 146–154. https://doi.org/10.1037/1040-3590.16.2.146

Doss, R. C., Chelune, G. J., & Naugle, R. I. (2004). WMS-III performance in epilepsy
patients following temporal lobectomy. *Journal of the International Neuropsychological Society, 10*(2), 173–179. https://doi.org/10.1017/S1355617704102026

Downes, J. J., Priestley, N. M., Doran, M., Ferran, J., Ghadiali, E., & Cooper, P. (1998).
Intellectual, mnemonic, and frontal functions in dementia with Lewy bodies: A comparison with early and advanced Parkinson's disease. *Behavioural Neurology, 11*,
173–183. https://doi.org/10.1155/1999/85186

Drew, M., Tippett, L. J., Starkey, N. J., & Isler, R. B. (2008). Executive dysfunction
and cognitive impairment in a large community-based sample with Multiple Sclerosis from New Zealand: A descriptive study. *Archives of Clinical Neuropsychology,
23*(1), 1–19.

Drozdick, L. W., Holdnack, J. A., & Hilsabeck, R. C. (2011). *Essentials of WMS®-IV
assessment*. Hoboken, NJ: John Wiley & Sons Inc.

Dujovne, B., & Levy, B. (1971). The psychometric structure of the Wechsler Memory
Scale. *Journal of Clinical Psychology, 27*, 474–482.

Dulay, M. F., Schefft, B. K., Testa, S. M., Fargo, J. D., Privitera, M., & Yeh, H. (2002).
What does the Family Pictures subtest of the Wechsler Memory Scale-III measure?

Insight gained from patients evaluated for epilepsy surgery. *The Clinical Neuropsychologist, 16*(4), 452–462. https://doi.org/10.1076/clin.16.4.452.13915

Efklides, A., Yiultsi, E., Kangellidou, T., Kounti, F., Dina, F., & Tsolaki, M. (2002). Wechsler Memory Scale, Rivermead Behavioral Memory Test, and Everyday Memory Questionnaire in healthy adults and Alzheimer's patients. *European Journal of Psychological Assessment, 18*, 63–77.

Eignor, D. R. (2013). *The standards for educational and psychological testing*. Washington, DC: American Psychological Association.

Eizadi-Mood, N., Akouchekian, S., Yaraghi, A., Hakamian, M., Soltani, R., & Sabzghabaee, A. M. (2015). Memory impairment following acute tricyclic antidepressants overdose. *Depression Research and Treatment, 2015*(Article ID 835786), 4. https://doi.org/10.1155/2015/835786

Ekman, P., & Friesen, W. V. (1976). *Pictures of facial affect*. Palo Alto, CA: Consulting Psychologists Press.

El-Missiry, A., Elbatrawy, A., El Missiry, M., Moneim, D. A., Ali, R., & Essawy, H. (2015). Comparing cognitive functions in medication adherent and non-adherent patients with schizophrenia. *Journal of Psychiatric Research, 70*, 106–112. https://doi.org/10.1016/j.jpsychires.2015.09.006

Emsaki, G., NeshatDoost, H. T., Tavakoli, M., & Barekatain, M. (2017). Memory specificity training can improve working and prospective memory in amnestic mild cognitive impairment. *Dementia & Neuropsychologia, 11*(3), 255–261. https://doi.org/10.1590/1980-57642016dn11-030007

Erickson, R. C., & Scott, M. L. (1977). Clinical memory testing: A review. *Psychological Bulletin, 84*(6), 1130–1149. https://doi.org/10.1037/0033-2909.84.6.1130

Ernst, J., Warner, M. H., Morgan, A., Townes, B. D., Eiler, J., & Coppel, D. B. (1986). Factor analysis of the Wechsler Memory Scale: Is the Associate Learning subtest an unclear measure? *Archives of Clinical Neuropsychology, 1*(4), 309–314. https://doi.org/10.1016/0887-6177(86)90134-4

Etherton, J. L., & Tapscott, B. E. (2015). Performance on selected visual and auditory subtests of the Wechsler Memory Scale-Fourth Edition during laboratory-induced pain. *Journal of Clinical and Experimental Neuropsychology, 37*(3), 243–252. https://doi.org/10.1080/13803395.2014.1002756

Ezzati, A., Katz, M. J., Zammit, A. R., Lipton, M. L., Zimmerman, M. E., Sliwinski, M. J., & Lipton, R. B. (2016). Differential association of left and right hippocampal volumes with verbal episodic and spatial memory in older adults. *Neuropsychologia, 93*(Part B), 380–385. https://doi.org/10.1016/j.neuropsychologia.2016.08.016

Farmer, J. E., & Eakman, A. M. (1995). The relationship between neuropsychological functioning and instrumental activities of daily living following acquired brain injury. *Applied Neuropsychology, 2*(3–4), 107–115. https://doi.org/10.1207/s15324826an0203&4_2

Fastenau, P. S., Denburg, N. L., & Abeles, N. (1996). Age differences in retrieval: Further support for the resource-reduction hypothesis. *Psychology and Aging, 11*(1), 140–146. https://doi.org/10.1037/0882-7974.11.1.140

Fazeli, P. L., Doyle, K. L., Scott, J. C., Iudicello, J. E., Casaletto, K. B., Weber, E. . . . Woods, S. P. (2014). Shallow encoding and forgetting are associated with dependence in instrumental activities of daily living among older adults living with HIV infection. *Archives of Clinical Neuropsychology, 29*(3), 278–288. https://doi.org/10.1093/arclin/acu009

Finkelstein, J. R. (1999). *Attention deficits in schizophrenia: Endophenotypic markers of vulnerability to the disorder?* ProQuest Information & Learning, US.

Fisher, D. C., Ledbetter, M. F., Cohen, N. J., Marmor, D., & Tulsky, D. S. (2000). WAIS-III and WMS-III profiles of mildly to severely brain-injured patients. *Applied Neuropsychology, 7*(3), 126–132. https://doi.org/10.1207/S15324826AN0703_2

Flynn, J. R. (2007). *What is intelligence?: Beyond the Flynn effect.* Cambridge: Cambridge University Press.

Flynn, J. R. (2009). Requiem for nutrition as the cause of IQ gains: Raven's gains in Britain 1938–2008. *Economics & Human Biology, 7,* 18–27.

Foley, J., Golden, C., Simco, E., Schneider, B., McCue, R., & Shaw, L. (2008). Pattern of memory compromise in chronic geriatric schizophrenia, frontotemporal dementia and normal geriatric controls. *Acta Neuropsychiatrica, 20*(1), 9–19. https://doi.org/10.1111/j.1601-5215.2007.00244.x

Foster, P. S., Yung, R. C., Drago, V., Crucian, G. P., & Heilman, K. M. (2013). Working memory in Parkinson's disease: The effects of depression and side of onset of motor symptoms. *Neuropsychology, 27*(3), 303–313. https://doi.org/10.1037/a0032265

Fox, D. D. (1994). Normative problems for the Wechsler Memory Scale-Revised Logical Memory Test when used in litigation. *Archives of Clinical Neuropsychology, 9*(3), 211–214. https://doi.org/10.1016/0887-6177(94)90026-4

Franzen, M. D., & Martin, N. (1996). Do people with knowledge fake better? *Applied Neuropsychology, 3*(2), 82–85. https://doi.org/10.1207/s15324826an0302_6

Franzen, M. D., Wilhelm, K. L., & Haut, M. W. (1995). The factor structure of the Wechsler Memory Scale-Revised and several brief neuropsychological screening instruments in recently detoxified substance abusers. *Archives of Clinical Neuropsychology, 10*(3), 193–204. https://doi.org/10.1016/0887-6177(94)E0036-O

Frerichs, R. J., & Tuokko, H. A. (2005). A comparison of methods for measuring cognitive change in older adults. *Archives of Clinical Neuropsychology, 20*(3), 321–333.

Frisby, C. L., & Beaujean, A. A. (2015). Testing Spearman's hypotheses using a bifactor model with WAIS-IV/WMS-IV standardization data. *Intelligence, 51,* 79–97. https://doi.org/10.1016/j.intell.2015.04.007

Frisby, C. L., & Kim, S. K. (2008). Using Profile Analysis via Multidimensional Scaling (PAMS) to identify core profiles from the WMS-III. *Psychological Assessment, 20*(1), 1–9. https://doi.org/10.1037/1040-3590.20.1.1

Frisch, S., Dukart, J., Vogt, B., Horstmann, A., Becker, G., Villringer, A. . . . Schroeter, M. L. (2013). Dissociating memory networks in early Alzheimer's disease and frontotemporal lobar degeneration: A combined study of hypometabolism and atrophy. *PLoS ONE, 8*(2): e55251. https://doi.org/10.1371/journal.pone.0055251

Fujimori, J., Nakashima, I., Baba, T., Meguro, Y., Ogawa, R., & Fujihara, K. (2017). Cognitive impairment in neuromyelitis optica spectrum disorders: A comparison of the Wechsler Adult Intelligence Scale-III and the Wechsler Memory Scale Revised with the Rao Brief Repeatable Neuropsychological Battery. *eNeurologicalSci, 9,* 3–7. https://doi.org/10.1016/j.ensci.2017.09.001

Gage, R., Burns, W. J., Sellers, A. H., Roth, L., & Mittenberg, W. (1995). Approaches to memory assessment in the chronic psychiatric elderly. *Applied Neuropsychology, 2*(3–4), 145–149. https://doi.org/10.1207/s15324826an0203&4_7

Gamito, P., Oliveira, J., Santos, N., Pacheco, J., Morais, D., Saraiva, T. . . . Barata, A. F. (2014). Virtual exercises to promote cognitive recovery in stroke patients: The comparison between head mounted displays versus screen exposure methods.

International Journal on Disability and Human Development, 13, 337–342. https:// doi.org/10.1515/ijdhd-2014-0325

Gass, C. S. (1995). A procedure for assessing storage and retrieval on the Wechsler Memory Scale-Revised. *Archives of Clinical Neuropsychology, 10*(5), 475–487. https://doi.org/10.1016/0887-6177(95)98192-G

Gass, C. S. (1996). MMPI-2 variables in attention and memory test performance. *Psychological Assessment, 8*(2), 135–138. https://doi.org/10.1037/1040-3590.8.2.135

Gass, C. S., & Ansley, J. (1994). MMPI correlates of poststroke neurobehavioral deficits. *Archives of Clinical Neuropsychology, 9*(5), 461–469. https://doi.org/10.1016/0887-6177(94)90008-6

Gass, C. S., Burda, P. C., Starkey, T. W., & Dominguez, F. (1992). MMPI interpretation of psychiatric inpatients: Caution in making inferences about concentration and memory. *Journal of Clinical Psychology, 48*(4), 493–499. https://doi.org/10.1002/1097-4679(199207)48:4<493::AID-JCLP2270480409>3.0.CO;2-P

Gass, C. S., Luis, C. A., Meyers, T. L., & Kuljis, R. O. (2000). Familial Creutzfeldt-Jakob disease: A neuropsychological case study. *Archives of Clinical Neuropsychology, 15*(2), 165–175.

Gass, C. S., & Russell, E. W. (1986). Differential impact of brain damage and depression on memory test performance. *Journal of Consulting and Clinical Psychology, 54*, 261–263.

Gass, C. S., Russell, E. W., & Hamilton, R. A. (1990). Accuracy of MMPI-based inferences regarding memory and concentration in closed-head-trauma patients. *Psychological Assessment: A Journal of Consulting and Clinical Psychology, 2*, 175–178. https://doi.org/10.1037/1040-3590.2.2.175

Gerstenecker, A., Myers, T., Lowry, K., Martin, R. C., Triebel, K. L., Bashir, K., & Marson, D. C. (2017). Financial capacity and its cognitive predictors in progressive multiple sclerosis. *Archives of Clinical Neuropsychology, 32*(8), 943–950.

Giovannetti, T., Lamar, M., Cloud, B. S., Swenson, R., Fein, D., Kaplan, E., & Libon, D. J. (2001). Different underlying mechanisms for deficits in concept formation in dementia. *Archives of Clinical Neuropsychology, 16*(6), 547–560.

Glisky, E., L., Polster, M. R., & Routhieaux, B. C. (1995). Double dissociation between item and source memory. *Neuropsychology, 9*, 229–235.

Glowinski, H. (1973). Cognitive deficits in temporal lobe epilepsy: An investigation of memory functioning. *Journal of Nervous and Mental Disease, 157*(2), 129–137. https://doi.org/10.1097/00005053-197308000-00005

Godding, P. R., Fitterling, J. M., Schmitz, J. M., Seville, J. L., & Parisi, S. A. (1992). Discriminative utility of a brief cognitive status assessment with alcoholics and the impact of cognitive status on acquisition of treatment-relevant information. *Psychology of Addictive Behaviors, 6*(1), 34–40. https://doi.org/10.1037/h0080602

Gold, J. M., Randolph, C., Carpenter, C. J., Goldberg, T. E., & Weinberger, D. R. (1992). The performance of patients with schizophrenia on the Wechsler Memory Scale-Revised. *Clinical Neuropsychologist, 6*, 367–373. https://doi.org/10.1080/13854049208401864

Golden, C. J. (2000). Wechsler Memory Scale. In *Encyclopedia of psychology* (Vol. 8). New York: Oxford University Press. https://doi.org/10.1037/10523-098

Goldstein, K. (1995). *The organism: A holistic approach to biology derived from pathological data in man.* New York: Zone Books.

Gomez, R. G., & White, D. A. (2006). Using verbal fluency to detect very mild dementia of the Alzheimer type. *Archives of Clinical Neuropsychology, 21*(8), 771–775.

Gonçalves, C., Pinho, M. S., Cruz, V., Gens, H., Oliveira, F., Pais, J. . . . Santos, J. M. (2017). Portuguese version of Wechsler Memory Scale-3rd edition's utility with demented elderly adults. *Applied Neuropsychology: Adult, 24*(3), 212–225. https://doi.org/10.1080/23279095.2015.1135440

Gonzales, M. M., Insel, P. S., Nelson, C., Tosun, D., Mattsson, N., Mueller, S. G. . . . Mackin, R. S. (2017). Cortical atrophy is associated with accelerated cognitive decline in mild cognitive impairment with subsyndromal depression. *The American Journal of Geriatric Psychiatry, 25*(9), 980–991. https://doi.org/10.1016/j.jagp.2017.04.011

Gorji, M. A. H., Ghahremanlu, H., Haghshenas, M., Sadeghi, M. R., & Gorji, A. M. H. (2012). Comparison of memory impairments among two groups of patients with diabetes with different disease durations. *BMC Research Notes, 5*, 1–3.

Government Printing Office. (1921). *Memoirs of the National Academy of Sciences.* Washington DC: Government Printing Office.

Granite, L. C. (2018). An examination of the Visual Working Memory Index of the WMS-IV: An investigation of construct validity. *Dissertation Abstracts International: Section B: The Sciences and Engineering, 79*(4-B(E)).

Grant, I., & Adams, K. (Eds.). (2009). *Neuropsychological assessment of neuropsychiatric and neuromedical disorders* (3rd ed.). New York: Oxford University Press.

Greve, K. W., Bianchini, K. J., Mathias, C. W., Houston, R. J., & Crouch, J. A. (2003). Detecting malingered performance on the Wechsler Adult Intelligence Scale Validation of Mittenberg's approach in traumatic brain injury. *Archives of Clinical Neuropsychology, 18*(3), 245–260.

Gronwall, D., & Wrightson, P. (1981). Memory and information processing capacity after closed head injury. *Journal of Neurology, Neurosurgery, and Psychiatry, 44*, 889–895.

Guilmette, T. J., & Rasile, D. (1995). Sensitivity, specificity, and diagnostic accuracy of three verbal memory measures in the assessment of mild brain injury. *Neuropsychology, 9*(3), 338–344. https://doi.org/10.1037/0894-4105.9.3.338

Guo, X., Zhang, Z., Wei, Q., Lv, H., Wu, R., & Zhao, J. (2013). The relationship between obesity and neurocognitive function in Chinese patients with schizophrenia. *BMC Psychiatry, 13*, 109. https://doi.org/10.1186/1471-244X-13-109

Haaland, K. Y., Linn, R. T., Hunt, W. C., & Goodwin, J. S. (1983). A normative study of Russell's variant of the Wechsler Memory Scale in a healthy elderly population. *Journal of Consulting and Clinical Psychology, 51*(6), 878–881. https://doi.org/10.1037/0022-006X.51.6.878

Halstead, W. (1947). *Brain and intelligence.* Chicago, IL: University of Chicago Press.

Hamby, S. L., Bardi, C. A., & Wilkins, J. W. (1997). Neuropsychological assessment of relatively intact individuals: Psychometric lessons from an HIV+ sample. *Archives of Clinical Neuropsychology, 12*(6), 545–556.

Haut, M. W., Young, J., Cutlip, W. D., Callahan, T., & Haut, A. E. (1995). A case of bilateral thalamic lesions with anterograde amnesia and impaired implicit memory. *Archives of Clinical Neuropsychology, 10*(6), 555–566.

Hawkins, K. A. (1999). Memory deficits in patients with schizophrenia: Preliminary data from the Wechsler Memory Scale-Third Edition support earlier findings. *Journal of Psychiatry & Neuroscience, 24*(4), 341–347.

Hawkins, K. A., Sullivan, T. E., & Choi, E. J. (1997). Memory deficits in schizophrenia: Inadequate assimilation or true amnesia? Findings from the Wechsler Memory Scale-Revised. *Journal of Psychiatry & Neuroscience, 22*(3), 169–179.

Hawkins, K. A., & Tulsky, D. (2001). The influence of IQ Stratification on WAIS-III/WMS-III FSIQ-General Memory Index discrepancy base-rates in the standardization sample. *Journal of the International Neuropsychological Society, 7*, 875–880.

Hebb, D. O. (1949). *The organization of behavior: A neuropsychological theory*. New York: John Wiley & Sons.

Heilbronner, R. L., Buck, P., & Adams, R. L. (1988). Factor analysis of the Wechsler Memory Scale (WMS) with the WAIS and the WAIS-R. *International Journal of Clinical Neuropsychology, 10*, 20–22.

Heilbronner, R. L., Buck, P., & Adams, R. L. (1989). Factor analysis of verbal and non-verbal clinical memory tests. *Archives of Clinical Neuropsychology, 4*(4), 299–309.

Heirene, R. M., John, B., & Roderique-Davies, G. (2018). Identification and evaluation of neuropsychological tools used in the assessment of alcohol-related brain damage: A systematic review. *Frontiers in Psychology, 9*, 2618.

Helmes, E., & Miller, M. (2006). A comparison of MicroCog and the Wechsler Memory Scale (3rd ed.) in older adults. *Applied Neuropsychology, 13*(1), 28–33. https://doi.org/10.1207/s15324826an1301_4

Herman, M. (2004). Neurocognitive functioning and quality of life among dually diagnosed and non-substance abusing schizophrenia inpatients. *International Journal of Mental Health Nursing, 13*, 282–291. https://doi.org/10.1111/j.1440-0979.2004.00346.x

Hill, R. D., Crook, T. H., Zadiek, A., Yesavage, J., & Sheikh, J. (1989). The effects of age on recall of information from a simulated television news broadcast. *Educational Gerontology, 15*, 607–614.

Hill, S. Y., Lichenstein, S. D., Wang, S., & O'Brien, J. (2016). Volumetric differences in cerebellar lobes in individuals from multiplex alcohol dependence families and controls: Their relationship to externalizing and internalizing disorders and working memory. *The Cerebellum, 15*, 744–754. https://doi.org/10.1007/s12311-015-0747-8

Hilsabeck, R. C., Schrager, D. A., & Gouvier, W. D. (1999). Cross-validation of the two- and three-subtest short forms of the Wechsler Memory Scale-Revised. *Applied Neuropsychology, 6*(4), 247–251. https://doi.org/10.1207/s15324826an0604_8

Hilsabeck, R. C., Thompson, M. D., Irby, J. W., Adams, R. L., Scott, J. G., & Gouvier, W. D. (2003). Partial cross-validation of the Wechsler Memory Scale-Revised (WMS-R) General Memory-Attention/Concentration Malingering Index in a non-litigating sample. *Archives of Clinical Neuropsychology, 18*(1), 71–79. https://doi.org/10.1016/S0887-6177(01)00180-9

Hinton-Bayre, A. D. (2016). Clarifying discrepancies in responsiveness between reliable change indices. *Archives of Clinical Neuropsychology, 31*(7), 754–768. https://doi.org/10.1093/arclin/acw064

Hiscox, L. V., Johnson, C. L., McGarry, M. D. J., Schwarb, H., Beek, E. J. R., Roberts, N., & Starr, J. M. (2018). Hippocampal viscoelasticity and episodic memory performance in healthy older adults examined with magnetic resonance elastography. *Brain Imaging and Behavior*. Advance online publication. http://doi.org/10.1007/s11682-018-9988-8

Hoelzle, J. B., Nelson, N. W., & Smith, C. A. (2011). Comparison of Wechsler Memory Scale-Fourth Edition (WMS-IV) and Third Edition (WMS-III) dimensional structures: Improved ability to evaluate auditory and visual constructs. *Journal of Clinical and Experimental Neuropsychology, 33*, 283–291.

Hoffman, R., & al'Absi, M. (2004). The effect of acute stress on subsequent neuropsychological test performance (2003). *Archives of Clinical Neuropsychology, 19*(4), 497–506. https://doi.org/10.1016/j.acn.2003.07.005

Hoffman, R. G., Tremont, G., Scott, J. G., Adams, R. L., & Mittenberg, W. (1997). Cross-validation of predicted Wechsler Memory Scale-Revised scores in a normative sample of 25- to 34-year-old patients. *Archives of Clinical Neuropsychology, 12*(7), 677–682. https://doi.org/10.1016/S0887-6177(97)00022-X

Holdnack, J. A., Zhou, X., Larrabee, G. J., Millis, S. R., & Salthouse, T. A. (2011). Confirmatory factor analysis of the WAIS-IV/WMS-IV. *Assessment, 18*(2), 178–191. https://doi.org/10.1177/1073191110393106

Hom, J. (1992). General and specific cognitive dysfunctions in patients with Alzheimer's disease. *Archives of Clinical Neuropsychology, 7*(2), 121–133.

Hopkins, M. W., & Libon, D. J. (2005). Neuropsychological functioning of dementia patients with psychosis. *Archives of Clinical Neuropsychology, 20*(6), 771–783. https://doi.org/10.1016/j.acn.2005.04.011

Hori, T., Sanjo, N., Tomita, M., & Mizusawa, H. (2013). Visual Reproduction on the Wechsler Memory Scale-Revised as a predictor of Alzheimer's disease in Japanese patients with mild cognitive impairments. *Dementia and Geriatric Cognitive Disorders, 35*, 165–176. https://doi.org/10.1159/000346738

Horton Jr., A. M. (1996). Neuropsychological findings in adult attention deficit disorder: A pilot study. *Applied Neuropsychology, 3*(3–4), 181–185. https://doi.org/10.1207/s15324826an0303&4_12

Howard, A. R. (1950). Diagnostic value of the Wechsler Memory Scale with selected groups of institutionalized patients. *Journal of Consulting Psychology, 14*(5), 376–380. https://doi.org/10.1037/h0058479

Howard, A. R. (1954). Further validation studies of the Wechsler Memory Scale. *Journal of Clinical Psychology, 10*, 164–167. https://doi.org/10.1002/1097-4679(195404)10:2<164::AID-JCLP2270100212>3.0.CO;2-M

Howard, A. R. (1966). A fifteen-year followup with the Wechsler Memory Scale. *Journal of Consulting Psychology, 30*(2), 175–176. https://doi.org/10.1037/h0023182

Hulicka, I. M. (1966). Age differences in Wechsler Memory Scale scores. *The Journal of Genetic Psychology: Research and Theory on Human Development, 109*, 135–145. https://doi.org/10.1080/00221325.1966.10533690

Ilonen, T., Mattlar, C.-E., & Salokangas, R. K. R. (1997). Rorschach findings and neuropsychological comparison of first-episode psychotic depression with first-episode nonpsychotic depression and schizophrenia: A preliminary report. *Rorschachiana, 22*(1), 198–210. https://doi.org/10.1027/1192-5604.22.1.198

Ingram, N. S., Diakoumakos, J. V, Sinclair, E. R., & Crowe, S. F. (2016). Material-specific retroactive interference effects of the Wechsler Adult Intelligence Scale-Fourth Edition on the Wechsler Memory Scale-Fourth Edition in a nonclinical sample. *Journal of Clinical and Experimental Neuropsychology, 38*(4), 371–380. https://doi.org/10.1080/13803395.2015.1119253

Ishikawa, S. S., Raine, A., Lencz, T., Bihrle, S., & Lacasse, L. (2001). Autonomic stress reactivity and executive functions in successful and unsuccessful criminal psychopaths from the community. *Journal of Abnormal Psychology, 110*(3), 423–432. https://doi.org/10.1037/0021-843X.110.3.423

Iverson, G. L. (2001). Interpreting change on the WAIS-III/WMS-III in clinical samples. *Archives of Clinical Neuropsychology, 16*(2), 183–191. https://doi.org/10.1016/S0887-6177(00)00060-3

Ivison, D. J. (1977). The Wechsler Memory Scale: Preliminary findings toward an Australian standardisation. *Australian Psychologist, 12*, 303–312. https://doi.org/10.1080/00050067708254291

Ivnik, R. J., Malec, J. F., Sharbrough, F. W., Cascino, G. D., Hirschorn, K. A., Crook, T. H., & Larrabee, G. J. (1993). Traditional and computerized assessment procedures applied to the evaluation of memory change after temporal lobectomy. *Archives of Clinical Neuropsychology, 8*(1), 69–81.

Ivnik, R. J., Smith, G. E., Malec, J. F., Petersen, R. C., & Tangalos, E. G. (1995). Long-term stability and intercorrelations of cognitive abilities in older persons. *Psychological Assessment, 7*(2), 155–161. https://doi.org/10.1037/1040-3590.7.2.155

Jacobs, D., Salmon, D. P., Tröster, A. I., & Butters, N. (1990). Intrusion errors in the figural memory of patients with Alzheimer's and Huntington's disease. *Archives of Clinical Neuropsychology, 5*(1), 49–57. https://doi.org/10.1016/0887-6177(90)90006-B

Jacobs, J. (1887). Experiments in prehension. *Mind, 12*, 75–79.

Johnson, D. E., Epstein, J. N., Waid, L. R., Latham, P. K., Voronin, K. E., & Anton, R. F. (2001). Neuropsychological performance deficits in adults with attention deficit/hyperactivity disorder. *Archives of Clinical Neuropsychology, 16*(6), 587–604.

Johnson, D. K., Storandt, M., & Balota, D. A. (2003). Discourse analysis of logical memory recall in normal aging and in dementia of the Alzheimer type. *Neuropsychology, 17*(1), 82–92. https://doi.org/10.1037/0894-4105.17.1.82

Johnson, J. L. (1994). Episodic memory deficits in Alzheimer's disease: A behaviorally anchored scale. *Archives of Clinical Neuropsychology, 9*(4), 337–346.

Johnson, J. L., & Lesniak-Karpiak, K. (1997). The effect of warning on malingering on memory and motor tasks in college samples. *Archives of Clinical Neuropsychology, 12*(3), 231–238. https://doi.org/10.1016/S0887-6177(96)00040-6

Johnstone, B., Erdal, K., & Stadler, M. A. (1995). The relationship between the Wechsler Memory Scale-Revised (WMS-R) Attention Index and putative measures of attention. *Journal of Clinical Psychology in Medical Settings, 2*(2), 195–204. https://doi.org/10.1007/BF01988643

Johnstone, B., Hogg, J. R., Schopp, L. H., Kapila, C., & Edwards, S. (2002). Neuropsychological deficit profiles in senile dementia of the Alzheimer's type. *Archives of Clinical Neuropsychology, 17*(3), 273–281.

Johnstone, B., Vieth, A. Z., Johnson, J. C., & Shaw, J. A. (2000). Recall as a function of single versus multiple trials: Implications for rehabilitation. *Rehabilitation Psychology, 45*(1), 3–19. https://doi.org/10.1037/0090-5550.45.1.3

Jordan, C. M., Whitman, R. D., Harbut, M., & Tanner, B. (1993). Neuropsychological sequelae of hard metal disease. *Archives of Clinical Neuropsychology, 8*(4), 309–326. https://doi.org/10.1016/0887-6177(93)90022-S

Jurden, F. H., Franzen, M. D., Callahan, T., & Ledbetter, M. (1996). Factorial equivalence of the Wechsler Memory Scale-Revised across standardization and clinical samples. *Applied Neuropsychology, 3*(2), 65–74. https://doi.org/10.1207/s15324826an0302_4

Kalska, H., Punamäki, R.-L., Mäkinen-Pelli, T., & Saarinen, M. (1999). Memory and metamemory functioning among depressed patients. *Applied Neuropsychology, 6*(2), 96–107. https://doi.org/10.1207/s15324826an0602_5

Kareken, D. A., & Williams, J. M. (1994). Human judgment and estimation of premorbid intellectual function. *Psychological Assessment, 6*(2), 83.

Karimian, N., Asgari, K., Neshat Doost, H. T., Oreizi, H. R., & Najafi, M. R. (2018). Investigating patterns of memory impairment in ischemic stroke in an Iranian population. *Applied Neuropsychology: Adult, 25*(5), 458–463. https://doi.org/10.1080/23279095.2017.132914

Kear-Colwell, J. J. (1973). The structure of the Wechsler Memory Scale and its relationship to "brain damage". *British Journal of Social & Clinical Psychology, 12*(4), 337–448. https://doi.org/10.1111/j.2044-8260.1973.tb00085.x

Kear-Colwell, J. J., & Heller, M. (1978). A normative study of the Wechsler Memory Scale. *Journal of Clinical Psychology, 34*(2), 437–442. https://doi.org/10.1002/1097-4679(197804)34:2<437::AID-JCLP2270340239>3.0.CO;2-K

Kelly, M. P., & Doty, R. E. (1995). Neuropsychological dysfunction: Research and evaluation. In *Managing chronic illness: A biopsychosocial perspective* (pp. 117–162). Washington, DC, US: American Psychological Association. https://doi.org/10.1037/10511-004

Kendall, B. S., Mills, W. B., & Thale, T. (1956). Comparison of two methods of electroshock in their effect on cognitive functions. *Journal of Consulting Psychology, 20*(6), 423–429. https://doi.org/10.1037/h0040610

Kent, P. L. (1993). *The theoretical adequacy of Wechsler's theory of memory and memory scales*. ProQuest Information & Learning, US.

Kent, P. L. (2013). The evolution of the Wechsler Memory Scale: A selective review. *Applied Neuropsychology: Adult, 20*(4), 277–291. https://doi.org/10.1080/09084282.2012.689267

Kent, P. L. (2017). Evolution of Wechsler's Memory Scales: Content and structural analysis. *Applied Neuropsychology: Adult, 24*(3), 232–251. https://doi.org/10.1080/23279095.2015.1135798

Kent, P. L. (2018). *Selected bibliography of the Wechsler Memory Scale 1945–2018*. Unpublished manuscript.

Kinno, R., Shiromaru, A., Mori, Y., Futamura, A., Kuroda, T., Yano, S. . . . Ono, K. (2017). Differential effects of the factor structure of the Wechsler Memory Scale-Revised on the cortical thickness and complexity of patients aged over 75 years in a memory clinic setting. *Frontiers in Aging Neuroscience, 9*. https://doi.org/10.3389/fnagi.2017.00405

Klawans, H. L. (2000). *Defending the cavewoman: And other tales of evolutionary neurology*. New York: W.W. Norton.

Kleinman, S. N., & Waber, D. P. (1994). Prose memory strategies of children treated for leukemia: A story grammar analysis of the Anna Thompson passage. *Neuropsychology, 8*(3), 464–470. https://doi.org/10.1037/0894-4105.8.3.464

Kolb, B., & Whishaw, I. Q. (1980). *Fundamentals of human neuropsychology*. San Francisco, CA: W. H. Freeman Co.

Kolb, B., & Whishaw, I. Q. (2015). *Fundamentals of human neuropsychology* (7th ed.). New York: Worth Publishers.

Kolb, B., & Whishaw, I. Q. (2008). *Fundamentals of human neuropsychology* (6th ed.). New York: Macmillan.

Korfine, L. (1998). *Memory functioning in borderline personality disorder*. ProQuest Information & Learning, US.

Koshiyama, D., Fukunaga, M., Okada, N., Ymashita, F., Yamamori, H., Yasuda, Y. . . . Hashimoto, R. (2018). Subcortical association with memory performance in schizophrenia: A structural magnetic resonance imaging study. *Translational Psychiatry*, *8*(20), 1–11.

Koziol, L. F., & Budding, D. E. (2009). *Subcortical structures and cognition: Implications for neuropsychological assessment*. New York: Springer Science & Business Media.

Krawiecki, J. A., Couper, L., & Walton, D. (1957). The efficacy of parentrovite in the treatment of a group of senile psychotics. *Journal of Mental Science*, *103*(432), 601–605. https://doi.org/10.1192/bjp.103.432.601

Kreiner, D. S., Ryan, J. J., & Miller, L. J. (2003). Predicting WMS-III performance from digit symbol incidental learning curves. *The Clinical Neuropsychologist*, *17*(1), 101–101.

Kremen, W. S., Panizzon, M. S., Franz, C. E., Spoon, K. M., Vuoksimaa, E., Jacobson, K. C. . . . Lyons, M. J. (2014). Genetic complexity of episodic memory: A twin approach to studies of aging. *Psychology and Aging*, *29*(2), 404–417. https://doi.org/10.1037/a0035962

Krop, H., Cohen, E., & Block, A. J. (1972). Continuous oxygen therapy in chronic obstructive pulmonary disease neuropsychological effects. In *Proceedings of the Annual Convention of the American Psychological Association*. American Psychological Association.

Ladowsky-Brooks, R. L. (2016). Four-hour delayed memory recall for stories: Theoretical and clinical implications of measuring accelerated long-term forgetting. *Applied Neuropsychology: Adult*, *23*, 205–212. https://doi.org/10.1080/23279095.2015.1030670

Lamb, Y. N., McKay, N. S., Singh, S. S., Waldie, K. E., & Kirk, I. J. (2016). Catechol-O-methyltransferase val[158]met polymorphism interacts with sex to affect face recognition ability. *Frontiers in Psychology*, *7*, 965.

Lamb, Y. N., Thompson, C. S., McKay, N. S., Waldie, K. E., & Kirk, I. J. (2015). The brain-derived neurotrophic factor (BDNF) val66met polymorphism differentially affects performance on subscales of the Wechsler Memory Scale-Third Edition (WMS-III). *Frontiers in Psychology*, *6*, 1212.

Langeluddecke, P. M., & Lucas, S. K. (2003). Quantitative measures of memory malingering on the Wechsler Memory Scale-Third edition in mild head injury litigants. *Archives of Clinical Neuropsychology*, *18*(2), 181–197. https://doi.org/10.1016/S0887-6177(01)00195-0

Larner, A. J. (2008). *Neuropsychological neurology: The neurocognitive impairments of neurological disorders*. Cambridge, UK: Cambridge University Press.

Larochette, A. C., Harrison, A. G., Rosenblum, Y., & Bowie, C. R. (2011). Additive neurocognitive deficits in adults with attention-deficit/hyperactivity disorder and depressive symptoms. *Archives of clinical neuropsychology*, *26*(5), 385–395.

Larrabee, G. J. (Ed.). (2007). *Assessment of malingered neuropsychological deficits*. New York: Oxford University Press.

Larrabee, G. J. (2015). The multiple validities of neuropsychological assessment. *American Psychologist*, *70*(8), 779–788.

Larrabee, G. J., Kane, R. L., & Schuck, J. R. (1983). Factor analysis of the WAIS and Wechsler Memory Scale: An analysis of the construct validity of the Wechsler Memory Scale. *Journal of Clinical Neuropsychology*, *5*(2), 159–168. https://doi.org/10.1080/01688638308401162

Larrabee, G. J., Trahan, D. E., & Curtiss, G. (1992). Construct validity of the continuous visual memory test. *Archives of Clinical Neuropsychology, 7*(5), 395–405.

Lawrence, C. (1984). Testing for memory disorder. *Australian and New Zealand Journal of Psychiatry, 18*, 207–210.

Lazar, R. M., Weiner, M., Wald, H. S., & Kula, R. W. (1995). Visuoconstructive deficit following infarction in the right Basal Ganglia: A case report and some experimental data. *Archives of Clinical Neuropsychology, 10*(6), 543–553.

Lee, P. W., Hung, B. K., Woo, E. K., Tai, P. T., & Choi, D. T. (1989). Effects of radiation therapy on neuropsychological functioning in patients with nasopharyngeal carcinoma. *Journal of Neurology, Neurosurgery & Psychiatry, 52*(4), 488–492. https://doi.org/10.1136/jnnp.52.4.488

Lees-Haley, P. R., Smith, H. H., Williams, C. W., & Dunn, J. T. (1996). Forensic neuropsychological test usage: An empirical survey. *Archives of Clinical Neuropsychology, 11*(1), 45–51. https://doi.org/10.1016/0887-6177(95)00011-9

Leonberger, F. T., Nicks, S. D., Larrabee, G. J., & Goldfader, P. R. (1992). Factor structure of the Wechsler Memory Scale-Revised within a comprehensive neuropsychological battery. *Neuropsychology, 6*(3), 239–249. https://doi.org/10.1037/0894-4105.6.3.239

Levy, B. (2006). Increasing the power for detecting impairment in older adults with the Faces subtest from Wechsler Memory Scale-III: An empirical trial. *Archives of Clinical Neuropsychology, 21*(7), 687–692.

Levy, L. H. (1963). *Psychological interpretation.* New York: Holt, Rinehart & Winston, Inc.

Lewis-Jack, O. O., Campbell, A. L., Ridley, S., Ocampo, C., Brown, A., Dennis, G. . . . Weir, R. (1997). Unilateral brain lesions and performance on Russell's version of the Wechsler Memory Scale in an African American population. *International Journal of Neuroscience, 91*(3–4), 229–240. https://doi.org/10.3109/00207459708986379

Lezak, M. (1976). *Neuropsychological assessment.* New York: Oxford University Press.

Lezak, M. (1983). *Neuropsychological assessment* (2nd ed.). New York: Oxford University Press.

Lezak, M. D. (1988). IQ: RIP. *Journal of Clinical & Experimental Neuropsychology, 10*, 351–361.

Lezak, M., Howieson, D. B., Bigler, E., & Tranel, D. (2012). *Neuropsychological assessment* (5th ed.). New York: Oxford University Press.

Lezak, M., Howieson, D. B., Loring, D. W., & Hannay, H. (2004). *Neuropsychological assessment* (4th ed.). New York: Oxford University Press.

Libon, D. J., Bogdanoff, B., Bonavita, J., Skalina, S., Cloud, B. S., Resh, R. . . . Ball, S. K. (1997). Dementia associated with periventricular and deep white matter alterations: A subtype of subcortical dementia. *Archives of Clinical Neuropsychology, 12*(3), 239–250.

Libon, D. J., Malamut, B. L., Swenson, R., Sands, L. P., & Cloud, B. S. (1996). Further analyses of clock drawings among demented and nondemented older subjects. *Archives of Clinical Neuropsychology, 11*(3), 193–205.

Libon, D. J., Swenson, R., Ashendorf, L., Bauer, R. M., & Bowers, D. (2013). Edith Kaplan and the Boston process approach. *The Clinical Neuropsychologist, 27*(8), 1223–1233.

Lichtenberger, E. O., Kaufman, A. S., & Lai, Z. C. (2002). *Essentials of WMS-III assessment.* New York: John Wiley & Sons.

Logue, P., & Wyrick, L. (1979). Initial validation of Russell's Revised Wechsler Memory Scale: A comparison of normal aging versus dementia. *Journal of Consulting and Clinical Psychology, 47*(1), 176–178. https://doi.org/10.1037/0022-006X.47.1.176

Lokken, K., Ferraro, F. R., Petros, T., Bergloff, P., Thompson, S., & Teetzen, M. (1999). The effect of importance level, delay, and rate of forgetting on prose recall in multiple sclerosis. *Applied Neuropsychology, 6*(3), 147–153. https://doi.org/10.1207/s15324826an0603_2

Loring, D. W., Lee, G. P., Martin, R. C., & Meador, K. J. (1989). Verbal and Visual Memory Index discrepancies from the Wechsler Memory Scale-Revised: Cautions in interpretation. *Psychological Assessment: A Journal of Consulting and Clinical Psychology, 1*(3), 198–202. https://doi.org/10.1037/1040-3590.1.3.198

Loring, D. W., & Papanicolaou, A. C. (1987). Memory assessment in neuropsychology: Theoretical considerations and practical utility. *Journal of Clinical and Experimental Neuropsychology, 9*(4), 340–358. https://doi.org/10.1080/01688638708405055

Louttit, C. M., & Browne, C. G. (1947). The use of psychometric instruments in psychological clinics. *Journal of Consulting Psychology, 11*, 49–54.

Lubin, B., Larsen, R. M., & Matarazzo, J. M. (1984). Patterns of psychological test usage in the United States: 1935–1982. *American Psychologist, 39*, 451–454.

Luria, A. R. (1976). *The neuropsychology of memory.* Washington, DC: Winston.

Luria, A. R. (1987). *The mind of a mnemonist.* Cambridge, MA: Harvard University Press.

Mack, J. L. (1986). Clinical assessment of disorders of attention and memory. *The Journal of Head Trauma Rehabilitation, 1*(3), 22–33. https://doi.org/10.1097/00001199-198609000-00006

Manglam, M. K., Ram, D., Praharaj, S. K., & Sarkhel, S. (2010). Working memory in schizophrenia. *German Journal of Psychiatry, 13*, 116–120.

Marson, D. C., Dymek, M. P., Duke, L. W., & Harrell, L. E. (1997). Subscale validity of the Mattis dementia rating scale. *Archives of Clinical Neuropsychology, 12*(3), 269–275.

Martin, P. K., & Schroeder, R. W. (2014). Chance performance and floor effects: Threats to the validity of the Wechsler Memory Scale-Fourth Edition Designs subtest. *Archives of Clinical Neuropsychology, 29*(4), 385–390.

Martin, P. K., Schroeder, R. W., Heinrichs, R. J., & Baade, L. E. (2015). Does true neurocognitive dysfunction contribute to Minnesota Multiphasic Personality Inventory-Restructured Form cognitive validity scale scores? *Archives of Clinical Neuropsychology, 30*(5), 377–386.

Maruff, P., & Darby, D. (2006). Age-related memory impairment. In P. J. Snyder, P. Nussbaum, & D. Robins (Eds.), *Clinical neuropsychology: A pocket handbook for assessment* (2nd ed., pp. 155–182). Washington, DC: American Psychological Association.

Masuda, H., Hirano, S., Takahashi, N., Hatsugano, E., Uzawa, A., Uchida, T. . . . Mori, M. (2017). Comparison of cognitive and brain grey matter volume profiles between multiple sclerosis and neuromyelitis optica spectrum disorder. *PLoS One, 12*(8), e0184012.

Matarazzo, J. D. (1972). *Wechsler's Measurement and Appraisal of Adult Intelligence* (5th and enlarged ed.). Baltimore, MD: The Williams and Wilkins Co.

Matarazzo, J. D. (1990). Psychological assessment vs psychological testing: Validation from Binet to the school, clinic and courtroom. *American Psychologist, 45*, 999–1017.

McCaffrey, R. J., Ortega, A., & Haase, R. F. (1993). Effects of repeated neuropsychological assessments. *Archives of Clinical Neuropsychology, 8*(6), 519–524. https://doi.org/10.1016/0887-6177(93)90052-3

McCarty, S. M., Ziesat, H. A., Logue, P. E., Power, D. G., & Rosenstiel, A. K. (1980). Alternate-form reliability, and age-related scores for Russell's Revised Wechsler Memory Scale. *Journal of Consulting and Clinical Psychology, 48*(2), 296–298. https://doi.org/10.1037/0022-006X.48.2.296

McDowell, B. D., Bayless, J. D., Moser, D. J., Meyers, J. E., & Paulsen, J. S. (2004). Concordance between the CVLT and the WMS-III word lists test. *Archives of Clinical Neuropsychology, 19*(2), 319–324. https://doi.org/10.1016/S0887-6177(03)00023-4

Meehl, P. E. (1954). *Clinical versus statistical prediction: A theoretical analysis and a review of the evidence*. St. Paul, MN: University of Minnesota.

Migoya, J., Zimmerman, S. W., & Golden, C. J. (2002). Abbreviated form of the Wechsler Memory Scale-III Faces subtest. *Assessment, 9*(2), 142–144. https://doi.org/10.1177/10791102009002004

Milanovich, J. R., Axelrod, B. N., & Millis, S. R. (1996). Validation of the Simulation Index-Revised with a mixed clinical population. *Archives of Clinical Neuropsychology, 11*(1), 53–59. https://doi.org/10.1016/0887-6177(95)00016-X

Miller, J. B., Axelrod, B. N., Rapport, L. J., Hanks, R. A., Bashem, J. R., & Schutte, C. (2012a). Substitution of California Verbal Learning Test, Second Edition for Verbal Paired Associates on the Wechsler Memory Scale, Fourth Edition. *The Clinical Neuropsychologist, 26*(4), 599–608.

Miller, J. B., Axelrod, B. N., Rapport, L. J., Millis, S. R., VanDyke, S., Schutte, C., & Hanks, R. A. (2012b). Parsimonious prediction of Wechsler Memory Scale, Fourth Edition Scores: Immediate and delayed memory indexes. *Journal of Clinical and Experimental Neuropsychology, 34*(5), 531–542. https://doi.org/10.1080/13803395.2012.665437

Miller, J. B., Axelrod, B. N., & Schutte, C. (2012). Parsimonious estimation of the Wechsler Memory Scale, Fourth Edition demographically adjusted index scores: Immediate and delayed memory. *The Clinical Neuropsychologist, 26*(3), 490–500. https://doi.org/10.1080/13854046.2012.665084

Miller, J. B., Millis, S. R., Rapport, L. J., Bashem, J. R., Hanks, R. A., & Axelrod, B. N. (2011). Detection of insufficient effort using the advanced clinical solutions for the Wechsler Memory Scale, Fourth Edition. *The Clinical Neuropsychologist, 25*(1), 160–172. https://doi.org/10.1080/13854046.2010.533197

Millis, S. R., Malina, A. C., Bowers, D. A., & Ricker, J. H. (1999). Confirmatory factor analysis of the Wechsler Memory Scale-III. *Journal of Clinical and Experimental Neuropsychology, 21*(1), 87–93. https://doi.org/10.1076/jcen.21.1.87.937

Milner, B. (1975). Psychological aspects of focal epilepsy and its neurosurgical management. *Neurosurgical Management of the Epilepsies. Advances in Neurology, 8*, 299–321.

Mirskey, A. F. (1989). The neuropsychological of attention: Elements of a complex behavior. In E. Perecman (Ed.), *Integrating theory and practice on clinical neuropsychology* (pp. 75–91). Hilsdale, NJ: Lawrence Erlbaum Associates.

Mitchell, M. (1987). Scoring discrepancies on two subtests of the Wechsler Memory Scale. *Journal of Consulting and Clinical Psychology, 55*(6), 914–915. https://doi.org/10.1037/0022-006X.55.6.914

Mitrushina, M., & Satz, P. (1991). Changes in cognitive functioning associated with normal aging. *Archives of Clinical Neuropsychology, 6*(1–2), 49–60.

Mittenberg, W., Azrin, R., Millsaps, C., & Heilbronner, R. (1993). Identification of malingered head injury on the Wechsler Memory Scale-Revised. *Psychological Assessment, 5*(1), 34–40. https://doi.org/10.1037/1040-3590.5.1.34

Mittenberg, W., Burton, D. B., Darrow, E., & Thompson, G. B. (1992). Normative data for the Wechsler Memory Scale-Revised: 25- to 34-year olds. *Psychological Assessment*, *4*(3), 363–368. https://doi.org/10.1037/1040-3590.4.3.363

Mittenberg, W., Malloy, M., Petrick, J., & Knee, K. (1994). Impaired depth perception discriminates Alzheimer's dementia from aging and major depression. *Archives of Clinical Neuropsychology*, *9*(1), 71–79.

Mittenberg, W., Theroux, S., Aguila-Puentes, G., Bianchini, K., Greve, K., & Rayls, K. (2001). Identification of malingered head injury on the Wechsler Adult Intelligence Scale. *The Clinical Neuropsychologist*, *15*(4), 440–445.

Mittenberg, W., Thompson, G. B., & Schwartz, J. A. (1991). Abnormal and reliable differences among Wechsler Memory Scale-Revised subtests. *Psychological Assessment: A Journal of Consulting and Clinical Psychology*, *3*(3), 492–495. https://doi.org/10.1037/1040-3590.3.3.492

Montgomery, V., Harris, K., Stabler, A., & Lu, L. H. (2017). Effects of delay duration on the WMS logical memory performance of older adults with probable Alzheimer's disease, probable vascular dementia, and normal cognition. *Archives of Clinical Neuropsychology*, *32*(3), 259–266. https://doi.org/10.1093/arclin/acx005

Moore, C. A., & Lichtenberg, P. A. (1996). Neuropsychological prediction of independent functioning in a geriatric sample: A double cross-validational study. *Rehabilitation Psychology*, *41*(2), 115–130. https://doi.org/10.1037/0090-5550.41.2.115

Moore, P. M., & Baker, G. A. (1996). Validation of the Wechsler Memory Scale-Revised in a sample of people with intractable temporal lobe epilepsy. *Epilepsia*, *37*, 1215–1220.

Moore, P. M., & Baker, G. A. (1997). Psychometric properties and factor structure of the Wechsler Memory Scale-Revised in a sample of persons with intractable epilepsy. *Journal of Clinical and Experimental Neuropsychology*, *19*(6), 897–905. https://doi.org/10.1080/01688639708403770

Moosavian, E., & Hadianfard, H. (2014). Investigating the role of facial emotion recognition as an independent function from cognitive performance in patients with schizophrenia. *Advances in Cognitive Science*, *15*, 1–8.

Muniyandi, K., Venkatesan, J., & Jayaseelan, V. (2012). Study to assess the prevalence, nature and extent of cognitive impairment in people living with AIDS. *Indian Journal of Psychiatry*, *54*(2), 149–153.

Mutchnick, M. G., Ross, L. K., & Long, C. J. (1991). Decision strategies for cerebral dysfunction IV: Determination of cerebral dysfunction. *Archives of Clinical Neuropsychology*, *6*(4), 259–270

Naugle, R. I., Chelune, G. J., Cheek, R., Lüders, H., & Awad, Issam A. (1993). Detection of changes in material-specific memory following temporal lobectomy using the Wechsler Memory Scale-Revised. *Archives of Clinical Neuropsychology*, *8*(5), 381–395. https://doi.org/10.1016/0887-6177(93)90002-I

Naugle, R. I., Cullum, C. M., Bigler, E. D., & Massman, P. J. (1986). Neuropsychological characteristics and atrophic brain changes in senile and presenile dementia. *Archives of Clinical Neuropsychology*, *1*(3), 219–230. https://doi.org/10.1016/0887-6177(86)90028-4

Nicks, S. D., Leonberger, F. T., Munz, D. C., & Goldfader, P. R. (1992). Factor analysis of the WMS-R and the WAIS. *Archives of Clinical Neuropsychology*, *7*(5), 387–393. https://doi.org/10.1016/0887-6177(92)90151-C

Niwa, F., Kondo, M., Sakurada, K., Nakagawa, M., Imanishi, J., & Mizuno, T. (2016). Reginal cerebral blood flow in ^{123}I-IMP single-photon emission computed tomography and the Wechsler Memory Scale-revised in nondemented elderly subjects with subjective cognitive impairment. *Internal Medicine, 55*, 3571–3578.

O'Carroll, R. E. (1995). Associative learning in acutely ill and recovered schizophrenic patients. *Schizophrenia Research, 15*(3), 299–301. https://doi.org/10.1016/0920-9964(94)00052-A

O'Connor, M. G., & Lafleche, G. (2006). Amnesic syndromes. In P. J. Snyder, P. Nussbaum, & D. Robins (Eds.), *Clinical neuropsychology: A pocket handbook for assessment* (2nd ed., pp. 463–488). Washington, DC: American Psychological Association.

O'Mahony, J. F., & Doherty, B. (1993). Patterns of intellectual performance among recently abstinent alcohol abusers on WAIS-R and WMS-R sub-tests. *Archives of Clinical Neuropsychology, 8*(5), 373–380. https://doi.org/10.1093/arclin/8.5.373

O'Shea, D. M., Langer, K., Woods, A. J., Porges, E. C., Williamson, J. B., O'Shea, A., & Cohen, R. A. (2018). Educational attainment moderates the association between hippocampal volumes and memory performances in healthy older adults. *Frontiers in Aging Neuroscience, 10*, 1–9. https://doi.org/10.3389/fnagi.2018.00361

O'Shea, M. F., Saling, M. M., Bladin, P. F., & Berkovic, S. F. (1996). Does naming contribute to memory self-report in temporal lobe epilepsy? *Journal of Clinical and Experimental Neuropsychology, 18*(1), 98–109. https://doi.org/10.1080/01688 639608408266

Oberlin, L. E., Manuck, S. B., Gianaros, P. J., Ferrell, R. E., Muldoon, M. F., Jennings, J. R. . . . Erickson, K. I. (2015). Blood pressure interacts with APOE ε4 to predict memory performance in a midlife sample. *Neuropsychology, 29*(5), 693–702. https://doi.org/10.1037/neu0000177

Osborne, D., & David, L. J. (1978). Standard scores for Wechsler Memory Scale subtests. *Journal of Clinical Psychology, 34*(1), 115–116. https://doi.org/10.1002/1097-4679(197801)34:1<115::AID-JCLP2270340126>3.0.CO;2-J

Özdemir, O., Özdemir, P. G., Boysan, M., & Yılmaz, E. (2015). The relationships between dissociation, attention, and memory dysfunction. *Nöropsikiyatri Arşivi, 52*(1), 36–41. https://doi.org/10.5152/npa.2015.7390

Palmer, B. W., Boone, K. B., Lesser, I. M., & Wohl, M. A. (1998). Base rates of "impaired" neuropsychological test performance among healthy older adults. *Archives of Clinical Neuropsychology, 13*(6), 503–511.

Paolo, A. M., Tröster, A. I., Axelrod, B. N., & Koller, W. C. (1995). Construct validity of the WCST in normal elderly and persons with Parkinson's disease. *Archives of Clinical Neuropsychology, 10*(5), 463–473.

Park, E., & Jon, D. (2018). Modality-specific working memory systems verified by clinical working memory tests. *Clinical Psychopharmacology and Neuroscience, 16*, 489–493.

Parker, J. W. (1957). The validity of some current tests for organicity. *Journal of Consulting Psychology, 21*, 425–428.

Patterson, C. H. (1946). The clinical psychologist in an army hospital. *American Journal of Orthopsychiatry, 16*, 215–221. https://doi.org/10.1111/j.1939-0025.1946.tb05375.x

Pauls, F., Petermann, F., & Lepach, A. C. (2013). Memory assessment and depression: Testing for factor structure and measurement invariance of the Wechsler Memory

Scale-Fourth Edition across a clinical and matched control sample. *Journal of Clinical and Experimental Neuropsychology, 35*(7), 702–717. https://doi.org/10.1080/13 803395.2013.820257

Pearson. (2009a). *Advanced clinical solutions for the WAIS-IV and WMS-IV.* San Antonio, TX: Author.

Pearson. (2009b). *Interpretive report of WMS-IV testing.* Retrieved from images.pearsonclinical.com/images/Assets/WMS-IV/WMSIV_Writer_Report_21yrMale.pdf

Pearson. (2011). *WMS-IV flexible approach quick reference.* Retrieved from https://images.pearsonclinical.com/images/Products/WMS-IV/4958-2010_WMS-IV_Flexible_Approach_FLY_rd4.pdf

Pearson. (2019). *2019 catalog: Psychological and educational assessments.* Retrieved from https://images.pearsonclinical.com/images/ca/catalogs/2019-Catalog/2019-Pearson-Catalog.pdf

Pearson. (n.d.a). *WMS-III to WMS-IV: Rationale for change.* San Antonio, TX: Author. Retrieved from https://images.pearsonclinical.com/images/Products/WMS-IV/WMS-RationaleforChange.pdf

Pearson. (n.d.b). *The Wechsler Memory Scale-IV.* Retrieved from www.pearsonclinical.com/psychology/products/100000281/wechsler-memory-scale-fourth-edition-wms-iv.html#tab-details

Pheley, A. M., & Klesges, R. C. (1986). The relationship between experimental and neuropsychological measures of memory. *Archives of Clinical Neuropsychology, 1*(3), 231–241.

Phillipou, A., Gurvich, C., Castle, D. J., Abel, L. A., & Rossell, S. L. (2015). Comprehensive neurocognitive assessment of patients with anorexia nervosa. *World Journal of Psychiatry, 5*(4), 404–411.

Pinkston, J. B., Wu, J. C., Gouvier, W. D., & Varney, N. R. (2000). Quantitative PET scan findings in carbon monoxide poisoning: Deficits seen in a matched pair. *Archives of clinical neuropsychology, 15*(6), 545–553.

Piotrowski, C., & Keller, J. W. (1989). Psychological testing in outpatient mental health facilities: A national study. *Professional Psychology: Research and Practice, 20,* 423–425. https://doi.org/10.1037/0735-7028.20.6.423

Pirkola, T., Tuulio-Henriksson, A., Glahn, D., Kieseppä, T., Haukk, J., Kapri, J. . . . Cannon, T. D. (2005). Spatial working memory function in twins with schizophrenia and bipolar disorder. *Biological Psychiatry, 58*(12), 930–936. https://doi.org/10.1016/j.biopsych.2005.05.041

Poon, L. W., Crook, T. E., Davis, K. L., Eisdorfer, C. E., Gurland, B. J., Kaszniak, A. W., & Thompson, L. W. (1986). *Handbook for clinical memory assessment of older adults.* Washington, DC: American Psychological Association.

Powel, J. (1988). Wechsler Memory Scale-Revised: David A. Wechsler. New York: Psychological Corporation. Harcourt Brace Jovanovich, Inc, 1987. 150 pp. *Archives of Clinical Neuropsychology, 3,* 397–403.

Powell, J. B., Cripe, L. I., & Dodrill, C. B. (1991). Assessment of brain impairment with the Rey Auditory Verbal Learning Test: A comparison with other neuropsychological measures. *Archives of Clinical Neuropsychology, 6*(4), 241–249.

Price, L. R., Tulsky, D., Millis, S., & Weiss, L. (2002). Redefining the factor structure of the Wechsler Memory Scale-III: Confirmatory factor analysis with cross-validation. *Journal of Clinical and Experimental Neuropsychology, 24*(5), 574–585. https://doi.org/10.1076/jcen.24.5.574.1013

Prifitera, A., & Barley, W. D. (1985). Cautions in interpretation of comparisons between the WAIS-R and the Wechsler Memory Scale. *Journal of Consulting and Clinical Psychology, 53*(4), 564–565. https://doi.org/10.1037/0022-006X.53.4.564

Prigatano, G. P. (1974). Memory deficit in head injured patients. In *Meeting of the Southwestern Psychological Association*, El Paso, TX.

Prigatano, G. P. (1977). Wechsler Memory Scale is a poor screening test for brain dysfunction. *Journal of Clinical Psychology, 33*(3), 772–777. https://doi.org/10.1002/1097-4679(197707)33:3<772::AID-JCLP2270330337>3.0.CO;2-Q

Prigatano, G. P. (1978). Wechsler Memory Scale: A selective review of the literature. *Journal of Clinical Psychology, 34*(4), 816–832. https://doi.org/10.1002/1097-4679(197810)34:4<816::AID-JCLP2270340402>3.0.CO;2-Q

Prigatano, G. P., Parsons, O., Levin, D. C., Wright, E., & Hawryluk, G. (1983). Neuropsychological test performance in mildly hypoxemic patients with chronic obstructive pulmonary disease. *Journal of Consulting and Clinical Psychology, 51*(1), 108–116. https://doi.org/10.1037/0022-006X.51.1.108

Psychological Corporation. (1997). *WAIS-III and WMS-III technical manual.* San Antonio, TX: Psychological Corporation.

Psychological Corporation. (2002). *WAIS-III WMS-III WIAT-II writer.* San Antionio, TX: Psychological Corporation.

Quadfasel, A. F., & Pruyser, P. W. (1955). Cognitive deficit in patients with psychomotor epilepsy. *Epilepsia, 4*(Ser. 3), 80–90. https://doi.org/10.1111/j.1528-1157.1955.tb03176.x

Quintart, J. C. (1959). Les troubles de la mémoire provoqués par l'électrochoc. [Memory losses caused by ECT.]. *Acta Neurologica et Psychiatrica Belgica, 59*, 625–637.

Rabin, L. A., Barr, W. B., & Burton, L. A. (2005). Assessment practices of clinical neuropsychologists in the United States and Canada: A survey of INS, NAN, and APA Division 40 members. *Archives of Clinical Neuropsychology, 20*(1), 33–65. https://doi.org/10.1016/j.acn.2004.02.005

Rabin, L. A., Paolillo, E., & Barr, W. B. (2016). Stability in test-usage practices of clinical neuropsychologists in the United States and Canada over a 10-year period: A follow-up survey of INS and NAN members. *Archives of Clinical Neuropsychology, 31*(3), 206. https://doi.org/10.1093/arclin/acw007

Randolph, C., Gold, J. M., Kozora, E., Cullum, C. M., Hermann, B. P., & Wyler, A. R. (1994). Estimating memory function: Disparity of Wechsler Memory Scale-Revised and California Verbal Learning Test indices in clinical and normal samples. *Clinical Neuropsychologist, 8*(1), 99–108. https://doi.org/10.1080/13854049408401547

Rawling, P., & Brooks, N. (1990). Simulation index: A method for detecting factitious errors on the WAIS-R and WMS. *Neuropsychology, 4*(4), 223–238. https://doi.org/10.1037/0894-4105.4.4.223

Rawling, P., & Lyle, J. G. (1978). Cued recall and discrimination of memory deficit. *Journal of Consulting and Clinical Psychology, 46*(6), 1227–1229. https://doi.org/10.1037/0022-006X.46.6.1227

Ready, R. E., & Veague, H. B. (2014). Training in psychological assessment: Current practices of clinical psychology programs. *Professional Psychology: Research and Practice, 45*, 278–282.

Riccio, C. A., Wolfe, M. E., Romine, C., Davis, B., & Sullivan, J. R. (2004). The Tower of London and neuropsychological assessment of ADHD in adults. *Archives of Clinical Neuropsychology, 19*(5), 661–671.

Rogers, S. A., McPherson, S., Lu, P. H., & Cummings, J. (2007). Discriminative ability of WMS-III norms among older adults. *The Clinical Neuropsychologist, 21*(4), 696–696.

Rosenfeld, B., Sands, S. A., & Van Gorp, W. G. (2000). Have we forgotten the base rate problem? Methodological issues in the detection of distortion. *Archives of Clinical Neuropsychology, 15*(4), 349–359.

Rosenzweig, S. (1949). Defect of function from neurologic damage. In S. Rosenzweig (Ed.), *Psychodiagnosis: An introduction to the integration of tests in dynamic clinical practice* (pp. 304–310). New York: Grune & Stratton. http://dx.doi.org/10.1037/10583-016

Ross, S. R., Putnam, S. H., Gass, C. S., Bailey, D. E., & Adams, K. M. (2003). MMPI-2 indices of psychological disturbance and attention and memory test performance in head injury. *Archives of Clinical Neuropsychology, 18*(8), 905–916. https://doi.org/10.1016/S0887-6177(02)00169-5

Russell, E. W. (1975). A multiple scoring method for the assessment of complex memory functions. *Journal of Consulting and Clinical Psychology, 43*(6), 800–809. https://doi.org/10.1037/0022-006X.43.6.800

Russell, E. W. (1988). Renorming Russell's version of the Wechsler Memory Scale. *Journal of Clinical and Experimental Neuropsychology, 10*(2), 235–249. https://doi.org/10.1080/01688638808408238

Russo, A. C. (2018). A practitioner survey of Department of Veterans Affairs Psychologists who provide neuropsychological assessments. *Archives of Clinical Neuropsychology, 33*(8), 1046–1059.

Ryan, C. M. (1990). Memory disturbances following chronic, low-level carbon monoxide exposure. *Archives of Clinical Neuropsychology, 5*(1), 59–67.

Ryan, J. J., Arb, J. D., & Ament, P. A. (2000). Supplementary WMS-III tables for determining primary subtest strengths and weaknesses. *Psychological Assessment, 12*(2), 193–196. https://doi.org/10.1037/1040-3590.12.2.193

Ryan, J. J., & Geisser, M. E. (1986). Validity and diagnostic accuracy of an alternate form of the Rey Auditory Verbal Learning Test. *Archives of Clinical Neuropsychology, 1*(3), 209–217.

Ryan, J. J., Kreiner, D. S., & Burton, D. B. (2002). Does high scatter affect the predictive validity of WAIS-III IQs? *Applied Neuropsychology, 9*(3), 173–178. https://doi.org/10.1207/S15324826AN0903_5

Ryan, J. J., Rosenberg, S. J., & Heilbronner, R. L. (1984). Comparative relationships of the Wechsler Adult Intelligence Scale-Revised (WAIS-R) and the Wechsler Adult Intelligence Scale (WAIS) to the Wechsler Memory Scale (WMS). *Journal of Behavioral Assessment, 6*(1), 37–43. https://doi.org/10.1007/BF01321459

Sabater, A., García-Blanco, A. C., Verdet, H. M., Sierra, P., Ribes, J., Villar, I. . . . Livianos, L. (2016). Comparative neurocognitive effects of lithium and anticonvulsants in long-term stable bipolar patients. *Journal of Affective Disorders, 190*, 34–40. https://doi.org/10.1016/j.jad.2015.10.008

Sacks, O. (1985). *The man who mistook his wife for a hat.* London: Duckworth.

Sahin, S., Onal, T. O., Cinar, N., Bozdemir, M., Cubuk, R., & Karsidag, S. (2017). Distinguishing depressive psuedodementia from Alzheimer Disease: A comparative study of hippocampal volumetry and cognitive tests. *Dementia and Geriatric Cognitive Disorders, 7*, 231–239.

Sapin, L. R., Frishberg, B. M., & Sherman, J. L. (1990). MRI and neuropsychological correlates of dementia in Binswanger's disease. *Archives of Clinical Neuropsychology, 5*(1), 89–97.

Sass, K. J., Sass, A., Westerveld, M., Lencz, T., Rosewater, K. M., Novelly, R. A. . . . Spencer, D. D. (1992). Russell's adaptation of Wechsler Memory Scale as an index of hippocampal pathology. *Journal of Epilepsy, 5*, 24–30. https://doi.org/10.1016/S0896-6974(05)80017-9

Sawada, H., Oeda, T., Kohsaka, M., Umemura, A., Tomita, S., Park, K. . . . Kawamura, T. (2018). Early use of donepezil against psychosis and cognitive decline in Parkinson's disease: A randomized controlled trial for 2 years. *Journal of Neurology, Neurosurgery, and Psychiatry, 12*, 1–9.

Saykin, A. J., Gur, R. C., Sussman, N. M., O'Connor, M. J., & Gur, R. E. (1989). Memory deficits before and after temporal lobectomy: Effect of laterality and age of onset. *Brain and Cognition, 9*(2), 191–200. https://doi.org/10.1016/0278-2626(89)90029-8

Scheltens, P., Prins, N., Lammertsma, A., Yaqub, M., Gouw, A., Wink, A. M. . . . Alam, J. (2018). An exploratory clinical study of p3α 8 kinase inhibition in Alzheimer's disease. *Annals of Clinical and Translational Neurology, 5*(4), 464–473.

Schmidt, M., Trueblood, W., Merwin, M., & Durham, R. L. (1994). How much do "attention" tests tell us? *Archives of Clinical Neuropsychology, 9*(5), 383–394. https://doi.org/10.1016/0887-6177(94)90002-7

Schneider, B. C., Thoering, T., Cludius, B., & Moritz, S. (2015). Self-reported symptoms of attention-deficit/hyperactivity disorder: Rate of endorsement and association with neuropsychological performance in an adult psychiatric sample. *Archives of Clinical Neuropsychology, 30*(3), 186–191.

Scholes, K. E., & Martin-Iverson, M. T. (2010). Cannabis use and neuropsychological performance in healthy individuals and patients with schizophrenia. *Psychological Medicine, 40*, 1635–1646. https://doi.org/10.1017/S0033291709992078

Schroeder, R. W., Buddin, W. N., Hargrave, D. D., VonDran, E. J., Campbell, E. B., Brockman, C. J. . . . Baade, L. E. (2013). Efficacy of Test of Memory Malingering Trial 1, Trial 2, the Retention Trial, and the Albany Consistency Index in a Criterion Group Forensic Neuropsychological Sample. *Archives of Clinical Neuropsychology, 28*(1), 21–29.

Schwartz, E. W. (1997). *Attention, concentration and memory in chronic daily headache patients.* ProQuest Information & Learning, US.

Scott, J. G., Krull, K. R., Williamson, D. J., Adams, R. L., & Iverson, G. L. (1997). Oklahoma premorbid intelligence estimation (OPIE): Utilization in clinical samples. *The Clinical Neuropsychologist, 11*(2), 146–154.

Scoville, W. B., & Milner, B. (1957). Loss of recent memory after bilateral hippocampal lesions. *Journal of Neurology, Neurosurgery, and Psychiatry, 20*, 11–21.

Seelye, A. M., Howieson, D. B., Wild, K. V, Moore, M. M., & Kaye, J. A. (2009). Wechsler Memory Scale-III Faces test performance in patients with mild cognitive impairment and mild Alzheimer's disease. *Journal of Clinical and Experimental Neuropsychology, 31*(6), 682–688. https://doi.org/10.1080/13803390802484763

Sherer, M., Nixon, S. J., Anderson, B. L., & Adams, R. L. (1992). Differential sensitivity of the WMS to the effects of IQ and brain damage. *Archives of Clinical Neuropsychology, 7*, 505–514.

Shimada, H., Kato, T., Ito, K., Makizako, H., Doi, T., Yoshida, D., . . . Suzuki, T. (2012). Relationship between atrophy of the medial temporal areas and cognitive functions in elderly adults with mild cognitive impairment. *European Neurology*, *67*(3), 168–177. https://doi.org/10.1159/000334845

Shin, M., Chey, J., Kim, J., Park, K., Hwang, S., & Hong, S. (2016). Impact of eduction on the Korean Wechsler Memory Scale IV performances. *Korean Journal of Clinical Psychology*, *35*, 585–599.

Shipley, W. C. (1940). A self-administered scale for measuring intellectual impairment and deterioration. *Journal of Psychology*, *9*, 371–377.

Shontz, F. C. (1957). Evaluation of intellectual potential in hemiplegic individuals. *Journal of Clinical Psychology*, *13*, 267–269. https://doi.org/10.1002/1097-4679 (195707)13:3<267::AID-JCLP2270130309>3.0.CO;2-Y

Shores, E. A., & Carstairs, J. R. (2000). The Macquarie University Neuropsychological Normative Study (MUNNS): Australian norms for the WAIS-R and WMS-R. *Australian Psychologist*, *35*, 41–59. https://doi.org/10.1080/00050060008257467

Siegler, I. C., McCarty, S. M., & Logue, P. E. (1982). Wechsler Memory Scale scores, selective attrition, and distance from death. *Journal of Gerontology*, *37*(2), 176–181. https://doi.org/10.1093/geronj/37.2.176

Skeel, R. L., Sitzer, D., Fogal, T., Wells, J., & Johnstone, B. (2004). Comparison of Predicted-difference, Simple-difference, and Premorbid-estimation methodologies for evaluating IQ and memory score discrepancies. *Archives of Clinical Neuropsychology*, *19*(3), 363–374.

Skillbeck, C. E., & Woods, R. T. (1980). The factorial structure of the Wechsler Memory Scale: Samples of neurological and psychogeriatric patients. *Journal of Consulting and Clinical Psychology*, *43*, 800–809.

Slick, D. J., & Craig, P. L. (1991). Neuropsychological assessment in public psychiatric hospitals: The changing state of the practice—1979 to 1989. *Archives of Clinical Neuropsychology*, *6*(1–2), 73–80.

Slick, D. J., Hinkin, C. H., van Gorp, W. G., & Satz, P. (2001). Base rate of WMS-R Malingering Index in a sample of non-compensation-seeking men infected with HIV-1. *Applied Neuropsychology*, *8*(3), 185–189. https://doi.org/10.1207/S153248 26AN0803_9

Slick, D. J., Sherman, E. M., & Iverson, G. L. (1999). Diagnostic criteria for malingered neurocognitive dysfunction: Proposed standards for clinical practice and research. *The Clinical Neuropsychologist*, *13*(4), 545–561.

Small, J. G., Milstein, V., & Stevens, J. R. (1962). Are psychomotor epileptics different?: A controlled study. *Archives of Neurology*, *7*, 187–194. https://doi.org/10.1001/archneur.1962.04210030025004

Smith, G. E., Ivnik, R. J., Malec, J. F., Kokmen, E., Tangalos, E. G., & Kurland, L. T. (1992). Mayo's Older Americans Normative Studies (MOANS): Factor structure of a core battery. *Psychological Assessment*, *4*(3), 382–390. https://doi.org/10.1037/1040-3590.4.3.382

Smith, G. E., Ivnik, R. J., Malec, J. F., Petersen, R. C., Kokmen, E., & Tangalos, E. G. (1994). Mayo cognitive factors scales: Derivation of a short battery and norms for factor scores. *Neuropsychology*, *8*(2), 194–202. https://doi.org/10.1037/0894-4105.8.2.194

Smith, G. E., Ivnik, R. J., Malec, J. F., & Tangalos, E. G. (1993). Factor structure of the Mayo Older Americans Normative Sample (MOANS) core battery: Replication in a clinical sample. *Psychological Assessment*, *5*(1), 121–124. https://doi.org/10.1037/1040-3590.5.1.121

Snow, W. G., & Sheese, S. (1985). Lateralized brain damage, intelligence, and memory: A failure to find sex differences. *Journal of Consulting and Clinical Psychology, 53,* 940–941.

Soble, J. R., Bain, K. M., Bailey, K. C., Kirton, J. W., Marceaux, J. C., Critchfield, E. A. . . . O'Rourke, J. J. (2018). Evaluating the accuracy of the Wechsler Memory Scale-Fourth Edition (WMS-IV) logical memory embedded validity index for detecting invalid test performance. *Applied Neuropsychology: Adult, 26*(4), 311–318. https://doi.org/10.1080/23279095.2017.1418744.

Soble, J. R., Eichstaedt, K. E., Waseem, H., Mattingly, M. L., Benbadis, S. R., Bozorg, A. M. . . . Schoenberg, M. R. (2014). Clinical utility of the Wechsler Memory Scale-Fourth Edition (WMS-IV) in predicting laterality of temporal lobe epilepsy among surgical candidates. *Epilepsy & Behavior, 41,* 232–237. https://doi.org/10.1016/j.yebeh.2014.10.014

Soble, J. R., Osborn, K. E., Mattingly, M. L., Vale, F. L., Benbadis, S. R., Rodgers-Neame, N. T., & Schoenberg, M. R. (2015). Utility of Green's Word Memory Test Free Recall Subtest as a measure of verbal memory: Initial evidence from a temporal lobe epilepsy clinical sample. *Archives of Clinical Neuropsychology, 31,* 79–87.

Spearman, C. G. (1904). "General intelligence," objectively defined and measured. *American Journal of Psychology, 15,* 201–209.

Spedo, C. T., Foss, M. P., Elias, A. H. N., Pereira, D. A., Santos, P. L. D., Ribeiro, G. N. D. A., . . . & Barreira, A. A. (2013). Cross-cultural adaptation of visual reproduction subtest of wechsler memory scale fourth edition (WMS-IV) to a Brazilian context. *Clinical Neuropsychiatry, 10,* 111–119.

Squire, L. R., & Butters, N. (Eds.). (1992). *Neuropsychology and memory* (2nd ed.). New York: Guilford Press.

Stambrook, M., Cardoso, E., Hawryluk, G. A., Eirikson, P., Piatek, D., & Sicz, G. (1988). Neuropsychological changes following the neurosurgical treatment of normal pressure hydrocephalus. *Archives of Clinical Neuropsychology, 3*(4), 323–330.

Standlee, L. S. (1953a). The Archimedes negative aftereffect as an indication of memory impairment. *Journal of Consulting Psychology, 17*(4), 317. https://doi.org/10.1037/h0060805

Standlee, L. S. (1953b). Validity of Archimedes spiral in discriminating memory ability of psychotics and of normals. *A.M.A. Archives of Neurology and Psychiatry, 71,* 648–650.

Stark, S., Fox, J., Roberts, C., Stewart, J., & Golden, C. (2014). Examining gender differences on tasks of episodic and working memory within a mixed clinical sample (Conference session abstract). 122nd American Psychological Association Annual Convention, Washington, DC. https://doi.org/10.1037/e548082014-001

Steinberg, B. A., Bieliauskas, L. A., Smith, G. E., & Ivnik, R. J. (2005). Mayo's Older Americans Normative Studies: Age- and IQ-adjusted norms for the Wechsler Memory Scale-Revised. *The Clinical Neuropsychologist, 19*(3–4), 378–463. https://doi.org/10.1080/13854040590945201

Stieper, D. R., Williams, M., & Duncan, C. P. (1951). Changes in impersonal and personal memory following electro-convulsive therapy. *Journal of Clinical Psychology, 7*(4), 361–366. https://doi.org/10.1002/1097-4679(195110)7:4<361::AID-JCLP2270070412>3.0.CO;2-K

Stone, C. P. (1947). Losses and gains in cognitive functions as related to electro-convulsive shock. *Journal of Abnormal and Social Psychology, 42,* 206–214.

Stone, C. P., Girdner, J., & Albrecht, R. (1946). An alternate form of the Wechsler Memory Scale. *The Journal of Psychology, 22*, 199–206. https://doi.org/10.1080/00 223980.1946.9917307

Stuss, D. T., Kaplan, E. F., Benson, D. F., Weir, W. S., Steven, C., & Sarazin, F. F. (1982). Evidence for involvement of orbitofrontal cortex in memory functions: An interference effect. *Journal of Comparative and Physiological Psychology, 96*(6), 913–925. https://doi.org/10.1037/0735-7036.96.6.913

Suchy, Y., & Sweet, J. J. (2000). Information/Orientation subtest of the Wechsler Memory Scale-Revised as an indicator of suspicion of insufficient effort. *The Clinical Neuropsychologist, 14*(1), 56–66. https://doi.org/10.1076/1385-4046(200002)14:1;1-8;FT056

Sullivan, E. V., Fama, R., Rosenbloom, M. J., & Pfefferbaum, A. (2002). A profile of neuropsychological deficits in alcoholic women. *Neuropsychology, 16*(1), 74–83. https://doi.org/10.1037/0894-4105.16.1.74

Sutker, P. B., Allain, A. N., Johnson, J. L., & Butters, N. M. (1992). Memory and learning performances in POW survivors with history of malnutrition and combat veteran controls. *Archives of Clinical Neuropsychology, 7*(5), 431–444. https://doi. org/10.1016/0887-6177(92)90156-H

Sutker, P. B., Galina, Z. H., West, J. A., & Allain, A. N. (1990). Trauma-induced weight loss and cognitive deficits among former prisoners of war. *Journal of Consulting and Clinical Psychology, 58*(3), 323–328. https://doi.org/10.1037/0022-006X.58.3.323

Tanner, B. A. (2009). The WMS Assistant: A Windows program to aid in writing WMS-III report. *The Open Psychology Journal, 2*, 8–11. https://doi.org/10.2174/ 1874350100902010008

Teraishi, T., Sasayama, D., Hori, H., Yamamoto, N., Fujii, T., Matsuo, J. . . . Kunugi, H. (2013). Possible association between common variants of the phenylalanine hydroxylase (PAH) gene and memory performance in healthy adults. *Behavioral and Brain Functions, 9*, 30 https://doi.org/10.1186/1744-9081-9-30

Terman, L. M., & Merrill, M. A. (1937). *Measuring intelligence.* Cambridge, MA: Riverside Press.

Thiruselvam, I., Vogt, E. M., & Hoelzle, J. B. (2015). The interchangeability of CVLT-II and WMS-IV Verbal Paired Associates Scores: A slightly different story. *Archives of Clinical Neuropsychology, 30*(3), 248–255.

Thurstone, L. L. (1936). The isolation of seven primary abilities. *Psychological Bulletin, 33*, 780–781.

Toal, R. (1957). Reliability (Internal Consistency) of the Wechsler Memory Scale and correlation with the Wechsler-Bellevue Intelligence Scale. *Journal of Consulting Psychology, 21*(2), 131–135. https://doi.org/10.1037/h0039695

Tomer, A., Larrabee, G. J., & Crook, T. H. (1994). Structure of everyday memory in adults with age-associated memory impairment. *Psychology and Aging, 9*(4), 606–615. https://doi.org/10.1037/0882-7974.9.4.606

Torkelson, R. M., Jellinek, H. M., Malec, J. F., & Harvey, R. F. (1983). Traumatic brain injury: Psychological and medical factors related to rehabilitation outcome. *Rehabilitation Psychology, 28*(3), 169–176. https://doi.org/10.1037/h0090992

Toulopoulou, T., Rabe-Hesketh, S., King, H., Murray, R. M., & Morris, R. G. (2003). Episodic memory in schizophrenic patients and their relatives. *Schizophrenia Research, 63*(3), 273–284. https://doi.org/10.1016/S0920-9964(02)00324-9

Trahan, D. E., & Quintana, J. W. (1990). Analysis of gender effects upon verbal and visual memory performance in adults. *Archives of Clinical Neuropsychology, 5*(4), 325–334. https://doi.org/10.1016/0887-6177(90)90012-E

Trahan, D. E., Quintana, J. W., Willingham, A. C., & Goethe, K. E. (1988). The Visual Reproduction subtest: Standardization and clinical validation of a delayed recall procedure. *Neuropsychology, 2*, 29–39.

Trahan, L. H., Stuebing, K. K., Hiscock, M., & Fletcher, J. M. (2014). The Flynn effect: A meta-analysis. *Psychological Bulletin, 140*, 1332–1260.

Tremont, G., Hoffman, R. G., Scott, J. G., Adams, R. L., & Nadolne, M. J. (1997). Clinical utility of Wechsler Memory Scale-Revised and predicted IQ discrepancies in closed head injury. *Archives of Clinical Neuropsychology, 12*, 757–762. https://doi.org/10.1016/S0887-6177(97)00049-8

Trenerry, M. R., Jack Jr., C. R., Cascino, G. D., Sharbrough, F. W., & Ivnik, R. J. (1996). Sex differences in the relationship between visual memory and MRI hippocampal volumes. *Neuropsychology, 10*, 343–351. https://doi.org/10.1037/0894-4105.10.3.343

Tröster, A. I., Woods, S. P., & Morgan, E. E. (2007). Assessing cognitive change in Parkinson's disease: Development of practice effect-corrected reliable change indices. *Archives of Clinical Neuropsychology, 22*(6), 711–718.

Trudel, T. M., Tryon, W. W., & Purdum, C. M. (1998). Awareness of disability and long-term outcome after traumatic brain injury. *Rehabilitation Psychology, 43*(4), 267–281. https://doi.org/10.1037/0090-5550.43.4.267

Trueblood, W., & Binder, L. M. (1997). Psychologists' accuracy in identifying neuropsychological test protocols of clinical malingerers. *Archives of Clinical Neuropsychology, 12*(1), 13–27.

Tuğal, Ö., Yazici, K. M., Yağcioğlu, A. E. A., & Göğüş, A. (2004). A double-blind, placebo controlled, cross-over trial of adjunctive donepezil for cognitive impairment in schizophrenia. *International Journal of Neuropsychopharmacology, 7*(2), 117–123. https://doi.org/10.1017/S1461145703004024

Tulsky, D. S., Chelune, G. J., & Price, L. R. (2004). Development of a new delayed memory index for the WMS-III. *Journal of Clinical and Experimental Neuropsychology, 26*, 563–576.

Tulsky, D. S., Chiaravalloti, N. D., Palmer, B. W., & Chelune, G. J. (2003). The Wechsler Memory Scale, Third Edition: A new perspective. In D. S. Tulsky, D. H. Saklofske, G. J. Chelune, R. K. Heaton, R. J. Ivnik, R. Bornstein, A. Prifitera, & M. F. Ledbetter (Eds.), *Clinical interpretation of the WAIS-III and WMS-III.* New York: Elsevier

Tulsky, D. S., & Ledbetter, M. F. (2000). Updating to the WAIS-III and WMS-III: Considerations for research and clinical practice. *Psychological Assessment, 12*, 253–262.

Tulsky, D. S., & Price, L. R. (2003). The joint WAIS-III and WMS-III factor structure: Development and cross-validation of a six-factor model of cognitive functioning. *Psychological Assessment, 15*(2), 149–162. https://doi.org/10.1037/1040-3590.15.2.149

Tulsky, D. S., Zhu, J., & Ledbetter, M. F. (2002). *WAIS—III/WMS—III technical manual (updated).* San Antonio, TX: Psychological Corporation.

Tuulio-Henriksson, A., Partonen, T., Suvisaari, J., Haukka, J., & Lönnqvist, J. (2004). Age at onset and cognitive functioning in schizophrenia. *The British Journal of Psychiatry, 185*, 215–219. https://doi.org/10.1192/bjp.185.3.215

Umfleet, L. G., Janecek, J. K., Quasney, E., Sabsevitz, D. S., Ryan, J. J., Binder, J. R., & Swanson, S. J. (2015). Sensitivity and specificity of memory and naming tests for identifying left temporal-lobe epilepsy. *Applied Neuropsychology: Adult, 22*, 189–196. https://doi.org/10.1080/23279095.2014.895366

Uttl, B., Graf, P., & Richter, L. K. (2002). Verbal Paired Associates tests limits on validity and reliability. *Archives of Clinical Neuropsychology, 17*(6), 567–581.

Vakil, E., Arbell, N., Gozlan, M., Hoofien, D., & Blachstein, H. (1992). Relative importance of informational units and their role in long-term recall by closed-head-injured patients and control groups. *Journal of Consulting and Clinical Psychology, 60*(5), 802-803. https://doi.org/10.1037/0022-006X.60.5.802

Vakil, E., Hoofien, D., & Blachstein, H. (1992). Total amount learned versus learning rate of verbal and nonverbal information, in differentiating left- from right-brain injured patients. *Archives of Clinical Neuropsychology, 7*(2), 111–120. https://doi.org/10.1016/0887-6177(92)90005-8

Van den Broek, A., Golden, C. J., Loonstra, A., Ghinglia, K., & Goldstein, D. (1998). Short forms of the Wechsler Memory Scale-Revised: Cross-validation and derivation of a two-subtest form. *Psychological Assessment, 10*(1), 38–40. https://doi.org/10.1037/1040-3590.10.1.38

Van Gorp, W. G., Miller, E. N., Satz, P., & Visscher, B. (1989). Neuropsychological performance in HIV-1 immunocompromised patients: A preliminary report. *Journal of Clinical and Experimental Neuropsychology, 11*(5), 763–773.

Vanderploeg, R. D., Goldman, H., & Kleinman, K. M. (1987). Relationship between systolic and diastolic blood pressure and cognitive functioning in hypertensive subjects: An extension of previous findings. *Archives of Clinical Neuropsychology, 2*(1), 101–109.

Varney, N. R., Campbell, D., & Roberts, R. J. (1994). Long-term neuropsychological sequelae of fever associated with amnesia. *Archives of Clinical Neuropsychology, 9*(4), 347–352.

Victor, M., Herman, K., & White, E. E. (1959). A psychological study of the Wernicke-Korsakoff syndrome: Results of Wechsler-Bellevue Intelligence Scale and Wechsler Memory Scale testing at different stages in the disease. *Quarterly Journal of Studies on Alcohol, 20*, 467–479.

Wachi, M., Tomikawa, M., Fukuda, M., Kameyama, S., Kasahara, K., Sasagawa, M. . . . Sohma, Y. (2001). Neuropsychological changes after surgical treatment for temporal lobe epilepsy. *Epilepsia, 42*(Suppl. 6), 4–8. https://doi.org/10.1046/j.1528-1157.2001.0420s6004.x

Wagner, M. T., & Bachman, D. L. (1996). Neuropsychological features of diffuse Lewy body disease. *Archives of Clinical Neuropsychology, 11*(3), 175–184.

Walker, A. J., Batchelor, J., & Shores, A. (2009). Effects of education and cultural background on performance on WAIS-III, WMS-III, WAIS-R and WMS-R measures: Systematic review. *Australian Psychologist, 44*(4), 216–223. https://doi.org/10.1080/00050060902833469

Walker, A. J., Batchelor, J., Shores, E. A., & Jones, M. (2009). Diagnostic efficiency of demographically corrected Wechsler Adult Intelligence Scale-III and Wechsler Memory Scale-III indices in moderate to severe traumatic brain injury and lower education levels. *Journal of the International Neuropsychological Society, 15*(6), 938–950. https://doi.org/10.1017/S1355617709990610

Wang, Y., Xu, X., Feng, C., Li, Y., Ge, X., Zong, G. . . . Zhang, P. (2015). Patients with type 2 diabetes exhibit cognitive impairment with changes of metabolite concentration in the left hippocampus. *Metabolic Brain Disease, 30*(4), 1027–1034. https://doi.org/10.1007/s11011-015-9670-4

Wannan, C. M. J., Bartholomeusz, C. F., Cropley, V. L., Van Rheenen, T. E., Panayiotou, A., Brewer, W. J. . . . Wood, S. J. (2018). Deterioration of visuospatial associative memory following a first psychotic episode: A long-term follow-up study. *Psychological Medicine, 48*(1), 132–141. https://doi.org/10.1017/S003329171700157X

Wasserman, J. D. (2012). A history of intellectual assessment: The unfinsihed tapestry. In D. P. Flanagan & P. L. Harrison (Eds.), *Contemporary intellectual assessment: Theories, tests, and issues* (3rd ed., pp. 3–22). New York: Guildford Press.

Watson, R. (1951). *The clinical method in psychology*. New York: Harper and Row.

The Wechsler Memory Scale-Third Edition-Abbreviated. (n.d.). Retrieved from http://clarionpsych.com/wms_iii.html

Wechsler, D. (1917). A study of retention in Korsakoff psychosis. *Psychiatric Bulletin of the New York State Hospitals, 11*, 403–451.

Wechsler, D. (1939). *The measurement of adult intelligence*. Baltimore, MN: Williams and Wilkins.

Wechsler, D. (1945). A standardized memory scale for clinical use. *The Journal of Psychology: Interdisciplinary and Applied, 19*, 87–95. https://doi.org/10.1080/0022398 0.1945.9917223

Wechsler, D. (1961). Intelligence, memory and the aging process. In P. H. Hoch & J. Zubin (Eds.), *Psychopathology of aging*. New York: Grune & Stratton.

Wechsler, D. (1963). Engrams, memory storage, and mnemonic storage. *American Psychologist, 18*, 149–153.

Wechsler, D. (1987). *The Wechsler Memory Scale-Revised manual*. San Antonio, TX: Psychological Corporation.

Wechsler, D. (1997). *The Wechsler Memory Scale-III administration and scoring manual*. San Antonio, TX: Pearson Assessments.

Wechsler, D. (2009a). *The Wechsler Memory Scale-IV*. San Antonio, TX: Pearson Assessments.

Wechsler, D. (2009b). *Wechsler Memory Scale-Fourth Edition (WMS-IV) technical and interpretive manual*. San Antonio, TX: Pearson.

Wechsler, D., & Stone, C. P. (1973). *Wechsler Memory Scale manual*. San Antonio, TX: Psychological Corporation.

Weingartner, H., Kaye, W., Smallberg, S. A., Ebert, M. H., Gillin, J. C., & Sitaram, N. (1981). Memory failures in progressive idiopathic dementia. *Journal of Abnormal Psychology, 90*(3), 187–196. https://doi.org/10.1037/0021-843X.90.3.187

Wells, F. L., & Martin, H. A. (1923). A method of memory examination suitable for psychotic cases. *American Journal of Psychiatry, 3*, 243–258.

Westervelt, H. J., Carvalho, J., & Duff, K. (2007). Presentation of Alzheimer's disease in patients with and without olfactory deficits. *Archives of Clinical Neuropsychology, 22*(1), 117–122.

Westervelt, H. J., Ruffolo, J. S., & Tremont, G. (2005). Assessing olfaction in the neuropsychological exam: The relationship between odor identification and cognition in older adults. *Archives of Clinical Neuropsychology, 20*(6), 761–769.

Whipple, G. M. (1915). *Manual of mental and physical tests: Part 2. Complex processes* (2nd ed.). Baltimore, MD: Warwisk & York.

White, D. A., & Murphy, C. F. (1998). Working memory for nonverbal auditory information in dementia of the Alzheimer type. *Archives of Clinical Neuropsychology, 13*(4), 339–347.

Whitmer, R. A. (2007). Type 2 diabetes and risk of cognitive impairment and dementia. *Current Neurology and Neuroscience Reports, 7*(5), 373–380.

Wilde, N. J., Strauss, E., Chelune, G. J., Hermann, B. P., Hunter, M., Loring, D. W. . . .
Sherman, E. (2003). Confirmatory factor analysis of the WMS-III in patients with
temporal lobe epilepsy. *Psychological Assessment, 15*, 56–63.

Wilhelm, K. L., & Johnstone, B. (1995). Use of the Wechsler Memory Scale-Revised
in traumatic brain injury. *Applied Neuropsychology, 2*(1), 42–45. https://doi.org/10.
1207/s15324826an0201_8

Wilk, C. M., Gold, J. M., McMahon, R. P., Humber, K., Iannone, V. N., & Buchanan, R. W.
(2005). No, it is not possible to be schizophrenic yet neuropsychologically normal.
Neuropsychology, 19(6), 778–786. https://doi.org/10.1037/0894-4105.19.6.778

Williams, D. L., Goldstein, G., & Minshew, N. J. (2005). Impaired memory for faces
and social scenes in autism: Clinical implications of memory dysfunction. *Archives
of Clinical Neuropsychology, 20*(1), 1–15. https://doi.org/10.1016/j.acn.2002.08.001

Williams, J. M. (1997). The prediction of premorbid memory ability. *Archives of Clinical Neuropsychology, 12*(8), 745–756.

Willson, D. F. (1997). *The nature of accelerated forgetting rates in schizophrenia:
Evidence for mediation by attention and executive control.* ProQuest Information &
Learning, US.

Woodard, J. L., & Axelrod, B. N. (1995). Parsimonious prediction of Wechsler Memory
Scale-Revised memory indices. *Psychological Assessment, 7*(4), 445–449. https://
doi.org/10.1037/1040-3590.7.4.445

Woodard, J. L., & Axelrod, B. N. (1996). "Parsimonious prediction of Wechsler Memory Scale-Revised memory indices": Correction. *Psychological Assessment, 8*(4),
382. https://doi.org/10.1037/1040-3590.8.4.382

World Health Center. (2012). *Dementia cases expected to triple by 2050 but still largely
ignored.* Retrieved from www.who.int/mediacentre/news/releases/2012/dementia_
20120411/en/

Xiang, Y. T., Shum, D., Chiu, H. F., Tang, W. K., & Ungvari, G. S. (2010). Association of demographic characteristics, symptomatology, retrospective and prospective
memory, executive functioning and intelligence with social functioning in schizophrenia. *Australian & New Zealand Journal of Psychiatry, 44*(12), 1112–1117.

Ylioja, S. G., Baird, A. D., & Podell, K. (2009). Developing a spatial analogue of the
Reliable Digit Span. *Archives of Clinical Neuropsychology, 24*(8), 720–739. https://
doi.org/10.1093/arclin/acp078

Young, J. C., Caron, J. E., Baughman, B. C., & Sawyer, R. J. (2012). Detection of suboptimal effort with symbol span: Development of a new embedded index. *Archives
of Clinical Neuropsychology, 27*(2), 159–164. https://doi.org/10.1093/arclin/acr109

Zagar, R., Arbit, J., Stuckey, M., & Wengel, W. W. (1984). Developmental analysis of the
Wechsler Memory Scale. *Journal of Clinical Psychology, 40*(6), 1466–1473. https://doi.
org/10.1002/1097-4679(198411)40:6<1466::AID-JCLP2270400635>3.0.CO;2-5

Zaidel, D., & Sperry, R. W. (1974). Memory impairment after commissurotomy in man.
Brain, 97(2), 263–272.

Zappert, L. N. (2008). *The effects of psychosocial stressors and reproductive life events
on the clinical course of major depression in women during the midlife.* ProQuest
Information & Learning, US.

Index

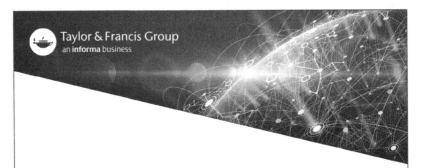

Printed in the United States
by Baker & Taylor Publisher Services